Persistence and Change:

*Bennington College and
Its Students
After Twenty-five Years*

Persistence and Change:

Bennington College and
Its Students
After Twenty-five Years

THEODORE M. NEWCOMB

> The University of Michigan

KATHRYN E. KOENIG

> York University

RICHARD FLACKS

> The University of Chicago

DONALD P. WARWICK

> The University of Michigan

JOHN WILEY & SONS, INC.   NEW YORK   LONDON   SYDNEY

Library of Congress Catalog Card Number: 67–12567

Printed in the United States of America

Preface

Two studies of change and persistence are reported here—one of a set of individuals and the other of the college within which they had been objects of study more than 20 years ago. The present inquiries are thus historically and institutionally related. More than that, they represent interdependent aspects of a common problem: How do the effects of a college, especially those that are relatively enduring, depend upon students' experiences that result from the nature of the institution?

These two investigations have been supported by grants from the National Institute of Mental Health, the United States Office of Education, and the Horace H. Rackham School of Graduate Studies of the University of Michigan. In a no less important sense they were made possible by the continuing help of students and staff members at Bennington College between 1959 and 1962. I wish, in particular, that it were still possible to thank the late president of the College, William C. Fels, for his unfailingly gracious and understanding involvement in the study. Much more recently President Edward J. Bloustein has consented, in the interests of accuracy, to read the manuscript; if errors have nevertheless crept in, they are, of course, not his.

It is no longer possible, as it was in the 1930's when the study reported in *Personality and Social Change* was conducted, to carry on such an extended enterprise with little or no financial, secretarial, or professional assistance. The present work has emerged very largely from the minds and the labors of three of my former graduate stu-

v

dents in social psychology. Dr. Kathryn Koenig took on the task of interviewing and sending questionnaires to the former students; Chapters 3, 4, 6, 7, and 8 are hers. Her experience as a teacher of psychology at Bennington also enabled her to be of special usefulness in planning the study of the college as of 1959–1962. Chapters 9 and 10, however, are the work of Dr. Donald P. Warwick, whose problem was the identification of the community norms during this period. Dr. Richard Flacks is responsible for Chapters 11 and 12, in which he reports his intensive studies of student subcultures, including deviate ones, during the same years. No investigator has had more responsible and astute collaborators, as together we drew out the essentials from our mass of data. Insofar as we have been able to illuminate the general problem, and to shed further light on the findings of the study of a quarter-century ago, it is largely because of their contributions.

Theodore M. Newcomb

Ann Arbor, Michigan
November 1966

Contents

Part Four: Then and Now

Appendices

Index

Persistence and Change:

*Bennington College and
Its Students
After Twenty-five Years*

PART ONE

Two Studies of Bennington College

1. Personality and Social Change: 1935–1939

This study is best understood in the light of an earlier one made during a period of rapid and controversial social change in America. It began during the year of the Wagner Labor Act and ended in the year of General Franco's military triumph that brought the end of the Spanish Civil War and the start of World War II. Nearly every one of some 550 students attending Bennington College in Bennington, Vermont, during those four years expressed her own views concerning various public issues that were then important to Americans—not once, but, typically, at several different times during her student days at the college. Thus for nearly all of them it was possible to observe whether there was attitude change over periods ranging from one to four academic years.

Change was observed, in fact, on the part of most of those students and, as in the case of the majority of their older contemporaries, its usual direction was toward the acceptance of policies identified with the New Deal. For the most part—or so the students believed, at any rate—it was in a direction away from their parents' convictions, for with few exceptions the daughters had come to college in general agreement with their parents, most of whom were reported as not pro–New Deal. They were orderly changes, usually continuing with the student's succeeding years in the college. They were not trifling ones—rarely extreme, but great enough to represent a genuine shift, and they were much more prominent than those of students, both male and female, at other colleges from families much like those whose daughters came to Bennington.

Such changes in attitude do not occur in a vacuum, and so they must be understood in terms of the social environment provided by the college at that time. It was a new, "experimental" college of 250 women students; it had been planned during the years of maximum enthusiasm over "progressive education," although it was not committed to the doctrines now associated with the phrase. It was still

3

new, its entering class having not yet graduated in 1935. Situated on a farm site among the Green Mountains, it was relatively isolated. Some of its salient characteristics are described as follows in the original report (Newcomb, 1943).

> Partly as an outgrowth of the college's educational plan, and partly because of the limitations of nearby extra-college attractions, the community at this time was, to a very unusual degree, self-sufficient and self-contained. Partly because of the youth of the institution, and partly because of the novelty of its plan, it was also rather self-conscious. Many of its critics would probably have labeled it self-satisfied. At any rate it was not only a highly integrated community, but its members always referred to it by precisely that term. No phrase was more constantly on our lips than "the college community." . . . The faculty, rather young and given to friendly, informal relationships with students, was almost universally described by those familiar with the college as "liberal" (doubtless in more than one sense). There were a few charges of "radicalism," but probably no more than were directed against many other college faculties (p. 8).

The college faculty of 50, mostly men, during these years was, as such bodies go, a relatively youthful group, mostly in their thirties. Most of these teachers (who had no other titles) lived on or near the campus, and students were often in their homes. Being for the most part of "liberal" persuasion concerning public issues of the day, they were inevitably in a position to exert influence upon their students toward their own positions. Deliberate efforts to do so were nevertheless carefully eschewed by faculty members, and charges of "propagandizing" were virtually unknown, even though many parents were disturbed by the trend of their daughters' thinking. Faculty members usually came to think of many of their students (a majority of whom came from private preparatory schools) as having led overprotected lives, and they included among their teaching responsibilities that of "introducing students to the rest of the world."

The original study documented in various ways the prevalence of community norms according to which nonconservative attitudes toward contemporary public issues were widely approved. Individuals (mainly older students) whose personal prestige was high were, year after year, typically those whose attitudes were, in fact, rather conspicuously liberal, and were so judged by other students who held them in esteem. Those generally regarded as "resistant to community expectations" usually held distinctively conservative attitudes, and were so perceived by their peers. Perhaps it is still more indicative that the general trend toward abandoning conservative attitudes represented a communitywide phenomenon; it was not (as at nearby Williams College) limited to those majoring in economics or political science, but characterized students in all major fields, for example, modern dance, literature, and science.

Although a large majority of students changed in ways that we have described, there was a sizable minority of those who did not. Most of these individuals turned out to have certain more or less distinctive personality characteristics of their own, together with their own ways of fitting into the community. Several of them were near-isolates socially, sometimes so out of touch as to be quite unaware of the existence of anticonservative norms. Others were regarded by the college psychiatrist as markedly overdependent upon parents. The nonchangers included a large proportion of those regarded by other students as rebellious or negativistic; norm-flouters were also generally in defiance of normative pressures away from conservative attitudes. Thus the nonchangers tended to fight the community, or to be so little a part of it as not to be aware of the norms concerning public issues, or they would recognize them without accepting them because of strong ties toward home and family.

Thus the patterns of changing and nonchanging attitudes, as observed in the original study, were outcomes of the interplay of forces stemming from the world at large, from the college community, and from individual personality characteristics. It is against this early background that the study made nearly a quarter-century later must be seen.

2. Persistence and Change: Late 1930's to Early 1960's

The changes manifested by Bennington students of three decades ago were not unique but, in degree at least, they were atypical (see P. E. Jacob, *Changing Values in College*, 1957, especially Chapter VI, "The Peculiar Potency of Some Colleges"). We have taken pains to point out that they occurred in a very particular time-space context, and this leads directly to the problems of individual and institutional change with which the present study is concerned. Briefly, these problems are as follows.

Individual Change

The situation in which students' changes occurred was only briefly experienced—four years at the most, as compared with some 18 previous years and more than 20 subsequently. Furthermore, their changes were of a kind that, although not uncommon on the part of late adolescents and very young adults, are often transitory; added years together with the assumption of adult responsibilities lead to the dilution or the abandoning of youthful "excesses," or even to reaction against them. Given such a temporary experience at a susceptible period of life in a somewhat secluded community, what is the subsequent fate of attitudes thus engendered? Under what conditions, if at all, would individuals maintain the kinds of attitudes with which they had left the college 20-odd years before, and under what conditions change them, in what directions? Thus our first problem deals with *individual* change and persistence of attitudes over a relatively long period of time.

Institutional Change

Insofar as the pattern of observed changes in the 1930's had, as one of its necessary preconditions, a distinctive institutional setting, it is hardly to be expected that similar patterns would continue if marked changes had occurred in that institution. If, on the other hand, the Bennington College of the early 1960's had remained essentially the same, we would expect more nearly similar patterns of change on the part of its students in the later period. Or, more realistically, since neither total change nor no change at all is very probable, it might be that analogous student changes, differing perhaps in degree or in content, but not essentially in pattern, might still be the rule. And so our second problem, briefly, was this: from the point of view of its effects upon students' attitudes, how different was the later Bennington College from the earlier one, and what were the effects of *institutional* changes (if any) upon individuals' changes during their college years?

The Interdependence of the Two Problems

On the surface, these are quite different problems, and altogether independent ones, although answers to each of them are worth having, in their own right. What has happened to women who left the college so long ago does not seem likely to have greatly affected, or been affected by, what has happened to the college itself during the same period.

From the point of view, however, of comprehending the processes by which colleges affect their students, or fail to do so, the two problems are closely related. First, we can understand the subsequent fate of the attitudes of the students of the 1930's no better than we understand the processes by which their attitudes developed during their college years. And, second, the limitations of the single, original study resulted in considerable uncertainty as to the particular features of the college, as of that time, that were peculiarly responsible for the observed changes. Thus there is an important sense in which, as we shall now try to show, the findings of the original study cannot be very fully accounted for without *both* strands of the later one.

It was for just this reason that we undertook the not inconsiderable task presented by the later one. We had, of course, a natural curiosity, kept alive by repeated inquiries over the years: "What ever happened to all those girls? Probably married conventional husbands and forgot about their wild days," or "I don't suppose that college is still having such dramatic effects; after all, times change and established colleges, like adult individuals, settle down." But beyond all that, we had both scientific and educational concerns that prodded us into planning the later study.

On the scientific side, the original study suffered from being a one-shot affair. Descriptively, its findings were dependable enough, having been shown to reappear in each of four consecutive years. But in the absence of systematic "controls" there was no way of isolating the essential ingredients, the crucial causative factors. The original report made no claims of universality; indeed, it stressed the probable uniqueness of both the world situation and the institutional setting. What a second study might show, as a single one could not, was that changes on the world scene together with identifiable institutional changes might produce different effects. Not that all of the possible changes of epoch and social setting could be disentangled, of course; but only that, with a bit of luck, certain known changes in the two settings could be related to the findings, whatever they turned out to be.

Somewhat more specifically, a failure to find attitudinal changes in the 1960's comparable with those of the 1930's could be related to known changes of the world scene and local setting, whereas a finding of similar attitude changes at the two times could be related to whatever constant features, world or local, could be detected. Without such comparisons over two points in time (widely separated, preferably), there was no way to distinguish, among all possible influences, those that were from those that were not effective in inducing changes at the earlier time. Such, in a very general sense, were the hypotheses underlying the present study: similarities between the two sets of findings could be accounted for in terms of world and local similarities, whereas different findings would call upon changes in either or both kinds of settings for explanation.

Concerning the mounting problems of higher education, our interests were quite different. On the one hand, college and university educators commonly insist that undergraduate education should include experiences that could have the effect of changing students' values—extending their horizons, increasing their interest in the new and unfamiliar, inculcating a sense of excitement in ideas for their own sake, for example. On the other hand, the growth of mammoth universities, and the increasing proportion of students in colleges that are urban if not commuter-like, appear to be creating an increased sense of impersonality and anonymity that contravene the traditional assumptions about the importance of the academic community in liberal education. These assumptions, whether or not explicit, are that the effectiveness of colleges in inculcating values depends rather heavily upon a sense of community that carries with it the exact opposite of impersonality and anonymity.

These assumptions have never adequately been put to the test, nor will the present study be in any way decisive. At least indirectly, however, we hoped that it might have some contribution to make toward that end. It might turn out that the early Bennington College and the recent one are alike in providing a social setting in which recognized kinds of values are developed and supported by community norms. If so, regardless of the content of those norms, then certain persisting features of the college might be identified as contributing, perhaps crucially, to the function of inculcating values, and whatever features of the college had changed would not be essential to the performance of that function. If, on the other hand, it should appear that the college had recently ceased to perform that function, then the fact that it had earlier done so could perhaps be accounted for in terms of institutional changes known to have occurred. In either instance, we ought to obtain a fuller explanation of the earlier findings.

❊   ❊   ❊   ❊

Such was our reasoning as we planned the following investigation. We could, at the very least, satisfy our own and many others' curiosity as to the persistence of rather remarkable individual changes incurred many years ago in a special historical and institutional setting. We could study the durability of that institution's effectiveness in facilitating such changes. We had a fairly good chance of contributing to the social-scientific understanding of the interplay of public, institutional, and personal factors in the modification of attitudes and in the persistence of those modifications. And, finally, we had at least a sporting chance of refining our own knowledge of those features, in one small college, that seem essential to its function of stimulating and supporting students' systems of values.

PART TWO

Restudying the Original Population

3. Population and Procedures

Nature of the Sample

The immediate problem in launching a follow-up study is to locate the people who had participated in the original study. Even though more than 20 years had elapsed since then, getting the married names and the addresses of the participants was relatively easy. Most of the women had kept in touch with the Alumnae Office of Bennington College and an accurate directory was available.* Of the 525 women who had participated in the original study, 15 were known to have died, and 24 had left no mailing address with the Alumnae Office. The remaining 486 women became the focus of the follow-up study.

The population of 486 women was small enough to make it reasonable to try to include everyone in the follow-up study. Of all the possible ways of getting information from each of them, a personal interview seemed to be the method which would provide the most information from the largest number of people, although it is also the most expensive and time-consuming method. We therefore decided to interview only those for whom the most data were available from the original study and to send questionnaires to the others, for whom we had less complete information as of the 1930's.

Members of the graduating classes of 1938, 1939, and 1940 had been studied for at least three years, and all others in the original study for only one or two years. Hence students who had graduated in these three years became our interview population. Of a total of 147 for whom current addresses were available, interviews were, in fact, held with 129, usually at their homes. It proved impossible to arrange interviews with the 16 others, several of whom were currently residing overseas, and so questionnaires (more fully described later) were mailed to them; nine of these were completed and returned. One graduate refused to be interviewed or to answer the questionnaire and, inadvertently, one of them was never asked to participate. Alto-

---

* We are grateful to Mrs. Helen Feeley and the members of her staff who helped us to reach almost every alumna who had been in the original study.

gether, almost 94% of the graduates (138 of 147) having known addresses participated.

Questionnaires were also mailed to all other former students who had in any way participated in the original study, and for whom a current address could be obtained. Some of them had attended the college for less than three years between 1935 and 1939, and some had graduated (in 1936, 1937, 1941, or 1942), but had participated in the study for less than three years. Of 329 questionnaires mailed to this population, 207 were returned in usable form, which is 62.9% of the total. As shown in Table 3.1, graduates were significantly more likely to submit replies than nongraduates. Less identification with the college and less involvement with the original study presumably contributed to the nongraduates' lack of interest in the follow-up study.

All of these women, when students at Bennington College, had completed a questionnaire on political and economic attitudes known as the PEP scale. A high score on this scale indicated "conservative" attitudes, according to standards of that time. A comparison of scores obtained as students on this scale (that is, in the 1930's) by the women who returned the follow-up questionnaire and by those who did not shows no meaningful difference in scores, either for subsequent graduates or for nongraduates, separately considered. We have no indication of any attitudinal bias related to participation or nonparticipation in the follow-up study. However, since we know nothing of the present attitudes and values of the women who failed to complete our questionnaire, we cannot assume that no present bias is present in the sample.

The information is most complete for women in the interview sample, next most complete for graduates in the questionnaire sample, and least complete for those who did not graduate from Bennington.

Table 3.1   Percentages of Graduates and Nongraduates Who Completed the Mailed Questionnaire

	Completed Questionnaire		Did Not Complete Questionnaire		Total
Graduates	117	73%	44	27%	161
Nongraduates	90	54%	78	46%	168
	207		122		329

Chi square = 12.05; $p < .001$

Therefore the study will have most to say about women who graduated from Bennington College in 1938, 1939, and 1940, and least to say about women who attended the college in the 1930's, but who left before they had completed their work for a degree. The major analyses will be derived from the information provided by the graduates.

Nature of the Interview

The interview was a structured one, lasting from one hour to 2½ hours, usually given in the respondent's home. Before the appointment was made, the respondent had received a letter from the investigators explaining the nature of the follow-up study, and requesting her to return a list of dates and times at which she might be interviewed it she were willing to participate in the study. A specific appointment was made when the interviewer arrived in the locality of the respondent.

The first part of the interview consisted of questions about the respondent's postcollege history. Each person was asked about the educational and professional training she had received since graduating from Bennington College and about the plans she may have made for future training. Each respondent was asked to describe the types of employment she had engaged in during the past 20-odd years and any future plans for working. If she was not currently employed, she was asked to speculate about the type of employment that she might possibly accept.

The next part of the interview was concerned with the organizational activities and interests of the respondent. She was asked to describe the activities and organizations she was involved in currently and to indicate what she thought was the most important activity or organizational work she had done since graduation. Since the principal concern of the investigators was the area of attitudes and behavior related to public issues, specific questions were asked regarding participation in political organizations, controversial issues, and community activities.

The largest section of the interview dealt with questions about the respondent's political, social, and economic attitudes, interests, and activities, both in the past and at present. The respondent was asked to recall her attitudes in these areas when she first enrolled in Bennington College, when she graduated from college, and at the current time. She was encouraged to describe the changes and development of such attitudes over this period of time and to describe what she considered to be the most important influences which contributed to her present point of view. In addition to general questions about the respondent's point of view in general terms, specific questions were asked regarding her behavior and attitudes in these areas. For example, she was asked to report her voting record since 1940; to indicate whether she had ever worked for a political candidate or party, and, if so, for whom; to express an opinion regarding major public figures such as President Roosevelt and General MacArthur, and to state how she felt about current issues, such as admitting Red China to the United Nations. Such questions were used to try to get a picture of how interested each woman was in public affairs, how active she was and had been in social and political causes, and what relevant opinions she held currently.

Each woman was asked a smaller number of questions about comparable attitudes and interests of her friends and, if she was married, about those of her husband. Our intent was to assess the amount of social support or opposition that each person recognized regarding her own point of view.

The last part of the interview dealt mainly with the respondent's identification and involvement with Bennington College. She was asked about the friendships with other alumnae that she had maintained over the years, her attitude toward the college, her assessment of her educational experience there, and her interest in the college today.

Finally, additional background questions were asked concerning the respondent's marital status, her husband's occupation, the number of children, and geographical mobility. (See Appendix A for the complete interview.)

Every woman who was interviewed was also given two short questionnaires to complete during the time of the interview: the Political Economic Progressivism (PEP) scale from the original study which she was asked to answer as she thought she had answered it when she was a senior in college; and a set of 45 items selected from the *Omnibus Personality Inventory* (OPI) * to measure "liberalism" and "nonauthoritarianism." The entire 20-item nonauthoritarianism scale (based upon the original "F-scale" of Adorno *et al.*, 1950) was included along with 25 items from the liberalism scale, selected as dealing with political liberalism in the public domain. (See Appendix A for the questionnaires.)

---

* *Omnibus Personality Inventory*—Form C. Center for the Study of Higher Education, University of California, Berkeley, California, 1959.

Nature of the Mailed Questionnaire

The questionnaire * was constructed to be similar to the interview schedule and included questions from the following areas: educational and vocational history, marital status, husband's education and occupation, organizational interests and activities, voting preferences for the elections from 1940 to 1960, husband's voting preferences, current issues, the PEP scale, 15 items from the OPI scales, and an evaluation of the respondent's educational experience at Bennington College. The questionnaire was much shorter than the interview, and in some areas the two are not directly comparable. Whenever possible the same categories were used in analyzing the questionnaires as in analyzing the interviews. (See Appendix A for the questionnaire.)

The 1964 Questionnaire

In late September of 1964 a one-page questionnaire was mailed to graduates of 1938, 1939, and 1940—the population nearly all of whose members had been interviewed three or four years earlier (see Appendix C). Of the 133 graduates for whom addresses were then available, all but nine (7%) returned the questionnaire—all before election day, except for three from overseas.

Respondents were asked to indicate their own preferred presidential candidates. The questionnaire provided for judgments of voting preferences of their husbands, and of their own and their husbands' brothers and sisters. It also asked for information as to whether their sisters and sisters-in-law had attended or graduated from Bennington College.

Data Available from the Original Study

Records from the original study in the 1930's were still available. Everyone who participated in the follow-up study had taken the PEP scale at least once while in college, and this score is the primary indicator of the respondent's conservatism while in college. All those who were interviewed had taken the PEP scale at least twice—once

---

* The phrases "the questionnaire" or "the mailed questionnaire" will always refer to this one, which dates from 1961. The 1964 questionnaire, described later, will always be so labeled.

early in the first year of college and again just before graduation. The PEP scale is the only measure from the first study for which there are complete records for everyone who participated in the follow-up study. Table 3.2 shows what other data were available for them from the original study.

Table 3.2   Information from the Original Study

	Number of Women for Whom There Was Information	
Type of Information	Interview Sample	Questionnaire Sample
1. Political party preference (1938)	101	189
2. Father's party preference in 1930's	96	122
3. Mother's party preference in 1930's	101	130
4. Information about public affairs	138	157
5. Religious preference as freshmen	138	–
6. Sociometric rating–friendship	128	40
7. Rating for "community representative"	128	47
8. "Guess Who" rating on 28 traits	129	26

The sociometric rating was the number of persons who had chosen each respondent as a friend in the 1930's. For most people there was a record of sociometric choice both in terms of who chose them and whom they chose. Sociometric ratings were also collected from the respondents in the interview and the questionnaire, so that it was possible to compare the patterns of choice in the 1930's with the patterns of choice in the follow-up study.

In addition to the friendship choices, there also are records of choices as "community representative." The students were asked to list at least two, and not more than five, persons whom they considered "most worthy to represent the college" at an intercollegiate gathering. The number of choices received as "community representative" was used as an indicator of prestige when the person was in college.

The "Guess Who" ratings provided a source of information about the reputed characteristics of the students. Each of 24 students, selected to represent every cross section and group of importance in the student community of that time, named three individuals from each of three classes of 1938, 1939, and 1940 who were reputedly most extreme on each of 28 traits, as listed in Appendix D. Examples of the items are the following.

Name three individuals who are

    most absorbed in social life, week ends, etc.

    most absorbed in national and international public affairs.

    least concerned about activities of student committees (E.P.C., etc.).

    least likely to lead a life of sheltered leisure.

In addition to the information collected specifically for the study, the college records were used to supplement information about the background of the respondent, or to fill in the missing data when the records from the study were incomplete.

Characteristics of the Participants in the Follow-up Study

The follow-up study was conducted in 1960–1961, 20 to 23 years after the women had graduated, so that most of them were in their early forties when they were interviewed. Among the graduates of 1938, 1939, and 1940, about 90% of the 138 had been married. At the time of the interview, 3% were widowed, 4% were divorced, and 3% were separated from their husbands. About 11% reported that they had been married more than once; 60% of the women who were married had three or more children, and 20% of the married women had at least one child who was younger than five in 1960–1961.

Most of the husbands had gone to college (90%); 40% had earned an advanced degree, and about half of them were graduates from "Ivy League" colleges. The husbands were employed in the following ways: 36% in the professions, such as medicine, law, and teaching; 33% were in business or management positions; 18% were in the fields of communication, entertainment, and the arts; about 7% held positions in government, most of them in the executive branch of the federal government; and the rest (6%) were involved in various other occupations.

Most of the respondents (71%) lived in the northeast United States. About 24% of the women had lived in the same area continuously since graduating from college.

A little over half of the graduates of 1938, 1939, and 1940 had done some graduate work (58%), but only 16% had continued long enough to earn an advanced degree. Only three of the 138 graduates in the study had a Ph.D. or an M.D. degree.

At the time of the interview, 43% of the women were employed either full time or part time. The largest category of employment was the arts, music, and dance, involving 34% of those who were employed. Table 3.3 shows the type of employment they were involved in at the time of the interview.

Only 10% of the women had never been employed since graduating from college. Most of the first jobs they had held were in the area of business, either selling or clerical work, although a few obtained positions in the arts. However, jobs in business were mentioned least often as the job which had been held for the longest period of time.

The most frequently mentioned leisure-time activity was reading, followed by such outdoor activities as sailing and hiking. The women in the interview sample read many magazines; 47% of them mentioned six or more magazines they read regularly. The most frequently mentioned were such current-events magazines as the *Sunday New York Times, Time,* and *Newsweek;* and literary magazines or commentaries, such as the *New Yorker, Atlantic Monthly,* and *Harpers.* Very few mentioned reading women's magazines which deal with fashion or homemaking and gardening.

In regard to politics, 62% of the 138 women preferred the Democratic party, 38% the Republican party. Most of them considered themselves

Table 3.3   Distribution of Employed Women in Various Occupations

	Present Occupation	*N*	Percent
Service	Therapy, social work, counselor, nurse, social-science research	8	13
Business	Public relations, sales, buyer, personnel, accountant, secretary	5	8
Science	Laboratory technician, medical research, specialist, doctor, research scientist	4	7
Communications	Editing, reporting, writing, commercial art, magazine layout	6	10
Education	Nursery school, elementary or high school teacher, school librarian	11	19
Education	College teaching	1	2
Arts	Creative artist, performer, composer, tutor, critic, museum curator	20	34
Self-employed enterprises		4	7
		59	100

liberal or left of center in their point of view. Sixty percent of them preferred John F. Kennedy in the 1960 election.

The characteristics of respondents answering the mailed questionnaire are very similar to those of the interview respondents. Forty-eight percent of the former had attended Bennington College for less than four years—11% for one year, 22% for two years, and 15% for three years. About the same proportion of women were married as among the interview respondents, but a slightly higher proportion of the husbands were in business (40%). Not as many of them had been employed since leaving Bennington College. Eighteen percent had never held a job. About 31% had done graduate work; five had earned a Ph.D. or an M.D. degree. The respondents tended to prefer the Democratic party, but only 52% of them preferred Kennedy (this relatively low figure being mainly attributable to nongraduates). The questionnaire respondents were less likely to call themselves liberal. They also listed fewer magazines that they read regularly. In other characteristics they were very much like the interview respondents.

Since the two samples do not differ greatly in terms of the basic characteristics of the respondents, most of the data presented in the following chapters are obtained from the interview respondents, from whom more complete and more extensive information is available. The questionnaire data provide a basis for comparing graduates and nongraduates, and also supplement some of the interview findings.

4. Change and Stability of Attitudes

A major problem of any study which attempts to compare attitudes toward public affairs over a long interval of time is that of finding comparable measures of attitudes. Attitude scales that were appropriate and valid in 1935 may be quite meaningless in 1960 because so many of the issues have changed. Many of the issues of social and economic reform, which formed the content of the major attitude scale used in the original study, are no longer controversial and they seem dated. None of the measurements of attitudes toward public affairs from the original study seemed appropriate for the follow-up study.

Even though the same attitude scales could not be used in the follow-up study, an attempt was made to build similar scales based on contemporary issues. A series of open-ended questions and Likert-type scales was constructed dealing with the subjects' attitudes about public events and persons. Where possible, the relative conservatism of the respondents with respect to each other is compared to their relative conservatism on analogous attitude scales when in college. The comparisons indicate whether the respondents who were most conservative in their attitudes in college are also the most conservative in their attitudes in 1960.

Among the data collected from the students in the 1930's, the following information was used in the present study: (1) their scores on the Political Economic Progressivism scale (PEP) when they entered college; (2) their scores on the PEP scale when they left college; (3) their changes, during college years, according to the same scale; and (4) their party preferences in 1938.

The following kinds of information were collected in the interview in 1960–1961. First, each woman was asked to describe her present political point of view, her interest, involvement, and preferences in politics. Second, each respondent was asked if she thought she had changed her political attitudes since graduating from college and, if so, what were the principal ways in which she had changed. Whether or not the respondent felt she had changed, she was asked to indicate

22

what she thought had been the important determinants of her present attitudes. All of these data depend on the person's own insight and impressions, and are supplementary to the more objective data.

Another group of questions measured the person's preferences, attitudes, and behavior. Her voting preference for each national election from 1940 to 1960 was obtained. Her feelings and comments with respect to ten public figures were recorded (F. D. Roosevelt, Taft, Truman, Joseph McCarthy, Reuther, Eisenhower, Kennedy, Nixon, MacArthur, and Stevenson). Finally, the attitudes of the women on seven public issues were measured. Using a five-point scale from "strongly approve" to "strongly disapprove," the respondents were asked to tell whether they approved or disapproved of the issues listed in Table 4.1 (see p. 25).

The items were scored by assigning five points for the most conservative response, four points for a moderately conservative response, three points for "no opinion" or "undecided," two points for a moderately nonconservative answer, and one point for the least conservative response. An index was constructed by combining the scores on all seven items. This index is referred to as the "1960 Political Conservatism Index."

An index of "favorability" to conservative and nonconservative figures was also devised. For every "favorable" and "very favorable" response to Taft, McCarthy, Eisenhower, Nixon, and MacArthur, one and two points, respectively, were assigned. These combined scores formed the index of favorability to conservative figures. Similarly, an index of favorability to nonconservative figures was formed from the responses to Roosevelt, Truman, Reuther, and Stevenson. The attitude toward Kennedy was not included in the index, but was used as a separate item.*

---

* Attitudes about Kennedy seemed to be very sensitive to immediate events and appeared to be very changeable. When the interviewing was begun in October, just before the national election, women who said they intended to vote for Kennedy expressed favorable attitudes about him and women who intended to vote for Nixon expressed unfavorable attitudes about Kennedy, as might be expected. Fourteen interviews and ten pretest interviews were given before election day. However, after the election there was an increasing number of women who said they had voted for Nixon and who expressed favorable attitudes about Kennedy. Those who were interviewed right after the inauguration were particularly favorable to Kennedy. However, after the "Bay of Pigs" incident in April 1961, many of the "liberal" respondents began to express doubts about Kennedy and to rate him unfavorably. Over the 12 months of the interviewing, from October 1960 to October 1961, the public image of John F. Kennedy was developing and changing, and the attitudes of the women in the study reflected this change.

The items from the 1960 Political Conservatism Index and the attitudes toward the ten public figures were put into a factor analysis. The factor loadings for a principal axes solution and for a varimax rotation are found in Appendix E. The first factor of the principal axes solution accounts for 84% of the common variance and all of the items contribute to this factor. The indices and the separate items were used in the analysis of the data.

To summarize, the principal measure of political attitudes in the 1930's was the PEP scale. The principal measures of political attitudes in 1960 were the indices of favorability to conservative and to nonconservative public figures, the conservatism index based on attitudes about public issues, and voting preferences over the past 20 years.

Political Attitudes and Activities in 1960

The majority of the graduates of 1938, 1939, and 1940 (including nine who responded by questionnaire) expressed a preference for the Democratic party over the Republican party on national issues, and, in the contest between Nixon and Kennedy, preferred Kennedy. (The percentages are 62%–Democrats, 38%–Republicans; 60%–Kennedy, 38%–Nixon, 2%–no preference.) * When asked to describe their present political points of view, 67% of the women said they were "liberal" or "left of center," 16% said they were in the middle of the road on most issues, and 17% said they were conservative or somewhat conservative.

A majority (57%) felt that they had not changed their points of view or their political attitudes significantly since graduating from college. Of those who felt they had changed, about equal proportions of women said that they had changed in liberal and in conservative directions.

Concerning the issues of the day, the majority of those who were interviewed expressed nonconservative attitudes and preferences. Table 4.1 shows the percentages who approved and disapproved of each issue.

The majority of the interview respondents expressed a favorable opinion of Roosevelt, Stevenson, Kennedy, Reuther, Truman, and Eisenhower, and an unfavorable opinion of McCarthy, Nixon, MacArthur, and Taft.

---

* In a brief questionnaire mailed to these women in October 1964, 90% of 124 respondents said that they preferred Johnson, 2% had no preference, and 8% preferred Goldwater (see Appendix C).

Table 4.1   Distribution of Opinion about Seven Issues

Issues	N	Approve	Disap-prove	No Opinion
* 1. The Supreme Court's decision about desegregation in schools	128	95%	3%	2%
2. The Eisenhower administration's handling of the U-2 incident	137	12%	82%	6%
* 3. Increasing Social Security taxes for medical needs of the aged	136	79%	17%	4%
* 4. Use of the Fifth Amendment in refusing to answer a Congressional Committee's questions about other people's allegedly subversive activities	127	70%	24%	6%
* 5. Admitting Red China to the United Nations	136	62%	29%	9%
* 6. Making greater concessions than the U. S. has offered toward the objective of nuclear disarmament	126	49%	36%	15%
* 7. Negro student sit-ins and picketing	85	85%	12%	3%

* Items for which approval was regarded as nonconservative.

Many of the women had done some work for political organizations or for candidates, or had become involved in some community project, cause, or protest. Sixty percent (79) of the interview sample reported having worked for a candidate or for a political organization at some time since graduating from college. The Democrats and other parties and candidates on the left had received help from most (52, or 66%) of these 79 women, whereas the Republicans and candidates and parties on the right were helped by only 21, or 27% of them. It was not ascertained what party or candidate the other six worked for. Two-thirds of those interviewed reported participating in at least one "liberal cause" or "liberal" organization.

The picture obtained from the interview sample is that of a group of women who favor a "liberal" political philosophy, are interested in public affairs, have become involved enough to have worked in some political capacity, prefer the Democratic party to the Republican party, and think of themselves as "liberal" rather than "conservative."

The results from the mailed questionnaire sample tend to support the picture from the interview sample, but they are less pronounced. A higher percentage of women in the questionnaire sample (although still not a majority, 34%) described themselves as "conservative." Likewise, more (48%) reported having voted for Nixon. Fewer women reported having worked for a political party or candidate (only 31%), and fewer approved of admitting Red China to the United Nations (55%). More of them described their husbands as being conservative (42%).

The questionnaire sample, unlike the interview sample, includes women who attended but did not graduate from Bennington College. Some of them may have left Bennington because they were not happy in the "unconventional, liberal" atmosphere. Whatever the factors involved, those who graduated from Bennington College tend to give fewer "conservative" responses than those who did not graduate. Table 4.2 compares the responses of the graduates and the nongraduates.

Every one of these eight comparisons is in the direction of less conservatism for the graduates. The probability that all eight differences would be in the same direction is less than .001 (by expanded binomial tables).

In describing their present points of view, 43% of the nongraduates described themselves as conservative; 51% described themselves as liberal. This compares to the 17% of the graduates who were inter-

Table 4.2   Percentage of Graduates and Nongraduates Favoring Each Public Figure

Attitude Toward	Graduates 1938, '39, '40		Graduates 1936, '37, '41, '42		Nongraduates 1936–1942	
	N	Percent *	N	Percent *	N	Percent *
Roosevelt	136	82	117	84	89	65
Truman	138	55	117	59	87	42
McCarthy	138	6	117	2	87	8
Eisenhower	137	53	117	55	90	68
Kennedy	136	83	117	84	86	80
Nixon	137	41	117	46	87	60
MacArthur	135	33	115	38	88	46
Stevenson	136	82	117	86	90	79

* The percent favoring the public figure.

viewed and the 32% of the graduates answering the questionnaire who described themselves as conservative. Each set of graduates is significantly less conservative than the nongraduates ($p < .01$ for questionnaire respondents and $<.001$ for interviewees).

The nongraduates also differed significantly ($p < .025$) from the rest of the women in the follow-up study in their voting preference in the 1960 election. Fifty-four percent of the nongraduates voted for Nixon as compared to 40% of the graduates responding by questionnaire or by interview.

In summary, the political attitudes of the majority of women in the interview sample and of the graduates in the questionnaire sample can be described as liberal or not conservative in 1960. The attitudes of the majority of the nongraduates are more conservative than those expressed by the graduates, but they cannot be characterized as conservative on all issues or questions.

The important emphasis of the follow-up study is on identifying change and persistence of attitudes over the period of more than 20 years, rather than just characterizing the political attitudes of the respondents at the later time. The following section deals with a comparison of the attitudes of the respondents in the 1930's and in 1960.

Conservatism on Leaving College and in 1960

The Interview Respondents

Each respondent completed the PEP scale when she first entered Bennington College and again during her final year. Her last PEP score is taken as an indicator of her political conservatism when she left college. The final PEP scores were correlated with respondents' scores on the 1960 Index of Political Conservatism, with a resulting coefficient of .47. Table 4.3 shows the chi-square distribution of the two indices of conservatism for the interview respondents.

The chi-square analysis and the product-moment correlation of .47 indicate that, with few marked exceptions, the respondents who were relatively conservative when they left college are relatively conservative today, and those who were nonconservative are still nonconservative. In general, political attitudes developed or maintained in college by these women persisted over the period between graduation and 1960 without major change.

Another indication of the relative stability of political attitudes during the interval between the two studies is the relationship between

Table 4.3   Relationship of Final PEP Score and 1960 Conservatism Index

Final PEP Score	1960 Conservatism Index		
	Above Median	Below Median	Total
Above median (conservative) *	43 (68%)	20 (32%)	63
Below median (nonconservative) *	23 (35%)	42 (65%)	65
	66	62	128

Chi-square = 13.2; $p < .001$

* Here and elsewhere in this chapter the median (63.5) is that of the total population of students, including interviewees, questionnaire respondents, and nonrespondents in 1960–1961, as of their final response to the PEP scale while in college.

college attitudes and the indices of favorability to conservative and nonconservative public figures. Table 4.4 indicates that women who were above the median in conservatism in the 1930's had significantly more favorable attitudes about the conservative public figures than did the women who scored below the median on conservatism in the 1930's. The product-moment correlation between the final PEP score and the Index of Favorability to Conservative Figures is .42. The women who were conservative when they graduated from Bennington are much more favorable to Taft, McCarthy, Eisenhower, Nixon, and MacArthur than are those who were nonconservative in college.

Analogous findings emerge concerning attitudes toward *non*conserva-

Table 4.4   Relationship of PEP Score to the Index of Favorability to Conservative Figures

Final PEP Score	Favorability to Conservative Figures			
	Above Median	Below Median	Total	Mean
Above median	44 (73%)	16 (27%)	60	3.5
Below median	22 (33%)	44 (67%)	66	1.4
	66	60	126	

Chi-square = 18.58; $p < .001$

$t = 5.0$
$p < .001$

Table 4.5 Relationship of PEP Score to the Index of Favorability to Nonconservative Figures

| Final PEP Score | Favorability to Nonconservative Figures | | | |
	Above Median	Below Median	Total	Mean
Above median	19 (32%)	41 (68%)	60	3.2
Below median	48 (72%)	18 (28%)	66	5.1
	67	59	126	

Chi-square = 19.7; $p < .001$ $t = 5.8$
                                                     $p < .001$

tive figures, as shown in Table 4.5. The correlation between final PEP score and the Index of Favorability to Nonconservative Figures is $-.45$, indicating that those who were conservative when they graduated are much less favorable to the nonconservative figures than those who were nonconservative when they graduated. Women who were nonconservative when they graduated were much more likely to be favorable to Roosevelt, Truman, Reuther, and Stevenson in 1960 than women who graduated from college relatively conservative.

Another indication of political attitudes in 1960 is the preference for presidential candidates in the national election. Although presidential choice may be determined by many factors other than political ideology, it can be taken as a crude indication of political attitudes. The distribution of votes for Nixon and Kennedy in the 1960 election is shown in Table 4.6. Only 18% of the women who scored below the

Table 4.6 Relationship between Final PEP Score and Vote in 1960 Presidential Election

| Final PEP Score | 1960 Vote | | | |
	Nixon	Kennedy	Other	Total
Above median	40 (61%)	24 (37%)	1 (2%)	65 (100%)
Below median	13 (18%)	59 (81%)	1 (1%)	73 (100%)
	53 (38%)	83 (60%)	2 (2%)	138

Chi-square (Nixon vs. Kennedy only) = 25.12; $p < .001$; 1 df median on conservatism in college voted for Nixon in 1960, as compared with 61% of those above the median.

The voting patterns of the alumnae who were interviewed are fairly consistent over the interval from 1940 to 1960. On the whole, those who were relatively conservative when they graduated voted for the Republican candidates and those who were relatively nonconservative at graduation voted for the Democratic candidates. There is a correlation of .48 between the final PEP score and the number of Republican presidential candidates voted for in the years 1940 to 1960. Table 4.7 shows the frequencies. (The complete voting pattern for all six elections is found in Appendix F.) The voting patterns of the women are highly consistent with their attitudes when they graduated from college.

Table 4.8 shows that respondents' self-descriptions, in terms of persistence of a liberal or conservative position or direction of change, were reasonably accurate—that is, in agreement with our indices based upon responses to many specific items. Except for the 23 individuals whose specific responses placed them in the objective category "Became more conservative," the typical self-report was in exact agreement with the objective category (as shown by the underlined figures in the table). Of 121 self-reports, 65 (54%) were "exact hits," the "errors" being thinly scattered among the remaining categories. In statistical terms, 65 exact hits exceeds the chance expectation of 30 at an enormously high level of significance.

These calculations are based upon dichotomies, so that the smallest objective changes are categorized with rather large ones. If we consider only those who were in the upper half of actual change in either direction (thus omitting what may be rather trivial changes), the level of accuracy becomes considerably higher. Of 24 individuals who

Table 4.7   Frequency of Voting Republican Since 1940

	Frequency of Republican Vote			
Final Pep Score	0–1	2–4	5–6	Total
Above median	21 (32%)	14 (22%)	30 (46%)	65 (100%)
Below median	52 (71%)	15 (21%)	6 (8%)	73 (100%)
	73	29	36	138

Chi-square = 28.65; $p < .001$; 2 df

Table 4.8　Relationship between Self-Report and Objective Measure of Change

Self-Report	Objective Measure of Change				
	Remained Liberal	Remained Con-servative	Became More Con-servative	Became More Liberal	Total
Remained liberal	28　(67%)	6　(14%)	8　(35%)	3　(16%)	45
Remained conservative	0	19　(44%)	3　(13%)	3　(16%)	25
Became more conservative	7　(17%)	8　(19%)	7　(30%)	1　(5%)	23
Became more liberal	6　(14%)	7　(16%)	4　(17%)	11　(58%)	28
Other	1　(2%)	3　(7%)	1　(4%)	1　(5%)	6
	42　(100%)	43　(100%)	23　(99%)	19　(100%)	127

had, clearly and unmistakably, become either more conservative or more liberal, 15 (62%) made estimates that were "direct hits," as compared with 6 (25%) that would have been expected by chance. This generally high level of accuracy is accompanied by some outright "errors": two of 11 individuals who had become much more conservative reported having become "more liberal," and one of 13 who had become much more liberal reported herself as becoming more conservative—four "clear misses," altogether.

At the time of the interview, most of the women described themselves as liberal and, in most instances, they felt that they were more liberal than most of the other people in their community. Table 4.9 shows the percentage of women who described themselves as conservative, middle of the road, or liberal.

In replying to the two questions about whether or not she had changed her political attitudes since college and what her present point of view was, each woman gave detailed discussions of her orientations in addition to trying to place herself on a continuum from conservative to middle of the road to liberal. Examples of some of the responses made to these questions follow. (In this summary, Quartile IV refers to the most conservative quarter of all interview respondents, at either time; Quartile III to all others in the more

Table 4.9   Description of Own Political Attitude (1960–1961)

Final PEP Score	Conserva-tive	Middle of road	Liberal	Total
Above median	19 (31%)	12 (20%)	30 (49%)	61 (100%)
Below median	4 (5%)	9 (12%)	61 (82%)	74 (99%)
	23 (17%)	21 (16%)	91 (67%)	135

Chi-square = 19.62; $p < .001$ (2 df)

conservative half; Quartile I to the most liberal quarter; and Quartile II to all others in the liberal half.)

Q60: Changed from Quartile IV (conservative) to II (liberal). "It is difficult to put attitudes into a category. At Bennington I was known as a conservative. Around here our neighbors think we have socialist literature. I have a brother-in-law in the CIA who feels that we are risking our necks to keep the *Progressive* around the house. It depends on who is looking at us whether we are thought to be conservative or liberal. From my own point of view I don't feel that I have changed particularly."

E90: Quartile III (conservative) at both times. "I have become more conservative. I am a registered Republican. I am slightly to the left of center. In the last election I voted for Kennedy. I don't necessarily vote Republican."

F32: Changed from Quartile IV to III (conservative). "I have voted Democratic all along. The Nixon vote wasn't a change in attitude at all. I was just on the fence and was conflicted. I was trying to understand the point of view of the two."

C32: Conservative shift from Quartile II to III. "About the events of that time (1938), my attitudes are not greatly different. I wouldn't any longer say that I was a simple left of center Democrat. Everything has become so complicated. It is no longer important to me to think whether I am taking a liberal or a reactionary position. If I had it to do over again, I would be involved again—you couldn't forsee how it would be. . . . I have voted for the Democrats, often without great joy. The Republicans are worse. I am left of center. I am not as interested in politics as I was in college."

Q35: Remained at Quartile IV (very conservative). "No, I haven't changed—I have always been a conservative and I always will be. I am really not involved in politics. I have no basis for judging who is doing what and why."

B72: Conservative shift from Quartile I to II. "I have remained the same, although I may have become more conservative. My friends think I am a radical. I would say I am an ardent Democrat, definitely liberal and involved in politics. I am more interested than I was in college and I have learned to make my opinions felt in the legislature."

Q21: Liberal shift from Quartile II to I. "I haven't changed a bit since college. I have always been a liberal Democrat. My friends tend to share my political attitudes. Only my relatives don't agree with me."

To summarize from all of the measures of current political belief (the attitudes toward current issues, favorability to conservative and nonconservative public figures, and voting preferences), the women who left college conservative tend to be conservative in 1960, and the ones who left college relatively nonconservative tend to give liberal responses today and tend to describe themselves as "liberal."

Change Comparisons Based on the Mailed Questionnaire

In all of the comparisons between indications of conservatism in the 1930's and the 1960's, responses from the mailed questionnaire correspond rather closely to the responses from the interview. Among both the graduates and the nongraduates, those who were conservative when they left college tend to give conservative responses to the questionnaire in 1961, and those who were not conservative when they left college tend not to give conservative responses to the 1961 questionnaire. (See Appendix F for the data tables.)

There is one exception to the parallel between the responses from the interviews and the responses from the questionnaires. Significantly larger proportions both of graduates and of nongraduates in the questionnaire sample described themselves as conservative than did the women who were interviewed (23%). Table 4.10, which is to be compared with Table 4.9, shows the self-judgments as related to PEP scores.

The data from both the interviews and the questionnaires support the interpretation that very little major change had taken place in the political attitudes of the respondents between the first study in the 1930's and the follow-up study in 1960–1961, as to *relative* standing. Nothing can be said, however, about common influences that may have similarly affected all or most of them—perhaps together with

Table 4.10   Description of Own Political Attitude (Mailed Questionnaire Sample)

Final PEP Score	Conserva-tive	Middle of Road	Liberal	Total
Graduates				
High *	24 (44%)	5 (9%)	26 (47%)	55 (100%)
Low*	2 (7%)	1 (4%)	24 (89%)	27 (100%)
	26 (32%)	6 (7%)	50 (61%)	82

Chi-square = 13.4; $p < .005$ (2 df)

Nongraduates				
Above median	28 (53%)	4 (7%)	21 (40%)	53 (100%)
Below median	6 (22%)	1 (4%)	20 (74%)	27 (100%)
	34 (43%)	5 (6%)	41 (51%)	80

Chi-square = 8.6; $p < .02$ (2 df)

* "High" and "Low" represent, respectively, scores above and below the median of the distribution (64 or above, and 63 or below) of the total population.

other women of their own generation who attended other colleges or who did not attend college.

Other Comparisons of Attitudes in 1938 and in 1961

Another indication of political attitude is the women's political party preference in 1938. Information about party preference in 1938 is missing from about one-fourth of the interview sample, and party preference can be taken as only a rough indication of political attitudes. In addition, the information was collected in 1938, so that some people in the sample indicated their preference when they were sophomores in college and others when they were juniors or seniors. Presumably those who indicated their preference when they were seniors were acting on a more stable and developed political point of view. In spite of these limitations, a comparison of party preference in 1938 and political attitudes in 1960–1961 shows much the same relationship as the comparisons made with the final PEP score. Table 4.11 compares the party preference of the women in

Table 4.11   Comparison of Party Preference in 1938 and 1960

Party Preference in 1938	N	Party Preference in 1960	
		Republican	Democratic
Republican	37	21 (57%)	16 (43%)
Democratic	45	13 (29%)	32 (71%)
Socialist, Communist *	9	1 (11%)	8 (89%)
	91	35 (38%)	56 (62%)

* If those who preferred the Socialist and Communist party in the 1930's are combined with those who preferred the Democratic party, a chi-square value of 7.5 is obtained, with a probability of <.01.

1938 and in 1960. Women who preferred the Republican party in 1938 tend to prefer the Republican party in 1960, and those who preferred the Democratic, Socialist, or Communist party in 1938 tend to prefer the Democratic party today.

The same type of relationship holds true for the women's preferences for president in 1960. Thus 61% of those who preferred the Republican party in 1938 preferred Nixon in 1960, and 73% of those who chose the Democratic, Socialist, or Communist party in 1938 preferred Kennedy in 1960.

Another example of the consistency of political outlook is found in the women's attitudes toward public issues in 1960. Again we find (see Table 4.12) that women who were Republican in 1938 tend to

Table 4.12   Relationship between Party Preference in 1938 and 1960 Conservatism Index

Party Preference in 1938	N	1960 Conservatism Index	
		Above Median	Below Median
Republican	36	24 (67%)	12 (33%)
Democratic	41	16 (39%)	25 (61%)
Socialist, Communist *	9	4 (44%)	5 (56%)

* When the people who preferred the Democratic party are combined with those who preferred the Socialist or Communist party, chi-square = 4.9, $p < .05$.

express conservative attitudes about issues in 1960–1961, and the women who identified with the Democratic, Socialist, or Communist party in 1938 tend not to express conservative attitudes about issues at the later time.

The same consistency in political outlook is found in the respondents' opinions of conservative public figures. Seventy-seven percent of those who preferred the Republican party in 1938 ($N = 34$) were very favorable to the conservative public figures, whereas only 36% of the women who preferred the Democratic, Socialist, or Communist party ($N = 47$) were very favorable to the conservative public figures. The relationship is significant at the .01 level.

Attitude Change in College and 1960 Conservatism

One group of women is of particular interest in the follow-up study —those individuals who changed their political attitudes in college from conservative to nonconservative. Was this change in attitude a stable one which persisted even after the women had graduated from college? Or did the women tend to go back to their original point of view after they had left college?

Using the median of the distribution of the final PEP scores of interview respondents as the criterion for defining conservatism and nonconservatism, we can identify four groups of women. (1) Those who first answered the PEP questionnaire with conservative answers (that is, they scored above the median), but, when answering it again as seniors, gave nonconservative answers (that is, they scored below the median). This is the group of women who changed from relatively conservative attitudes to relatively nonconservative attitudes while in college. (2) Those who were relatively nonconservative on the first administration of the PEP and who remained so on the last test. (3) Those who were relatively conservative on both the first and last administration of the PEP scale. (4) A few who at first answered the questionnaire in a relatively nonconservative way and changed to more conservative answers at the last administration of the PEP. Table 4.13 shows the distribution of scores on the 1960 Political Conservatism Index for each of these four groups of respondents.

The women who became less conservative in college are significantly less conservative in 1960 than the women who remained conservative in college ($t = 3.89$, $p < .001$). A comparison of the 41 women who became less conservative in college with the 20 women who remained

Table 4.13   Relationship between Change in Attitude in College and the
1960 Political Conservatism Index

Attitude Change in College	1960 Political Conservatism Index			
	Above Median	Below Median	Total	Mean
No change, remained conservative	36 (67%)	18 (33%)	54 (100%)	24.8
No change, remained nonconservative	6 (30%)	14 (70%)	20 (100%)	19.0
Became less conservative	15 (37%)	26 (63%)	41 (100%)	19.7
Became more conservative	4 (67%)	3 (33%)	7 (100%)	21.0
	61	61	122	

nonconservative shows that the two groups are very similar in their political attitudes in 1960.

Perhaps the most interesting comparison in this table is between those among initial conservatives who, by the present criterion, remained so in college (54 of them) and the 41 who became less so. In 1960 the former were still significantly more conservative (chi-square = 7.28, $p < .01$). All these comparisons indicate that there was no appreciable tendency for the women who had become less conservative in college to become more conservative again after they left college

Other data which support this conclusion show the relationship of change and persistence of attitude in college to the preference for presidential candidate in 1960 and to the 1960 party preference. In both instances, the women who became less conservative in college resemble the women who remained nonconservative in college in their 1960 preferences and they are significantly different from the women who remained conservative throughout their college years. Tables 4.14 and 4.15 show these relationships. The chi-squares of the difference between those women who remained conservative in college and those who became less conservative are 14.9 (Table 4.14) and 15.4 (Table 4.15), both significant at the .001 level.

These persisting effects of within-college change may also be shown by comparing the predictive value of earliest and latest PEP scores. The correlation between the former and 1960 conservatism scores is

Table 4.14   Relationship between Change in College and 1960 Candidate
Preference

	1960 Candidate Preference		
Change in College	Nixon	Kennedy	Total
No change, remained conservative	35 (65%)	19 (35%)	54 (100%)
No change remained nonconservative	3 (14%)	18 (86%)	21 (100%)
Became less conservative	9 (22%)	31 (78%)	40 (100%)
Became more conservative	2 (33%)	4 (67%)	6 (100%)
	49 (40.5%)	72 (59.5%)	121

only .29, as compared with a highly significant .47 between latest
PEP and 1960 scores. If the effects of later PEP score are "held
constant" by partial correlation, the correlation between initial PEP
and 1960 scores is .01. If the effects of earliest PEP score are similarly
held constant, the correlation between latest PEP and 1960 scores
still remains significant at .39. For the great majority of those whose
attitudes changed during college years, final position in college is a
much better predictor of attitude in 1960 than is initial position.

Table 4.15   Relationship between Change in College and 1960 Party
Preference

	1960 Party Preference		
Change in College	Republican	Democratic	Total
No change, remained conservative	34 (62%)	21 (38%)	55 (100%)
No change remained nonconservative	3 (14%)	18 (86%)	21 (100%)
Became less conservative	8 (19%)	33 (81%)	41 (100%)
Became more conservative	3 (50%)	3 (50%)	6 (100%)
	48 (38%)	75 (62%)	123

Summary: Late 1930's to Early 1960's

When the graduates of 1938, 1939, and 1940 were interviewed in 1960–1961, the majority of them described themselves as liberal rather than conservative in political point of view. Many of them were interested enough in public affairs to have worked in some political capacity. Most of them preferred the Democratic to the Republican party on national issues and expressed liberal attitudes on a number of these issues.

Those women who were relatively conservative in college tended to be relatively conservative in 1960–1961, as measured by their attitudes toward issues, their voting preferences, their opinions of public figures, and their party identifications. Similarly, those women who were relatively nonconservative when they graduated were relatively nonconservative in 1960–1961. Whether or not they had changed their political attitudes while in college, the point of view which characterized them as seniors fairly accurately characterized them in 1960–1961. Thus changes that had taken place in college tended to persist for the next 20-odd years. These conclusions, derived from the interview sample, also apply to the graduates in the questionnaire sample and to a lesser degree to the nongraduates. The general trend is the same, but there are more exceptions to the trend in the questionnaire sample.

Duration and Timing of College Experience

There follow some comparisons of responses in the late 1930's and in the early 1960's in certain categories which revealed attitude differences at the earlier time. They are designed to show that the category differences are still, many years later, associated with attitude differences. We shall show, moreover, that this is true for different kinds of categories that classify the same respondents in totally different ways.

Length of Time Spent in College

It was reported in the original study that the degree of conservatism expressed by students who left the college after two years or less during the 1930's was consistently greater at the time of their departure than that of those who departed after more than two years there (nearly all of whom graduated). Table 4.16 summarizes the

Table 4.16   Mean PEP Scores as of 1930's

	N	Latest Year in College	Mailed Questionnaire
One year in college	18	69.5	77.8
Two years in college	43	70.7	71.2
Three–four years in college	124	62.6	61.9

findings for former students who replied to a questionnaire mailed in 1939 to all students who had been in the college between 1935 and 1938, but were no longer there. Of those who had been in college one to two years, 56% replied, and of those who had been there three to four years, 83%. (High scores on this scale represented relative conservatism.)

Comparable data from all students responding in the 1930's (whether or not they were later to drop out) reveal the same trend. If we assume that responses made in the early autumn reflect the effects of all previous years spent in the college, this is shown by decreases, with added years, in the following mean PEP scores in the autumns of 1935, 1936, 1937, and 1938:

241 sophomores	69.4
166 juniors	65.9
155 seniors	62.4

These values do not differ significantly from those of the freshman and sophomore dropouts. A detailed comparison of continuing and noncontinuing subjects, moreover, indicates that the two groups differed hardly at all in PEP scores (Newcomb, 1943, p. 200). Whether comparing the same individuals as sophomores and, later, as seniors, or comparing sophomores and senior respondents at the same time, all PEP scores decreased significantly during this two-year period.

As to short-range effects, then, it is clear that the longer students remained in college the less conservative their attitudes. Table 4.17, based upon all interview and questionnaire responses in 1960–1961, shows that, in general, these effects persisted. On four of five "issues," as shown in this table, there are significant differences between the four-year and the two-year groups, the latter being more conservative. In view of the fact that the drop-outs, when last responding in college, did not differ significantly in PEP scores from their contemporaries who were later to graduate, it may be concluded not only that

Table 4.17   Percentages Expressing Various Attitudes in 1961 *

| | Years in College | | | Signifi- |
	Four Years	Three Years	One–two Years	cance Levels †
Republican preference, 1960	40.2	44.0	56.7	.05
Voted Republican five or six times, 1940–1960	29.6	40.0	58.0	.001
Opposed to Medicare	25.6	32.8	44.0	.01
Opposed to Red China in U.N.	31.9	60.0	42.0	NS
Opposed to sit-ins	16.3	8.0	36.4	.001

* N's vary only slightly from the following: 255 at 4 years; 25 at 3 years; 66 at 2 years or less.

† Comparing 4 years and 2 years or less.

continued college experiences had a "deconservatizing" effect, but also that this effect persisted.

Table 4.18 presents a more detailed breakdown for nongraduates for whom PEP scores were available shortly before they left the college, with respect to presidential preferences in 1960. The progressive increase in "conservatism" with length of time in college, as reflected both in the 1960 vote and in PEP scores in the 1930's, further illustrates the "deconservatizing" effect of continued years at the college, as shown both then and later.

The differences appearing in Tables 4.17 and 4.18 represent not merely the effects of time spent on the campus, presumably. Actually, in general, juniors and seniors became more caught up in the culture; they constituted a one-third minority who were expected to be "responsible"; they occupied positions (most commonly informal ones)

Table 4.18   Nongraduates' Preferences for Nixon in 1960, and Their Last Available PEP Scores in College

Years in College	N	Percent for Nixon	Mean PEP
3	13	46	65.2
2	37	49	68.8
1	34	62	72.4

of leadership and prestige. They were older, moreover, closer to years of marriage and relative independence from parents, and thus freer to act independently in ways that included differing from their parents in attitudes toward contemporary public affairs in a time of rapid social change.

Early and Late Years of College Experience

In the original study, respondents were students from seven consecutive classes entering from 1932 to 1938. The later classes among them showed some evidence of lesser attitude change during the years covered by the study than the earlier classes. Table 4.19 presents the summarized evidence, based on class averages of changes in PEP scores, for this conclusion. With a single minor exception (sophomore-junior changes on the part of the classes entering in 1934 and in 1935), every possible comparison shows lesser change on the part of the later class. The probability that nine of ten changes would all be in the same direction is less than .001. (It should be noted that these left-to-right comparisons involve totally different individuals.)

Turning now to the responses made in the early 1960's, Table 4.20 shows that the same kinds of differences appear for the graduates, although not for the two-year students. Of ten comparisons of graduates from successive sets of classes (two for each of five "issues"), all but two show the expected differences: later classes make more conservative responses than earlier ones. The probability that 8 of 10 differences will be in the same direction (according to binomial expansions, when there are equal possibilities of differences in the two directions) is .055.

The expected differences also appear for graduates, but not for two-year students as they recall their party preferences in 1940, and

Table 4.19   Mean Changes in PEP Scores

	Class Entered				
	1933	1934	1935	1936	1937
Freshman-Sophomore			6.0	3.8	2.5
Freshman-Junior			10.8	7.3	3.8
Sophomore-Junior		4.2	4.4	3.9	
Sophomore-Senior		6.6	5.8	3.8	
Junior-Senior	8.5	2.4	0.9		

Table 4.20 Political Attitudes Reported in 1960–1961, Categorized by Early and Late Years of College Attendance

Years of College Attendance	As of 1940		As of 1960	
	N	Percent	N	Percent
I. Percent of Preferences for Republican party				
Four years, entered				
1932 or 1933	60	40.0	64	31.2
1934–1936	138	49.3	138	38.0
1937 or 1938	40	67.5	47	53.2
One–two years, entered				
1934–1936	30	73.3	31	51.6
1937 or 1938	25	56.0 *	29	62.1

	N	Percent
II. Voted Republican Five or Six Times, 1940–1960		
Four years, entered		
1932 or 1933	64	21.9
1934–1936	138	26.1
1937 or 1938	48	39.5
One–two years, entered		
1934–1936	32	62.5
1937 or 1938	30	56.2 *

	Opposed Medicare		Opposed Red China in UN		Opposed Sit-ins	
	N	Percent	N	Percent	N	Percent
III. Miscellaneous Issues						
Four years, entered						
1932 or 1933	64	25.0	64	32.8	64	10.5
1934–1936	136	17.0 *	136	29.5 *	85	11.8
1937 or 1938	48	31.0	48	42.9	48	22.9
One–two years, entered						
1934–1936	36	38.9	36	47.2	36	36.1
1937 or 1938	30	40.4	30	46.8 *	30	36.2

* Reversals of the secular trend.

as they report their husbands' political preferences. The two-year students, however, show very small differences, and both are subject to distortion in the reporting (after 20 years, in the one instance, and for another person in the other).

It is hardly surprising that the effects of two years or less at the college, more than 20 years earlier, are about the same regardless of when those years occurred. Indeed, it may be argued that the surprising thing is that even for graduates these effects remain.

We have no objective evidence, unfortunately, as to why change away from conservatism was more pronounced during the early rather than the late years of the 1930's. Two kinds of reasons seem plausible, however. First, the earlier years were characterized by a rather remarkable cohesiveness and *esprit de corps,* almost certainly due in part to the college's newness. (When the original study began, the first entering class was beginning its senior year; its experiences, as its members knew, would never be repeated by anyone else.) These characteristics on the part of any group are commonly associated with susceptibility to influence by group norms.

The second plausible reason has to do with the content of the PEP scale, upon which most of our evidence for within-college changes rests: it dealt almost exclusively with the domestic issues that were made prominent by the depression (at its height when the college opened, and still with us when the study began) and by the advent of the New Deal. By the later 1930's, the "psychology of the *fait accompli*" was becoming evident in the college as elsewhere, with an associated decline of controversy and concern over these kinds of issues. Furthermore, international issues, beginning with the civil war in Spain and soon followed by Hitler's international forays, were beginning to supersede concern over domestic controversies.

Whatever the reasons, it is almost certain that community concern was pointed less in the late 1930's than it had been previously toward the kinds of issues tapped by the PEP scale. The fact that these differential concerns persisted, in the sense that earlier graduates were still less conservative about domestic political issues after more than 20 years than later ones, strongly suggests that the political attitudes of Bennington graduates, as of the early 1960's, were in part an outcome of their membership in the college community many years before.

5. Bennington Graduates Compared with Women Like Them in Other Respects

This chapter deals with a single question: How do our Bennington graduates (especially those of 1938, 1939, and 1940, who constituted our interview population) now compare with other women who resemble them as closely as possible *except* in having graduated from Bennington some two decades ago? The greater the differences in contemporary attitudes between our graduates and "control" populations, the more surely we can attribute to the former some continuing effects of their years at Bennington.

The 1960 Election

The availability of national election statistics in the presidential election of 1960 provides a basis of comparison with the preferences of our respondents, although not in any simple, direct way. For example, the 60–40% preference for Kennedy on the part of all the responding graduates of the classes of 1936 through 1942 is significantly greater (at the level of .001) than if they had shown the 50–50% division of the national election returns. But this fact is almost irrelevant to the question of whether these women's preferences were different from those of their non-Bennington peers. We must therefore examine some of the complicating factors.

Most important are the facts that (1) our respondents typically fall well within the top 1%, socio-economically, of the American population; (2) they are nearly all from Protestant backgrounds; and (3) nearly two-thirds of them are urban or suburban dwellers in the northeastern part of the country. Moreover, our respondents were women in their fifth decade of life, most of them college graduates. All of these considerations necessarily affect any estimates of the voting preferences of "non-Bennington women otherwise like our respondents."

We have obtained (from the Survey Research Center of the University of Michigan, 1965) actual frequencies of expressed preferences of a national sample of American adults, both before and after each of two elections. But the frequencies of respondents within these samples who are adequately matched with our own are pitifully small. For example, the 1960 national sample included five women in their forties reporting some college education who grew up outside the South (four of whom preferred Nixon). Such scanty information is altogether undependable for our purposes, and we have therefore examined the national data in several different ways, in order to answer the question: How did non-Bennington women, otherwise resembling our respondents, actually vote in 1960 and in 1964? Since the determinants of preferences in these two elections were different in important ways, we treat them separately.

The Michigan Survey Research Center's 1960 national sample *
provides breakdowns according to nine demographic variables, in all of which our population differs from the total adult population in America. In addition, all comparisons are separately presented for voters and for nonvoters. In view of the fact that 90% of all college-educated respondents are reported as actual voters (as compared with 74% of all others), we shall henceforth compare the Bennington population with actual voters only.

Within the voting segment of the national sample, only two of the nine demographic variables were clearly associated with significantly greater or lesser preference for Kennedy than the 50% that he received at the polls. The other seven are as follows (described in terms of the category most representative of our Bennington population):

> Female
> White †
> In the highest quarter of income level
> In the 35–44 age bracket
> Employed in a professional or managerial capacity ‡

---

* According to this sample, 49% of all actual voters (46% of women) preferred Kennedy. Of all voters whose votes were ascertained, and were not for a minor candidate, more than 49% were for Kennedy. We are indebted to Dr. Philip E. Converse for these data.

† Whites did not differ significantly from the 50% that Kennedy actually received.

‡ Refers to husbands, in the case of married women.

Living in a metropolitan area
Living in the Northeast

The remaining two variables, both characteristic of Bennington graduates, that did distinguish them from the national sample were as follows:

College graduates   35% of national sample for Kennedy
Protestants   36% of national sample for Kennedy

We do not have a breakdown for individuals who were both college graduates and Protestants, but since the two variables are by no means perfectly correlated, their preferences for Kennedy would almost certainly be less than 30%.

Two joint breakdowns are available from the national sample, however. First, in the northeastern states no more than 15% of Protestant voters preferred Kennedy (as compared with 65%, 51%, and 58% in the Midwest, South, and West, respectively). The finding is relevant because 64% of our Bennington interviewees lived in the ten northeastern states, and nearly all of them came from Protestant families.

Second, among national-sample respondents in the metropolitan areas of New York and Boston, 62% of the voters chose Kennedy. This finding is not inconsistent with the preceding one. Together, they probably stem from the facts that (1) the populations of greater New York and greater Boston are (relative to other metropolitan areas in the Northeast) heavily Catholic; and (2) Catholics in all regions preferred Kennedy by large margins (82% of the total sample, as compared with 36% of Protestants). In any case, it is quite clear that the Bennington graduates whom we interviewed are, demographically, much more like the subpopulation "Northeast, Protestant, college-educated" than like "Northeast, metropolitan, relatively heavily Catholic, predominantly noncollege." In short, 15% of Kennedy preferences (northeastern Protestants) is a closer estimate for our purposes than 62% (northeastern metropolitan).

By way of informal support, rather than as "proof," we cite the following small-number breakdowns from the 1960 national-sample study.

	Percent preferring Kennedy
Nonsouthern women, completed college	17% ($N = 30$)
Nonsouthern women, some college, age 40–49	26% ($N = 19$)
Nonsouthern women, some college, age 40–49, Northeast	0% ($N = 5$)

These various findings, no one of which is conclusive in itself, lead us to conclude that no more than 30% of "women like our Bennington graduates of 1938, 1939, and 1940" voted for Kennedy in 1960. This is about half of the 60% of our interview respondents, all of whom were Bennington graduates in the late 1930's, who preferred Kennedy.

The 1964 Election

According to the national sample data for the 1964 election, no single demographic variable accounted for as much deviation from the actual election returns as did Protestant affiliation or college education in 1960. The following three of them, however, showed deviations of nine or more percentage points from the 62% of the vote that President Johnson actually received in 1964.

	Johnson preference
All college educated	53%
All metropolitan residents	71%
All respondents in Northeast states	73%

Among Protestants in the Northeast, the figure was 58% and, in metropolitan areas of the Northeast, 76%. We have indicated, in considering the 1960 election, why our Bennington population seems to resemble the former of these populations more closely than the latter.

Turning to the small-number data in the subcategories that most closely correspond to our Bennington population, the following are relevant for Protestant women who grew up outside the South.

	Johnson preference	
	N	Percent
Completed college	27	41
Any college education, age 40–49	14	36

We have been cautioned * not to put much confidence in these latter figures, which are, in fact, more characteristic of the Midwest and Far West than of the Northeast. We are assured that "the rest of the data make it clear that college graduates in the Northeast of northeastern background voted very heavily for Johnson, despite a typical Republican background."

---

* We are particularly grateful to Dr. Philip E. Converse for his expert help in assessing the national sample data.

Another analysis by Converse (unpublished) leads us to the same conclusion. He shows that not only college education but also "quality" of college attended was associated with preference for Johnson over Goldwater. (His index, as developed by the American Association of University Professors, is now a fairly standard one.) Among graduates of colleges rated A and B, 20 of 34 (59%) were "particularly unhappy" at the selection of Goldwater as the Republican nominee, as compared with 24 of 60 (40%) of graduates from colleges rated C to G. "Among college graduates in the Northeast," he observes, "the large majority come from the first class of schools." These considerations suggest that a figure between 76% (all metropolitan residents of the Northeast) and 53% (all college graduates) is the most likely estimate of preferences by a population like our respondents except in attendance at Bennington College. Our best estimate is that about two-thirds of the total population of "women like our graduates of the late 1930's" voted for Johnson, as compared with 90% of our interview sample.

There is probably no population more closely resembling our interviewees than their sisters and sisters-in-law. * We have therefore compared this population, distinguishing between those who did and those who did not attend Bennington, with our interviewees on preferences just before the 1964 election (comparable data were not obtained in 1960). Bennington graduates among these female relatives very closely resemble the interviewees' 90% preference for Johnson, whereas those who attended but did not graduate from Bennington are much like those who never attended. The preferences of these several populations are shown in Tables 5.1 and 5.2.

The implications of Table 5.1 are consistent with our maximum estimates, based on national samples, of the preferences of women like our interview respondents except in having graduated from Bennington. Women who graduated in 1938, 1939, and 1940 (together with one-fifth as many who graduated a very few years earlier or later) were clearly and significantly less favorable to Goldwater, 25 years later, than other women closely resembling them in family backgrounds who never attended Bennington, or who were non-graduating students there.

One other question remains. Did our Bennington graduates come from families which, in spite of demographic similarities, were somehow different from the families of their sisters-in-law? Their families

---

* Including both brothers' wives and husbands' sisters. See Appendix C for 1964 questionnaire.

Table 5.1   Bennington Graduates Compared with Other Female Relatives
of Interviewees *

1964 Preference	Graduates	All Others	Total
Johnson	134 (89%)	177 (73%)	311 (79%)
Not Johnson	17 (11%)	66 (27%)	83 (21%)
	151 (100%)	243 (100%)	394 (100%)

Chi-square = 14.12; $p < .001$; 1 df

* The 151 graduates include 124 "own" responses by interviewees; all others in this table are judgments by the latter about their relatives.

might, in particular, have been more venturesome, more "progressive," more open to new experience than those of their sisters-in-law. If so, then their distinctiveness in 1964 might be attributable to family backgrounds rather than to four years of Bennington experience. Our 1964 data provide no support for this possibility. Table 5.2 shows that sisters and sisters-in-law hardly differed at all, either for Bennington graduates (85% vs. 86%) or for others (75% vs. 72%) in 1964 preferences.

In summary, our interview respondents, their sisters, and their sisters-in-law who have graduated from Bennington differ significantly from respondents' sisters and sisters-in-law who have not graduated from Bennington. Furthermore, questionnaire respondents who were Bennington graduates differed in about the same ways from nongraduates in 1960. The 1964 responses showed that Bennington gradu-

Table 5.2   Comparison of Sisters and Sisters-in-Law

	Johnson	Not Johnson	Total
Own Sisters			
Bennington graduates	17 (85%)	3 (15%)	20 (100%)
Others	40 (75%)	13 (25%)	53 (100%)
	57 (78%)	16 (22%)	73 (100%)
Sisters-in-law			
Bennington graduates	6 (86%)	1 (14%)	7 (100%)
Others	137 (72%)	53 (28%)	190 (100%)
	143 (73%)	54 (27%)	197 (100%)

ates resembled nonsiblings who were also graduates more closely than they resembled their own sisters who were nongraduates.

We therefore conclude either that self-selection on the part of *individuals* who went and stayed at Bennington—not selection of families from which they came—and/or spending four years there had effects that were still discernible after 25 years. As to the former possibility, we have no direct evidence. It is conceivable that, within families of sisters, those who were somehow predisposed to become and/or remain "liberal" were more likely than their sisters with lesser predispositions of the same kind to go to Bennington and to graduate.

It is possible, however, to test the more general hypothesis that Bennington students who were later to graduate were more predisposed to adopt liberal attitudes than were those who were later to drop out of college. If the latter, while they were still in college, had been less influenced in the nonconservative direction than the former, then we might infer that both leaving college in the 1930's and relative conservatism in the 1960's stemmed from a common predisposition. If, however, the drop-outs-to-be were indistinguishable, as long as they were in college, from those who were later to graduate, then the latters' relative liberalism could more probably be attributed to spending more time at Bennington.

The relevant evidence is provided by PEP scores in 1936 and 1937. Mean scores in *previous* years can be compared for in-college respondents and for those no longer in college in each of these years. As shown in Table 5.3, neither in 1936 nor in 1937 did the two groups differ at all.

Insofar as these findings apply to those particular students within the population of drop-outs who happened to be sisters or future sisters-in-law of other Bennington students, we can at least conclude

Table 5.3 Comparisons of Earlier PEP Scores for Drop-outs and Continuing Students

	Mean Score in Previous Years	
	N	Mean
Still in college in 1936	154	70.3
No longer in college in 1936	55	70.3
Still in college in 1937	99	70.6
No longer in college in 1937	63	71.2

that, at the time of leaving college, the nongraduating sisters and future sisters-in-law had been affected by their years at Bennington in the same ways as those who were later to graduate. At least for the drop-out students, whose 1964 attitudes were reported as being very similar to those of female relatives who never attended Bennington, the available evidence does not support the hypothesis that our interview population was self-selected for special susceptibility to liberal political attitudes.

Neither families from which our Bennington graduates came nor self-selection within those families appears to account for the continuing "liberalism," after 25 years, of the graduates of 1938, 1939, or 1940. We therefore conclude that the simple fact of four years of experience in the college had a good deal to do with it.

6. Factors Associated with Change: Social Support during Post-College Years

This chapter is devoted mainly to the human environments of our interview respondents since graduation from college. We shall, in general, be comparing women who showed noticeable changes during this period with those who did not.

We had predicted that those women who had experienced a large change in political attitudes while in college would tend to maintain that change. The assumption was that large changes during the college years were likely to have been accompanied by a reorganization of important values sufficiently extensive to support persistence. It was further assumed that this new value system would be important enough to influence post-college interests, jobs, community participation, and the choice of friends, including those from whom husbands were selected. If so, these students would tend to create for themselves a social environment which would nurture and reinforce the value systems with which they left college.

To the extent that we can assess the characteristics of post-college social environments, it appears that most of the women had just this sort of experience, though in varying degrees. Those who were able to maintain attitudes similar to the ones with which they left college were, by and large, women who lived in social environments which supported those attitudes, and those who changed their attitudes since college were primarily individuals who associated with others who held different opinions. The data presented in this chapter in support of these conclusions were obtained in interviews with the graduates of 1938, 1939, and 1940.

We look first at the prediction that those women, among the 129 interviewed, who had experienced a large change in political attitudes while in college would tend to maintain that change after college. Of these, 43 had scored at least 13 points lower on the PEP scale as

53

seniors than as freshmen in college. This represents a relatively large drop in "conservatism," amounting to a change of one standard deviation or more. Even with such a large change, 10 of these 43 still had higher scores on the PEP scale as seniors than most of their peers in college. In 1960–1961, 28 of these 43 (65%) were below the median on conservatism, and 15 (35%) were above the median. Of the 15 who became much less conservative in college and were relatively conservative in 1960–1961, 11 were married to someone who was conservative, or, if not married, had mainly conservative friends. For the other four, the political attitudes of husbands or friends were not ascertained.

Of the 28 who became much less conservative in college and were relatively nonconservative in 1960–1961, 24 were married to someone who was nonconservative, or, if not married, had friends who were predominantly nonconservative. For three of them, the political attitudes of friends and husbands were not ascertained. Only one woman from this group of 28 was known to be married to someone who was relatively conservative.

These figures suggest first that the majority who experienced a large change toward nonconservatism while in college held nonconservative political attitudes when surveyed in 1960–1961. Second, the data suggest that those who maintained nonconservative attitudes over the years lived in social environments which supported their nonconservatism; and, conversely, those who became more conservative again after college lived in social environments which supported conservatism.

The rest of the chapter will be devoted to exploring the relationship between political attitudes and social support for all of the women in the study. Eighty-six others were included in the study who, as college students, did not experience such large changes in political attitudes as the 43 just described. We shall also examine their current political attitudes, as related to the points of view of their husbands and their associates.

Attitudes of Husbands

The most important and influential member of the social environment for most of these women is her husband. Ideally, we would have interviewed the husbands, independently of the wives, but it was economically impractical and too difficult to arrange. Instead, each woman was asked to report how her husband felt about various political questions, what he thought about the issues, his opinion of the public figures, and how he had voted in the last 20 years. In some cases, the wives did not know how their husbands felt about the issues, and a few of them refused to answer for their husbands.

Since all of our information about the husband's political attitudes comes from the wife's report, there is a possibility of bias and distortion. There may be a tendency for the respondents to underestimate the differences in opinion between themselves and their husbands. In any case there is close agreement between the political attitudes of the women in our sample and reported political attitudes of their husbands. The product-moment correlation between the 1960 Conservatism Index reported for the husband and the 1960 Conservatism Index of the wife is .85. Ninety-one percent of 113 married couples, according to respondents, voted for the same candidate in the 1960 election, and 90% of 103 in 1964; 58% of the couples voted for the same candidate in all of the six presidential elections from 1940 through 1960.

Husbands' Attitudes as Related to Wives' Histories

Table 6.1 shows the relationship between the husband's political conservatism and the change or persistence of the wife's attitude since leaving college. The mean conservatism score of the husbands of the 30 women who remained conservative after college (Group a)

Table 6.1 Relationship of Wife's Change in Attitude and Husband's Political Conservatism

Final PEP Score in College †	1960 Conservatism Index †	Husband's 1960 Conservatism Index *			
		Above Median	Below Median	Total	Mean
(a) Above median	Above median	29	1	30	29.8
(b) Above median	Below median	1	13	14	17.2
(c) Below median	Above median	15	1	16	27.2
(d) Below median	Below median	6	24	30	18.1
		51	39	90	

* The husband's attitudes were reported by the wife.

† The median of final PEP scores is that of the total population of students replying in college, as in Chapter 4. The median for 1960 Conservatism Index is that of interviewees only.

is 29.8 as compared to a score of 17.2 for the husbands of the 14 women who became less conservative since college (Group b); $t = 6.6$, $p < .001$.

The average score of the husbands of the 16 women who became more conservative since college (Group c) is significantly higher than the mean score of the husbands of the 30 who remained nonconservative (Group d); $t = 4.7$, $p < .001$. The difference in mean scores of the husbands whose wives became more conservative (Group c) and the husbands of those who became less conservative (Group b) is also statistically significant; $t = 4.8$, $p < .001$. It is clear from Table 6.1 that the women who became less conservative after college were married to men who were on the average less conservative than the husbands of those who remained conservative over the years. Similarly, the women who became more conservative since college were married to men who were reported as more conservative than the husbands of the women who remained nonconservative after college. (See p. 61 for an analysis of predictability from final PEP score and from husbands' 1960 attitudes.)

Although there is a statistically high degree of agreement between spouses, such differences as do exist turn out not to be random. A pair-by-pair comparison shows that wives tend to report their husbands as more conservative than themselves. The mean difference in scores on the 1960 Political Conservatism Index is 1.4; $t = 3.51$, and $p < .001$ with 89 df.

When the sample is broken down into the four groups—those who remained conservative, those who remained nonconservative, those who became conservative, and those who became nonconservative after college—one finds some differences in the tendency to attribute greater conservatism to their husbands than to themselves. Table 6.2 shows that the husbands of those who remained conservative and the husbands of the women who remained nonconservative are reported by their wives to be more conservative than themselves, on the average. It is only with the group of women who became less conservative after college that we find virtually no such differences. The fact remains, however, that the attitudes reported for husbands were relatively nonconservative. The average differences in scores were small, even though statistically significant.

Each wife was also asked to report how her husband felt about a number of public figures (see Chapter 4); these responses were scored in the same manner as for the women themselves. Using the median obtained from the combined distribution of the couples'

Table 6.2   Degree of Husbands' Conservatism Relative to Four Groups
of Wives

	Mean Difference	t-value	p	N
(a) Wife conservative in college, also in 1960–1961	1.6	2.11	.05	30
(b) Wife conservative in college, not conservative in 1960	0.3	0.42	n.s.	14
(c) Wife not conservative in college, conservative in 1960	1.9	1.88	.10	16
(d) Wife not conservative in college, nor in 1960	1.4	2.19	.05	30
				90

scores, the men were divided into two groups, those who scored above this median and those who scored below this median on favorability to conservative figures. As shown in Table 6.3, a relatively high proportion of the husbands of the women who remained conservative favor the conservative public figures (for Groups a and b; chi-square = 19.5, $p < .001$). Other differences in this table are not significant.

Table 6.3   Husband's Favorability to Conservative Figures, as Related
to Wife's Change in Attitude

Final PEP Score in College	1960 Conservatism Index	Husband's Favorability to Conservative Figures *		Total
		Above Median †	Below Median †	
(a) Above median	Above median	31 (97%)	1 (3%)	32 (100%)
(b) Above median	Below median	5 (33%)	10 (67%)	15 (100%)
(c) Below median	Above median	11 (55%)	9 (45%)	20 (100%)
(d) Below median	Below median	12 (37%)	20 (63%)	32 (100%)
		59	40	99

* The husband's attitudes were reported by the wife.
† Median was determined from the combined distribution of scores for men and women.

Table 6.4   Husband's Choice in 1960 Election as Related to Wife's Change in Attitude

Final PEP Score in College	1960 Conservatism Index	Husband's Choice in 1960 Election *		
		Nixon	Kennedy	Total
(a) Above median	Above median	29 (88%)	4 (12%)	33 (100%)
(b) Above median	Below median	3 (20%)	12 (80%)	15 (100%)
(c) Below median	Above median	11 (55%)	9 (45%)	20 (100%)
(d) Below median	Below median	6 (19%)	25 (81%)	31 (100%)
		49	50	99

* The husband's choice is reported by the wife.

Table 6.4, in similar fashion, shows the relationship between husbands' voting preferences in 1960 and the relative stability of their wives' attitudes since college. A greater proportion of the husbands of the women who remained conservative since college preferred Nixon than of the husbands of those who became less conservative; chi-square $= 18.4, p < .001$. And the husbands of the women who became more conservative since college (Group c) were more likely to prefer Nixon than the husbands of the wives in Group d who remained nonconservative; chi-square $= 6.9, p < .01$.

This relationship is true not only of the 1960 election, but of the other elections from 1940 through 1960, as shown in Table 6.5, in which exactly the same pattern appears as in Table 6.4.

Table 6.5   Relationship of Wife's Change in Attitude and the Voting Pattern of Husband

Final PEP Score in College	1960 Conservatism Index	Number of Times Husband Voted Republican * 1940–1960			
		0–1	2–4	5–6	Total
(a) Above median	Above median	3 (9%)	8 (24%)	22 (67%)	33 (100%)
(b) Above median	Below median	8 (54%)	5 (33%)	2 (13%)	15 (100%)
(c) Below median	Above median	9 (45%)	3 (15%)	8 (40%)	20 (100%)
(d) Below median	Below median	22 (71%)	6 (19%)	3 (10%)	31 (100%)
		42	22	35	99

Chi-square $= 33.7, p < .001$, 6 df
Comparison of Groups a and b; chi-square $= 14.6, p < .001$, 2 df
Comparison of Groups c and d; chi-square $= 6.6, p < .05$, 2 df

* The voting pattern of the husband is reported by the wife.

Similar results are found when a switch in party preference is used as the indicator of change in political point of view. Thus the husbands of the women who switched from the Republican to the Democratic party are much less conservative than the husbands of those who were Republican in 1938 and also in 1960. Likewise the husbands of the women who were Democrats in 1938 and Republicans in 1960 are much more conservative than the husbands of the wives who remained Democrats over the years.

Spouses' Influence upon Each Other

One cannot safely infer from close agreements that wives changed their political attitudes to agree with their husbands' points of view. It is also possible that (1) the women married men of the same political orientation as themselves; or (2) the wives changed their political opinions after marriage; or (3) the husbands changed their political opinions after marriage. By comparing the voting preferences of the women before and after marriage with the reported voting preferences of the husband before and after marriage, a more detailed picture of their interaction regarding political attitudes can be obtained.

Complete information about voting preferences is available for only 68 couples. In this subsample, 63% (43) of the women married men with the same voting preferences as themselves; 37% of the women (25) married men with a preference for the opposing party. The subsequent data on these two groups are shown in Table 6.6. The

Table 6.6   Change and Stability of Party Preference on the Part of Husbands and Wives

I. Married man with same party preference	43
1. Neither wife nor husband changed parties after marriage 39	
2. Both husband and wife changed parties after marriage 2	
3. Wife changed parties after marriage, husband did not 2	
II. Married man with different party preference	25
4. Wife changed to husband's party after marriage	
(7 Democratic, 7 Republican) 14	
5. Husband changed to wife's party after marriage	
(6 became Democratic, 2 Republican) 8	
6. Husband and wife continued to have different party preferences (wives Democratic, husbands Republican, in all cases) 3	

Table 6.7   Husband-Wife Similarity in Party Preference

I. Women who remained in the same party 1940–1960		41
1. Married man of same party preference	31	
2. Married man of different party preference, husband changed to wife's party	7	
3. Married man of different party preference, husband and wife continued with different parties (husband Republican, wife Democratic, in all cases)	3	
II. Women who changed party preference 1940–1960		27
4. Wife changed to same party as husband after marriage (7 Democratic, 7 Republican)	14	
5. Wife changed before marriage, married man who shared new party preference	8	
6. Wife changed before marriage, married man of opposite party, husband changed to wife's new party preference	1	
7. Married man who shared party preference, both switched after marriage	2	
8. Married man of same party, wife changed, husband did not change	2	

same data, differently organized, appear in Table 6.7, in which women who remained in the same political party are compared with those who changed.

Among the 68 couples for whom full information is available, all but five were in agreement in 1960–1961, although 25 of them had differed at the time of marriage. Fourteen wives changed to agree with husbands, eight husbands to agree with wives, and two wives in initial agreement changed although their husbands did not. Considering also the three couples who continued to differ, it may be concluded that wives "followed" husbands in 14 instances (category 4 in Table 6.7), and were "independent" in 13 instances (categories 2, 3, 6, 8), whereas 41 couples were "collaborative." Of the 27 wives who changed party preferences, 22 changed to agree with their husbands—14 after marriage and 8 before (although we cannot be sure that the premarriage shifts represent influence by fiancés).

Wives' Attitudes in College as Related to Husbands' Present Attitudes

Husbands' attitudes in 1960–61 are also related to their wives' attitudes as of more than 20 years earlier. Thus, for example, 67%

of the women who scored above the median on conservatism in college were married to men who preferred Nixon in the 1960 election, whereas only 33% of the women who scored below the median on conservatism in college were married to men who preferred Nixon. The chi-square value of this relationship is 9.04, with a p value of less than .005. Thus in two-thirds of all cases it would have been possible to predict correctly, 20-odd years ago, whether a future husband's attitudes would be in the more or the less conservative half of the 1960–1961 distribution, simply by knowing in which half of the distribution the future wife belonged in the 1930's.

This rather strong relationship rests, of course, *both* upon the persistence of most women's attitudes over the years and upon their tendency to select and be selected by men having attitudes like their own. These two processes, as many lines of evidence suggest, are interdependent. That is, the persistence of their attitudes during late college and early postcollege years had something to do, directly or indirectly, with their "choice" of husbands who, typically, in turn helped to provide an environment supportive of those attitudes.

Attitudes of Friends

We hypothesized that friends were another important influence upon respondents' attitudes. It was not possible to interview their friends (with rare exceptions later noted). Hence our information about friends' attitudes comes only from respondents, each of whom was asked how most of her close friends felt about the several current issues and public figures. About 40% of the interviewees reported that they did not know how their friends felt, and were not willing to guess. An analysis of responses by the 60% who did reply shows that in all four groups—those who had remained conservative, remained nonconservative, become more conservative, or become less conservative since college—women reported significantly more conservatism on the part of their friends than on their own part. (See Appendix H for analysis of these data.)

Table 6.8 shows a distribution of scores on the 1960 Political Conservatism Index for the friends of the women in each of the four groups of attitude change or persistence. Respondents who became less conservative after college report attitudes for their friends that are significantly lower on conservatism than those reported for the friends of the women who remained conservative ($t = 4.16, p < .005$). Also women who became more conservative after college report

Table 6.8   Relationship of Respondent's Change in Attitude and Friends' Political Conservatism

Final PEP Score in College	1960 Conservatism Index	Friends' 1960 Conservatism Index [*]		Mean
		Above the Respondents' Median	Below the Respondents' Median	
(a) Above median	Above median	27	0	30.2
(b) Above median	Below median	5	10	22.0
(c) Below median	Above median	14	0	27.3
(d) Below median	Below median	11	20	19.7
		57	30	

[*] The friends' attitudes are reported by the respondent.

attitudes for their friends that are significantly more conservative than the attitudes of the friends of those who remained nonconservative ($t = 3.37$, $p < .005$).

Even though most of the women report attitudes for their friends that are more conservative than their own, they do tend to see some similarity between their own and their friends' beliefs. Friends of women who are not conservative are reported to be much less conservative than are the friends of the women who are conservative (chi-square = 37.9, $p < .001$). The ability of the respondents to report accurately how their friends feel about various issues probably varies with the frequency with which they discuss political issues, how important politics is to them, and how important it is for them to find support and agreement for their own points of view among their associates. Whether or not the reports are accurate, they are useful indicators of how the respondents perceive their friends. Only 8% of the women reported attitudes for their friends that were less conservative than their own.

Some of the close friends of the women in the study were other Bennington College alumnae who were also participants in the follow-up study. It is therefore possible to compare the attitude scores of the respondents with those of these friends. On the basis of the 1960 Conservatism Index our procedure was to classify the respondents in three groups: (1) those more than half of whose friends scored above the median on conservatism; (2) those more than half of whose friends scored below the median on conservatism; (3) those half of whose friends scored above the median and half below the median on conservatism. The proportion of women whose friends were classified in each of these groups is shown in Table 6.9. There is a tendency for those who became conservative since college to have friends from Bennington who are also conservative and for the women who became less conservative to have friends from Bennington who are not conservative. These findings are independent of respondents' judgments.

The relationship between respondents' conservatism and that of their Bennington friends in 1960 can most easily be shown by combining the first and third rows of Table 6.9, and comparing them with the second and fourth rows, assigning half of the cases in the third column to the first and half to the second column, as follows:

	Friends at or above median	Friends at or below median	Total
Respondents above median	34	24	58
Respondents below median	20.5	29.5	50
	54.5	53.5	108

The chi-square value of this distribution is 4.06, significant at less than .05. Thus there is a clear tendency, although not a marked one, for the respondent's own degree of conservatism to be associated with similar attitudes on the part of her Bennington friends.

This finding has special importance since it provides the only evidence we have that attitude scores obtained by report from the respondent about her friends and from those friends themselves tend to be congruent. All other comparisons of attitudes between the respondent and significant members of her social environment are based

Table 6.9   Relationship of Respondent's Attitude Change to the Attitudes of the Majority of Her Bennington Friends

Final PEP Score in College	1960 Conservatism Index	Actual Scores of Friends from Bennington on the 1960 Conservatism Index			
		More than Half of Friends Above Median	More than Half of Friends Below Median	Half Above, Half Below Median	Total
Above median	Above median	18 (46%)	15 (38%)	6 (15%)	39 (99%)
Above median	Below median	3 (19%)	8 (50%)	5 (31%)	16 (100%)
Below median	Above median	12 (63%)	5 (26%)	2 (11%)	19 (100%)
Below median	Below median	13 (38%)	17 (50%)	4 (12%)	34 (100%)
		46	45	17	108

on the respondent's report alone. Thus it appears that there is both an actual and a perceived congruence in political attitudes among the respondent and members of her social environment.

For the most part it appears that the graduates of the classes of 1938, 1939, and 1940 selected and moved into—and perhaps in some degree, created—a social environment which tended to support and reinforce the value systems with which they had left college. However, as we have seen, some of these women did not find support for their points of view in the associations they made after college. In some instances, too, their political attitudes were presumably not important enough to them or well enough developed to have influenced their post-college interests, selection of friends, or participation in activities.

Self-Reports of Interests and Influences

One of the ways in which the students who maintained conservative political attitudes in college during the 1930's differed from the students who became less conservative is that many of them were not as interested in politics and were not involved at that time. The women who were interviewed in 1960 were asked how frequently they discussed politics. Sixty-eight percent of the women who became *less* conservative after college said that they discussed politics frequently, whereas only 47% of the women who remained conservative said that they discussed politics that often. On the other hand, 61% of the women who became *more* conservative after college discussed politics frequently, and 71% of those who remained nonconservative said that they discussed them as often. There is thus some tendency for the people who remained conservative to discuss politics less frequently than any others, suggesting either personal indifference or a social environment of indifference, or both.

Each woman was asked why she had changed her political attitudes, or, if she had not changed them, what were the important influences which helped to shape her political point of view.

The most frequently mentioned reason for becoming more conservative was "getting older," and the most frequently mentioned reason for becoming less conservative was "I'm better informed now." From the relationships reported earlier in the chapter it appears that the husbands were an important influence on the women's political attitudes. However, only a small percentage of the women interviewed mentioned their husbands as an important influence on their political thinking. They felt that the major influences had been new information and new responsibilities.

The women were also asked to indicate the important influences on their political points of view. About 20% of them mentioned their husbands, 27% mentioned other relatives, 26% mentioned friends, and 25% mentioned work associates. Twenty percent mentioned their education at Bennington, Bennington classmates, or faculty. Almost everyone mentioned some interpersonal influence.

Overview: Supportive Social Environments

Change in political attitude after college is associated with many interpersonal and intrapersonal factors. In some instances, the changes in point of view were quite self-conscious, the result of much thinking, and something felt to be very important. In other cases, the person had changed her point of view without being aware of it, and was not involved with political orientations, nor did she consider politics an important part of her life.

Husbands' influence upon wives' attitudes most frequently appears to be indirect—by way of providing support for wives' existing attitudes—rather than direct, in the sense of influencing wives to change. Spouses' histories of stability and change suggest "independence" from their husbands about as often as "dependence" upon them, although more of the wives (about one-fifth) changed toward agreement with their husbands than the other way around (about one-eighth). Very few couples, as of 1960–1961, held opposing preferences for political parties.

Women who had friends who were interested in public affairs and who agreed with their own points of view tended to maintain their previous political orientations. Those who had friends who disagreed with them tended to defend and question their points of view, and sometimes changed them. In general, respondents tended to report that most of their friends had political orientations similar to their own. When the attitudes of the respondents who named each other as friends were compared, most pairs of ex-Bennington friends expressed similar attitudes about public issues.

The women who had not changed their political attitudes since college had, to a greater extent, moved into a social environment which supported their existing political viewpoints. In some instances, change was deliberate and self-conscious; in others, we have no evidence that change was determined by their interest in public affairs. On the other hand, those who changed their attitudes after college had moved into social environments which tended to oppose their points of view, or at least not support them. However, lack of social support was not sufficient to produce changes in attitudes in some women, and some of them changed their points of view even though there was a good deal of support for their original attitudes; events, new information, and new problems had arisen which initiated a re-evaluation of their positions.

7. Participation, Involvement, Personal Characteristics

In this chapter, we shall consider the personal histories and characteristics of the graduates of 1938, 1939, and 1940 who were interviewed.

Participation and Involvement

Mervin Freedman, in a chapter in the *American College* (Sanford, 1962), reviewed many of the studies of college alumni and found some general consistencies among them. Most of the alumni were rather passive politically, he reports.

> The lives of alumni were pretty much centered in the "private" sphere, with the family, work, and recreation as the predominant interests. The alumni voted, and were interested in governmental policies, but tended to be rather passive politically. Intellectual and esthetic pursuits did not loom large in their lives, a fact which led Pace to suggest that "colleges may not be producing the cultural values they so frequently claim." The chief differences between graduates and the people who dropped out of college were in the vocational realm. . . . Otherwise, differences were inconsequential. Thus, for example, the level of reading matter was not appreciably higher for the graduates than for the dropouts . . . (pp. 848–849)
>   . . . of the alumni figuring in the *Time Magazine* survey of 1947, fewer than one-third signed petitions, fewer than one-quarter sent telegrams or letters to office-holders, and fewer than one-fifth contributed money to political causes. Only about 20% of the alumni could be considered truly active politically. (p. 860)

Respondents in the present study were expected to be somewhat more active and interested in politics than the alumni Freedman describes. Many of the women had been actively concerned with political issues and causes when they were students, and they probably would maintain some of this interest.

Degree and Kind of Participation

The women in the study were involved in many different kinds of organizations, causes, and committees. As part of the interview, they were asked to list all of the organizations and all of the committee work in which they were currently active. Only 12% of the women said that they had not been active in any organization. In general, the Bennington College graduates who were interviewed were active in more organizations than a sample of women of comparable social class who participated in a study for the League of Women Voters (Slater et al., 1957). Slater reported that 29% of the women from the highest social class participated in no organizations, and 18% participated in four or more. In the Bennington sample, 36% of the women participated in four or more organizations, and only 12% participated in none.

If the respondent mentioned more than one organization, she was asked to indicate which of them was most important to her, or in which one she was most active. About 18% of the women mentioned a political organization as being most important, 19% mentioned an educational organization, and 15% selected a cultural organization. Six percent of them thought that none of the organizations that they belonged to was important to them, and 9% mentioned a social or recreational group as the one in which they were most interested. Most of the women were active in organizations that were community-centered or concerned with important institutions in the community.

The respondents were also asked about their involvement in committees and causes. Table 7.1 shows the proportion of respondents active in each of the various causes and committees.

Even though many women were active in organizations and causes, it was not uncommon for them to express a determination to limit their commitment to organizations, or to say that they were not as active as they had once been. Many women expressed a desire to focus their activities more, either by limiting themselves to a few, or by becoming more professional. In some instances, becoming professional meant additional training and in others it meant being paid for work which they used to do as volunteers. Two questions in the interview revealed the respondents' present feelings about work in organizations and committees and their plans for the future in regard to their interests and activities. A few quotes from the interviews will give some indication of the frequently expressed need to find a focus, to be professional, or to return to school for additional training.

Table 7.1   Percentage of Women Active in Causes

Type of Cause or Committee	Number and Percent Active	
1. Political party or candidate	79	60%
2. Educational groups	65	49%
3. Fund raising	54	41%
4. Cultural	47	36%
5. Civic improvement	34	26%
6. Racial integration	14	11%
7. Civil liberties	11	8%
8. Church	11	8%
9. Disarmament	5	4%
10. Civil defense	3	2%
No cause or committee	4	3%

(*P34*)   No, I'm not more active now than when I was in Bennington. I needed organizations as a social outlet when the kids were small. Now they bore me to tears. I need to feel professional.

(*P16*)   I was always interested in activities while at Bennington. Since then I have selected more carefully the things that are worth doing. . . . I have no plans for the next ten years. I will play it by ear. Not quite willing to have the children take care of themselves. I probably will get a degree or a year of graduate work or get a job. It depends on the amount of energy I have. I think going back to a learning situation is very important at this age. I would like to reach out more.

(*P26*)   When I first left college I was active. Within the last five years I am extremely disinterested. I am not really active in anything now. I was active in volunteer work for the state hospital. . . . (What are your plans for the next ten years?) I have thought about it a lot. I am quite concerned about it. I don't know what, but I will have to do something definite and interesting. I am trying to decide whether to return to school to get a Master's. I'm afraid of it. I would like to become skilled in one activity.

(*P27*)   I am through with activities now—I'm burned out, for a while. I am always like that. I have no special plans for the future. I am determined to stay with some form of interest. I don't want to atrophy. I would like to do what I am doing right now. [Currently she is working part time as an administrative assistant to a professor of area development.]

(*P6*) I have never been interested in women's organizations. I hate to get involved in a lot of different things. I would much rather work on one thing—less diverse things. I have given a lot of thought to what I would like to do in the next ten years. I thought I might go into teaching and I have looked into the program. Kind of postponed the thought of teaching. I may continue to work with retarded children.

(*P1*) I have not become more active since college. For one thing I feel that women's clubs—to me it's a waste of time. I don't feel like getting involved in something that isn't going to accomplish something for somebody. In the next ten years I would like to get into some kind of activity as much for my family's sake as for my own. It can't be frivolous.

We asked, "Have you thought about what you would like to do in the next ten years or so? What are your plans?" The responses were categorized and tabulated and the following distribution was obtained. (Responses total more than 100% because several respondents gave more than one answer.)

Would like to pursue goals which were interrupted, take additional courses or additional training	28%
Would like to do something in the arts, music, writing, or creative pursuits	28%
Would like to get a job, follow a career, find a continuing interest	25%
Would like to do some type of service, volunteer work, or "helping others"	20%
Would like to have no commitments, travel, do what they like	20%
Had no plans, or did not know	12%
Would like to become more active in their communities, run for office	10%
Would like to continue what they were doing, or would like to concentrate on family and children	9%

About one-fifth of the women had made very specific plans. As might be expected, women who still had small children generally had not made very definite plans for their own time during the next ten years.

Reading Habits

In addition to being interviewed about their organization and committee work, each respondent was asked about the magazines she read. The magazines were classified in several ways, for example, content, such as current events, women's magazines, fashion, literary topics, homemaking, and so on; and the "seriousness" of the magazines. "Serious" magazines were those which treat current events as well as broader intellectual issues at a deeper level than that found in the high-circulation weeklies. They also include any magazines that are related to an academic field or profession, for example, *Dance.* Eighty-nine percent of the sample mentioned at least one serious magazine in her list of magazines read regularly.

Table 7.2 Relationship between Magazine Preference and Political Attitudes

	Number of "Serious" Magazines	
1960 Political Conservatism	0–2	3 or More
Above the median	44 66%	23 34%
Below the median	20 33%	41 67%

Chi-square = 12.5; $p < .001$

Table 7.2 shows the relationship between reading serious magazines and political liberalism; the women who scored above the median on the 1960 Political Conservatism Index tended to read few serious magazines, whereas those who scored below the median on the index tended to read several of them.

Table 7.3 Political Attitudes and Preference for Serious Over Nonserious Magazines

	Ratio of Serious to Nonserious		
1960 Political Conservatism	More Serious than Nonserious	Equal	More Nonserious than Serious
Above the median	19 29%	9 14%	38 58%
Below the median	44 71%	8 13%	10 16%

Table 7.4   The Relationship between Change in Political Attitude and Magazine Preference

Final PEP Score in College	1960 Political Conservatism Index	Number of "Serious" Magazines				More Serious than Nonserious	
		0–2		3 or More		Total	
(A) Above	Above median	29	67%	14	33%	43 (100%)	7	16%
(B) Above	Below median	7	35%	13	65%	20 (100%)	14	70%
(C) Below	Above median	15	65%	8	35%	23 (100%)	12	52%
(D) Below	Below median	13	31%	29	69%	42 (100%)	30	71%
		64		64		128		

Difference between Groups A and B, $x^2 = 4.1$, $p < .05$; difference between Groups C and D, $x^2 = 5.44$, $p < .02$.

The women who scored above the median on the 1960 Political Conservatism Index also tend to read more "nonserious" magazines than "serious" magazines, whereas those who scored below the median read more "serious" than "nonserious" magazines. This association, significant at less than .001, is shown in Table 7.3.

The alumnae who remained conservative over the years are less likely to mention serious magazines than those who became less conservative since 1938–1939, or those women who were nonconservative at both times. Those who became more conservative since 1938–1939 read fewer serious magazines than the women who remained nonconservative over the years. These relationships are found in Table 7.4.

The women who became more conservative since college (Group C) for the most part read more serious than nonserious magazines. The women in Group A, the ones who remained conservative, are distinctive for reading more nonserious than serious magazines; 77% are so classified. In this sample, political conservatism appears to be related to "light" reading.

Pregraduation Characteristics

In the late 1930's, 24 students, carefully selected to represent every cross section and grouping of importance within the college community, were asked to name three students from each of the classes of 1938, 1939, and 1940 who were reputedly most extreme in each of 28 characteristics related to community citizenship. Several of these ratings were selected as possible predictors of community activity in 1960. (See Appendix D.)

The first of these is the rating of "who was most absorbed in college community affairs." The respondents who received no nominations for this characteristic were compared to the respondents who received at least one nomination. These two groups of women did not differ in the number of organizations they were participating in at the time of the interview. Thirty-three percent of those nominated as "most absorbed in college community affairs" considered their activities in educational organizations as the most important activity, whereas only 18% of the rest of the women listed an educational organization as the most important. Otherwise the patterns of participation between the two groups did not differ greatly.

Another characteristic on which the students were rated in the late 1930's was "Who is most anxious to hold positions of community responsibility?" Comparing the women who received no nominations with those who received at least one nomination, we find a tendency for the latter group to be more active in organizations in 1960. Sixty-three percent of the women who were nominated as "most anxious to hold positions in the community" were active in three or more organizations in 1960. Only 45% of the other women were active in that many organizations. The difference is statistically significant ($p < .05$). The category mentioned most often as important by those frequently nominated was "cultural activity."

Pregraduation Orientation to the College Community

In the original study, two aspects of individual orientation to the college community were found to be useful in accounting for students' change, or lack of it, with respect to the attitudes measured: awareness of own attitudinal position, as related to those of other students; and community reputation for "cooperativeness" as opposed to "negativism." For purposes of this analysis, a special sample of students was considered, consisting of approximately the most conservative sixth and the least conservative sixth (according to PEP scores) of all students graduating in 1938, 1939, and 1940. Since the members of this population were interviewed 20-odd years later, it is possible to relate the pregraduate dimensions of awareness and cooperativeness-negativism to subsequent attitude change.

Oversimplifying somewhat, "awareness" represents the degree to which relatively extreme conservatives and nonconservatives recognized their own relative deviance from community norms. Unawareness represents the belief that one's own rather extreme attitudes are typical of the community. "Negativism" reflects a reputation among peers for opposition to community norms, and "non-negativism" simply an absence of such a reputation. "Cooperativeness" refers to a reputation for active and enthusiastic involvement in whatever the college stands for, and "noncooperativeness" merely its absence.

The most conservative and nonconservative sixths have each been divided into four analogous categories. (The terms negativistic and non-negativistic were applied only to conservatives, because no members of the somewhat extreme group of nonconservatives were reputedly negativistic; correspondingly, none of the conservatives was reputedly cooperative, and so that term was reserved for the nonconservatives. See Newcomb, 1943, for fuller statements.)

The following thumbnail sketches of the eight categories of students, abstracted from the 1943 study, will suggest some of the "person-in-community dynamics" that then appeared to be related to their attitudinal histories in college. They also provide certain leads for predictions concerning postcollege change.

1. Conservative, negativistic, aware. The majority of this group were considered timid and insecure in social relationships. They were unsatisfied with the level of social success achieved in college and had a good deal of resentment against the student leaders. They were dependent on their parents. Two out of four students said that if the prevailing attitude in the college were conservative they would become more radical.

2. Conservative, negativistic, unaware. Members of this group were considered timid, more timid than the previous group, and inhibited. They seem to be more satisfied with their friendships and social success, which was small, than the previous group. They expressed no resentment against community leaders. They were extremely dependent on parents.

3. Conservative, non-negativistic, aware. This group was described as eager and enthusiastic. They had some prestige in the community. They had strong ties with their parents and felt that loyalty to parents was the main reason why they had remained conservative in college.

4. Conservative, non-negativistic, unaware. Members of this group were described by faculty as plodding and conscientious. They were overdocile and uncritical of authority. They also were dependent on parents. Most of them were bothered by feelings of inferiority, and had no prestige in the community. They hardly entered into community life at all.

5. Nonconservative, noncooperative, unaware. These people were hard-working, eager, enthusiastic. In the first two years they were unsure of themselves and dependent on instructors. They were eager to please instructors and become more self-dependent. Their major ambition on entering college was friendship and they saw their own attitude change as one aspect of being accepted. Three out of four felt that in a conservative college they would follow the trend of the majority.

6. *Nonconservative, noncooperative, aware.* These seniors were described as being highly independent. They were judged by faculty to have a high level of critical-mindedness. Four out of five felt that in a conservative college they would be even more radical. Their major ambition was intellectual prestige.

7. *Nonconservative, cooperative, aware.* These were highly independent and curious-minded students. They were described as being meticulous and perfectionistic. Five out of seven said they would be liberal in a conservative college. They felt that their present attitudes were a result of a hard-won victory—that they had fought hard for their intellectual and attitudinal independence.

8. *Nonconservative, cooperative, unaware.* They were described by faculty as enthusiastic, plugging, industrious, and conscientious. They were not overdependent on parents. They were more anxious to please than the "awares" and also were more in need of guidance by the instructors. Four out of six said that in a conservative college they would have drifted along with the majority.

The two groups of conservatives who were unaware of their relative conservatism seem to have been absorbed in their own personal problems or their own interests, so that they did not enter into community life. This group, the unawares, for whom political activity was relatively unimportant, should be *least* likely to change conservative attitudes after college because they are unlikely to be concerned with politics and political discussion, which, it is assumed, would continue to be a nonrelevant part of their lives. (It is possible, of course, that if they should be confronted with political issues, perhaps through persons of special importance to them, they might be very amenable to change because they had held no well-formulated set of political attitudes previously.) Among the unaware conservatives, those who were also negativistic should be least likely to change political attitudes after college.

The two groups of conservative and aware people had some interest in politics; they were aware of the college community trend and resisted it. The aware and non-negativistic are most likely to change because they were accepting of the college and they had prestige, but did not change attitudes, typically, because of their loyalty to their parents. With decreasing dependence on parents, they would be amenable to change. Because of their interest in politics they would probably become involved in political discussions and expose themselves to new and conflicting information.

The negativistic and aware group, on the other hand, felt rejected by the Bennington community, resented the college leaders, and felt that they would be in the minority no matter what the prevailing norms might be. They had thought about their conservatism and rationalized it. They would be likely to expose themselves to political information and probably least likely to be influenced by associates.

Among the conservatives it seems reasonable to predict that the group of women most likely to become more liberal after college would be the awares because they were interested in politics and were less absorbed in themselves than the unawares. The non-negativistic would also be likely to become more liberal because they were less resistant to influence. Table 7.5 compares various categories of change for the conservatives, as of the late 1930's, and the proportion of women who changed their attitudes.

Although the number of cases is very small, there is some support for the prediction that the conservative and aware women would be more likely to become liberal after college than the conservative and unaware women.

Table 7.5   Comparison of Categories of Conservative Students, as of the 1930's, with Respect to Postcollege Change

	Total N	N Becoming Less Conservative	Percent Changing
All "aware"	8	4	50
All "unaware"	8	1	12.5
All "negativistic"	8	2	25
All "non-negativistic"	8	3	37.5
Aware and also non-negativistic *	5	3	60
Unaware and also negativistic *	5	1	20
All individuals	16	5	33

* Other combined categories include only three cases each.

Looking now at the nonconservative women, it seems likely that the unaware group would be more likely to change than the aware group. The liberalism of the unaware group appeared to be an instrument in their search for acceptance, and their political orientation was not necessarily integrated into their intellectual lives; they were not necessarily committed to it for its own sake. The awares were confronted with the choice, and had consciously adopted a liberal point of view. Similarly the awares were concerned with being independent and hence would be less likely to be influenced by associates. The noncooperatives were most concerned to achieve their goals through individual efforts; the cooperatives were concerned to achieve their goals through communitywide efforts. Again, the cooperatives, because of their involvement with communitywide issues, would be more likely to change attitudes after college than the noncooperatives. The relevant findings appear in Table 7.6.

The women rated as cooperative (having community wide interests) were more likely to become conservative than the noncooperatives (having individualistic interests). But the awares, as a total group, were not much different from the unawares in tendency to become conservative. Only in combination with cooperativeness, in the case of these somewhat extreme nonconservatives, did the awareness dimension appear to make a difference; students who were both unaware and cooperative later showed the highest rate of change within this small population.

Table 7.6 Comparison of Categories of Nonconservative Students, as of the 1930's, with Respect to Postcollege Change

	Total N	N Becoming More Conservative	Percent Changing
All "aware"	12	3	25
All "unaware"	10	3	33
All "cooperative"	13	5	38
All "noncooperative"	9	1	11
Unaware and cooperative	6	3	50
Unaware and noncooperative	4	0	0
Aware and cooperative	7	2	29
Aware and noncooperative	5	1	20
All individuals	22	6	27

Nonauthoritarianism

Because it appeared that one of the personality characteristics that was related to change in attitudes in college was the student's relationship to parental authority, it seemed likely that authoritarianism might be more characteristic of the students who remained conservative in college than of those who became less conservative. No measure of authoritarianism was available for the original study, but such a scale was included in the follow-up study.

The scale which was selected was the Nonauthoritarianism (NA) scale taken from the OPI-Form C. It is a 20-item scale, originally constructed by Christie (1958), and was described by the authors of the OPI in the following manner:

> These items were originally abstracted from the California Authoritarianism (F) scale.* High scorers tend to be free from authoritarian thinking and are more democratic in their beliefs. Low scorers are generally conventional, rigid, prejudiced, and emotionally suppressed. †

The women who were interviewed were given the 20-item scale at the end of the interview, completing it while the interviewer waited. When there was not enough time to complete it at the end of the interview, the questions were left with the respondent to answer and return by mail. Twenty-two women did not complete the scale or left questions blank so that the scores were invalid. These 22 women gave slightly more conservative answers to the political issues raised in the interview than did the 106 women who completed the NA scale. However, this difference between the two groups was not large enough to be significant.

The scores on the nonauthoritarianism scale were related to measures of political attitudes collected in 1938–1939 and in 1960. Looking first at the relationship between nonauthoritarianism and final PEP scores, we find that there is a correlation of −.44 between the two. Women who were conservative when they left college tended to score low on the nonauthoritarianism scale in 1960, indicating a relationship between authoritarianism and conservatism. Table 7.7 shows this association.

---

* This and all other work on "the authoritarian personality" stems from the original book by that title by Adorno et al., 1950.

† Omnibus Personality Inventory—Research Manual. Center for the Study of Higher Education, University of California, Berkeley, California, 1962.

Table 7.7   Final PEP Score and Nonauthoritarianism in 1960–1961

| Final PEP Score | Nonauthoritarianism in 1960 | | | |
	Above Median	Below Median	Total	Mean
Above median (conservative)	20 (36%)	36 (64%)	56 (100%)	14.0
Below median	29 (58%)	21 (42%)	50 (100%)	15.7
	49	57	106	

Chi-square = 4.61, $p < .05$; $t = 2.96$, $p < .01$

Nonauthoritarianism is also related to change in political attitudes since college. Those women who became less conservative after leaving college score higher on nonauthoritarianism than the women who remained conservative, and the women who became more conservative since college score lower on nonauthoritarianism than the women who remained nonconservative in their attitudes. Table 7.8 shows this relationship.

As shown in Table 7.9, women who switched from the Republican to the Democratic party after leaving college were, on the average, higher on the nonauthoritarianism scale than those who remained Republicans over the years, whereas those who switched from the Democratic party to the Republican party were somewhat lower on the NA scale than the women who remained Democrats.

The nonauthoritarianism score is, in fact, related to every measure

Table 7.8   Nonauthoritarianism and Change in Political Attitude Since College

| Final PEP Score in College | 1960 Conservatism Index | Nonauthoritarianism in 1960 | | | |
		Above Median	Below Median	Total	Mean
Above median	Above median	10 (27%)	27 (73%)	37 (100%)	13.3 *
Above median	Below median	10 (53%)	9 (47%)	19 (100%)	15.8 *
Below median	Above median	5 (28%)	13 (72%)	18 (100%)	14.3 †
Below median	Below median	24 (75%)	8 (25%)	32 (100%)	16.5 †
		49	57	106	

* t test of the difference in means = 3.42; $p < .01$
† t test of the difference in means = 3.57; $p < .01$

Table 7.9   Nonauthoritarianism and Change in Party Preference

1938 Party Preference	1960 Party Preference	Nonauthoritarianism in 1960			
		Mean	N	t-value	p
Republican	Republican	13.4	18		
				3.97	.01
Republican	Democratic	16.6	14		
				2.29	.05
Democratic	Republican	13.9	9		
				2.15	.05
Democratic	Democratic	15.9	25		

of political attitude obtained in 1960–61. Correlations are as follows: −.67 with 1960 Political Conservatism Index; .54 with the Index of Favorability to Nonconservative Figures; −.50 with the Index of Favorability to Conservative Figures; and .52 with the number of Democratic presidential candidates preferred in the six elections from 1940 to 1960. Women who preferred Kennedy in 1960 averaged higher scores on this scale than women who preferred Nixon, and those who preferred the Democratic party in 1960 scored higher than those who preferred the Republican party.* All of these data seem to indicate that the women who are characterized by nonconservatism in political attitudes tend to be "more free from authoritarian thinking," as described by the originators of the concept, and as here measured, than the conservatives.

Although the items on the nonauthoritarianism scale are intended to tap "contentless" aspects of personality, rather than ideology, there are indirect ways in which opinions may influence replies. In any case we cannot assume that the women who became more conservative after college did so because they had developed more authoritarian personalities, or that the women who became less conservative after college changed because they were not authoritarian; the relationship may also operate the other way around. Although the relationships with nonauthoritarianism do not explain why the women did or did not change attitudes after college, they are consistent with the descriptions of conservatives and nonconservatives presented in the original study and in other college studies (Milton, 1952; Gump, 1953; Simos, 1956; Handlon et al., 1955).

---

* In the 1964 election, all of the women who preferred Goldwater and who had completed the NA scale scored below the median on NA.

Summary

The Bennington College graduates described in this study appear to be more active in organizations and causes than a comparable group of women who participated in a study of the League of Women Voters (Slater, 1957).

Sixty percent of the women who were interviewed reported having worked for a political party or candidate, with the Democrats and the "liberal" groups receiving more help than the Republicans and the "conservative" groups. Women who were nonconservative tended to read more "serious" magazines than the others. The women who remained conservative tended to read more nonserious magazines than any other group of women.

The pattern of participation and involvement in organizations and causes is very complex. Many of the women are active in their communities. The types of activities they were currently most involved in reflected their own interests and the needs of the community. Very few of the measures collected in college predicted to the type of activity or involvement in 1960. Political attitudes predicted to the type of participation, but not well to the amount of participation. The type and amount of participation is affected a good deal by the number and ages of the respondents' children. There were not enough cases in each category to control for the number and ages of the children.

Interestingly, activities and involvement in the college community did not predict well to later participation and involvement in the home community. Perhaps because Bennington College had so few formal organizations, there is little basis for comparison between the college situation and the contemporary one. Perhaps it is generally true that students who are active in their colleges do not become particularly active in their communities.

Many of the women who had been very active in organizations and committees expressed a wish to limit themselves to fewer activities, to focus their energies more. For many the emphasis on careers or part-time jobs seemed to be an answer: 43% of the sample were in 1960–1961 employed in part-time or full-time jobs, and 53% of the respondents mentioned a career, or additional training which would lead to a career, as part of their plans for the next ten years or so.

Although many expressed a wish to be less active in formal organizations, some of them at the same time mentioned a desire to be more active in their communities. They did not want to be tied down to organizational work, but they did want to have an influence on their communities. Some of the women became more selective in the types of work they did, limiting themselves to political, civic, or educational activities. It is difficult to assess in tabular form the influence of these women on their communities, but it appears to be considerable.

The individual's personality characteristics probably affected the degree to which she was subject to personal influence, or was likely to conform, or was open to new and conflicting information. Thus the women who, as students, were most open to information about the conflict between their political attitudes and the attitudes of the majority appeared to be open to new information after college, and changed their attitudes more than those women who were not aware, as students, of being opposed to the majority trend. Likewise those women who were rated as most individualistic as students were less likely to change attitudes after college than the other women.

Change in attitudes was also related to nonauthoritarianism, according to a scale designed to measure personal tendencies to be open to nonconformist influences and other, hypothetically related, characteristics. Those who became more conservative were more authoritarian, in this sense, and those who became less conservative were less so than the ones who did not change.

8. Individual Case Studies

In the previous chapter we looked at some of the general trends related to attitude change and persistence. For the majority of women who lived in social environments that minimized disturbing or opposing influences and provided reinforcing ones, political attitudes remained relatively unchanged during the interim between the two studies. Those whose husbands and friends agreed with their points of view were likely to maintain that point of view unchanged, whereas those who associated primarily with people whose attitudes were in opposition to their own were more likely to change. Some of them moved into environments supportive of their existing orientations.

There follow a number of individual case studies describing in detail some of the women who had maintained their political attitudes unchanged since college, and some of those who had not. The interviews were selected either because of the unusual amount of detail in them, or because of the unusual amount of information available about these individuals from the original study.

Nonconservatives Who Remained Nonconservative

The first three cases are of women who were relatively nonconservative when they graduated from Bennington College and were still relatively so when interviewed in 1960 or 1961.

Q72 was one of the group of students who were originally classified as nonconservative, cooperative, and unaware of their relative nonconservatism when they were in college. In her interview in 1939, she said that she "had been completely revolutionized in college." In her first year she was "shaken up" and became "terrifically skeptical about everything." During her summer vacations and her winter work periods she became an active worker for labor unions and "at first thought that they were perfect." By the time she was a junior she had become somewhat disillusioned by the methods the unions used and she felt that she could no longer be an "honest crusader for them now." By her senior year she had become a little more cautious.

After she graduated, Q72 went into government service and married someone who was also working for the government. Throughout the period after graduation she maintained an interest in politics and public affairs. She reports that since leaving Bennington she has been active in the American Civil Liberties Union, the Americans for Democratic Action, the League of Women Voters, civic committees, and campaign committees. Recently she has done work for racial integration.

In speaking of her years as a student at Bennington, Q72 recalled in 1961 that even though she had come from a liberal background, she had become more liberal in college, but "never became a member of the Communist party." She attributed her increase in interest and liberalism regarding public affairs to the nature of the college. "The college challenged you and your point of view and you had to discover something which was all your own thinking. There was so much individual attention. The atmosphere of the place was charged with intellectual curiosity. The excitement of discovery was there."

In regard to any change in attitude since college, Q72 felt in 1961 that fundamentally she had not changed. She may have "changed shades . . . from being radical to being liberal, but certainly not conservative." She felt that events had proved to her that her liberal attitudes were right. She and her husband are very interested in public affairs. In fact she feels that she is even more interested in public affairs at the present time than when she was a student.

Most of her friends tend to agree with her and her husband regarding political matters, although Q72 has "made an effort to get together with Republican groups." Both she and her husband have voted for the Democratic candidates in every presidential election since 1940, and they both are very favorable to the nonconservative public figures.

Q72 no longer keeps in touch with her friends from college. Not many of them live close to her, but she does see the Bennington alumnae in her area. She has become friends with several women from Bennington whom she has met since she graduated.

When asked about her assessment of her education at Bennington, Q72 expressed a great deal of satisfaction, although she felt that there are "terrible gaps" in her knowledge and that she was never exposed to many subjects. However, she reports, "I learned to tackle problems, and nothing has seemed too hard for me later. The excitement and stimulation of the place triggered everyone. There was an outstanding faculty and methodology and I was ripe for this. . . ."

Her husband, an Ivy League graduate, is no longer in the government, but now is engaged in business. He shares in her point of view and interest in public affairs.

Q72 was nonconservative when she graduated, began to work and study in the area of public affairs, met her husband who was also active in government and was also nonconservative, and has continued to maintain such interests over the years. Her associates, her activities, and her interests are all consonant with a liberal political orientation.

❋   ❋   ❋   ❋

L91 is another example of a woman who has remained non-conservative over the years, having come from a nonconservative background and having had her attitudes reinforced by the Bennington community. In her 1961 interview, she expressed the feeling that as a student she had been politically naive and quite unaware. She said that she had come from a liberal background and had remained the same in college, with most of her interest and excitement coming from the courses she was taking. She had belonged to a liberal group but had not given it much thought. She remembers "being shocked at the conservatism of the Bennington students." She had waited on tables in the student dining room and it had at first seemed to her that "all of the students were Republicans and conservatives."

L91 thought she had gone through a cycle since college as far as her political attitudes were concerned. She mentioned that her husband had noticed this change in her point of view too. When she graduated she had a strong social conscience and was "terribly serious and interested in the social problems of the country." During this period she moved to the left in her political orientation. She married soon after graduation and went to New York and joined a very exciting group in the performing arts. Many of her associates from this group were from "the left." Later she found out that the performing group had some sort of "tie-up with the Communist party." She left the group and her professional interests changed. Sometime after this (she did not specify the time) her political attitudes changed again. At the present time she says she is "back to where I was destined to be before I went to college."

L91 is a Democrat and has worked for the party and its candidates. She considers herself liberal and very involved in politics. She has even "toyed with the idea of running for office." Since graduation she has become much more active in the area of public affairs, and she stated that "at least one or two nights a week we are at some public affairs meeting." *L91* reports that her husband is very well informed about public affairs and that she tends to "lean on him," getting most of her information second-hand from him. Most of her friends are liberal and both she and her husband have always voted for the Democratic candidate in the presidential elections.

Both she and her husband come from politically active families. Her father had worked for the government during the Roosevelt administration, and her husband's father actively campaigned for the Democratic candidate for president. She reports that since graduating she has been active in the American Civil Liberties Union and the League of Women Voters; she has been a precinct committee-woman for the Democratic party and a member of the Democratic Women's Club; she has conducted a leaders' training program in discussion of foreign policy; and she has supported the Urban League. Her father was attacked by an extreme right-wing group that was attempting to blackball him, and *L91* helped to fight for him. Perhaps as a result of this experience, she has been very active in the cause of individual liberties.

L91 is another woman who has been active and involved in politics and causes since college. Her husband shares her interest and involvement and agrees with her point of view. With social support from her husband, family, and friends, she has maintained a nonconservative point of view since graduation.

❋   ❋   ❋   ❋

The third example of a nonconservative who remained nonconservative after college is a little different from the previous two cases. *Q61* came from a very conservative background and became relatively nonconservative during her years at Bennington. Since graduating she has become still less conservative, although she feels social opposition from her associates for this change.

In her interview in 1939, *Q61* offered a "pendulum" analogy to describe the changes that had taken place in her political attitudes since coming to Bennington. She said that she had been very conservative when she came to college, then went to the other extreme, and then swung part of the way back. She felt that "all attitudes are for one day only—you change them when you get evidence. You shouldn't be proud of them or ashamed of them." She had acquired an "attitude about attitudes" in college.

In her 1960 interview, *Q61* said that she had started out in college being the standard bearer of the Republican party and that she did not change perceptibly. She felt that only a slight change, not a broad one, had taken place in college because there was a force against change from home. However, she "had begun to get out of the cocoon at college and had begun to see the larger picture."

After college her political attitudes and opinions developed, she went on to say. "The awareness that developed at college bore fruit. Finally, I voted for Stevenson, not because I became a Democrat, but because I felt that he would move us in the directions I thought we should go—world peace, civil rights, underdeveloped countries, disarmament, these seem to be the Democratic platform rather than the Republican platform." *Q61* explained that the changes in her political point of view came about as a result of becoming aware of the political points of view of people from other countries. She also credits a thinking pattern which was set up at Bennington with giving her the tools to make her awareness broader. The atomic bomb was a crucial event in the development of her new political orientation in that it made control and conscience so important. All of these experiences, plus the practical political experiences coming from working on school committees, have helped to shape her political point of view.

She and her husband voted for the Republican candidates in the four national elections from 1940 to 1952. In 1956 both voted for Stevenson and in 1960 they both voted for Kennedy. *Q61* reports that they took a "great deal of taunting from their friends when they came out for Stevenson." Most of their close friends are more conservative than they. *Q61* goes on to say that she and her husband are "something of a fringe element in their community now." She said that it "took even more strength to vote for Kennedy than to vote for Stevenson."

Q61 and her husband discuss politics a great deal. It is an interest of theirs. She describes her point of view as "tending to be liberal in the area of public affairs. I tend to feel it is human life we are being casual about, really human life on the planet. I have not thought deeply about the way things are moving. I tend to be an Albert Schweitzer addict. . . . I would like to push issues more deeply."

Q61 has been active in the American Civil Liberties Union, the United World Federalists, the League of Women Voters, youth groups, and education committees. She has held positions of leadership in many of the organizations and committees she has worked for. Her involvement in committee work and her eagerness to learn from the situations in which she is working have influenced her attitudes by exposing her to new information. On the basis of her new information and new interests, she has become less conservative since college. In 1960, *Q61* was relatively nonconservative compared to her peers from Bennington. Her husband agreed with her point of view, but most of her friends and associates did not support her new orientation. Both she and her husband developed new political attitudes since 1940, even though they found some social opposition to their new positions.

       ❋   ❋   ❋   ❋

All three of these women, *Q72*, *L91*, and *Q61*, were active in public affairs and participated in their communities after graduation. Each of them married someone who shared her relatively non-conservative political beliefs. *Q72* and *L91* had social support for nonconservatism from their families, their background, and their associates, whereas *Q61* came from a conservative family and lived in a conservative community. With the important exception of her husband, *Q61* had little support for her beliefs from her friends and relatives. Although the local community was conservative, her interests took her beyond her local community into national committees where she found support for her nonconservative attitudes.

Conservatives Who Remained Conservative

Q70, who was conservative in college and has remained so, reported in her interview in 1939 that during college years she had not changed her attitudes regarding public affairs. The only change had been that she had become much more intellectual. She had become very interested and involved in her major. When asked to describe what had happened to most students at Bennington, she said in 1939 that the typical student at Bennington was "influenced by the socialistic and communistic pressure here." Freshmen and sophomores were much more interested than juniors and seniors in public affairs. "Juniors and seniors were too busy with their own work and interests . . . they didn't have time to send telegrams, etc. . . . I think it is silly—it won't do any good." Only freshmen were that enthusiastic. *Q70* had concentrated her efforts on the achievement of intellectual goals and had discovered that she could enjoy her work. In her senior year interview she described herself as a staunch Republican.

In her 1961 interview, *Q70* recalls that as a student she had not changed her political attitudes. She had come from a very conservative community and had not been exposed to liberal-minded people before.

After college she became active in community projects, committees, and politics. She had worked for bond issues for schools and projects in her local community. In the 1950's she became active in national politics and became a Republican National Committeewoman. Q70 felt that she had not changed her political attitudes since college and that over the years her family had been the major influence on her political beliefs. She felt that she had been on the right side of things all along. Her husband also was a Republican, although he was not active in politics. Most of her friends were similar to her in orientation. She has not kept in touch with many of her friends from Bennington.

Q70 became more interested and involved in politics after college and has continued with a relatively conservative point of view, associating mainly with people who agreed with her. She reported very few influences in her life which might cause her to change her point of view.

* * * *

Q47 was also classified as conservative in college, and remained relatively so. In her 1961 interview, Q47 recalled that she had her political attitudes crystallized at Bennington because she matured. She became much more interested in politics as a student, but she felt that this would have happened anywhere.

Q47 feels that her opinions haven't changed since college. She has patterned her political beliefs after a group of people whose ideas she respects (she did not mention who these people were). She describes herself as a "Barry Goldwater Republican." Most of her friends and her husband are Republicans also. Both she and her husband have preferred the Republican candidates in every election since 1940. All of her friends from Bennington are relatively conservative, but she has not kept in close touch with them. She has moved about a good deal.

More recently she has become active in local organizations. She has worked for the school libraries, helped with the Brownie troops, and done home nursing. Her only political activity has been to chauffeur people to the polls on election day.

Q47 mentioned reading two magazines regularly: the *Saturday Evening Post* and the *Freeman*. In discussing what she read, she said that she was upset by the lead article in a recent Bennington Alumnae magazine which was a description of a "peace group's" protest against nuclear arms and was written by another alumna. Q47 felt that the position of the article in the magazine and the commentary gave the impression that Bennington College endorsed the views expressed in the article. She felt that more care should be taken to avoid giving this impression.

Q47 is and has been more conservative than most of her peers from Bennington. She had maintained her conservative point of view over the years. She had married someone who is conservative and associated with people who also were conservative. Like *Q70*, she had not been exposed to many counter-influences to her point of view.

Conservatives Who Became Nonconservative

Q28 graduated relatively conservative, but in 1961 was relatively nonconservative. She recalls in her 1961 interview that as a student she "was extremely conservative. In fact I was involved in a torch light parade where we burned Roosevelt in effigy, I am ashamed to say." She feels that she did not change her political attitudes in college because she revolted against all the radicalism in college. She didn't become interested in politics until she moved to her present community.

She states directly in her interview that she has become less conservative since college. Her husband is a Democrat and she says that he has influenced her a good deal. She goes on to describe the forces helping to shape her viewpoint by saying, "I was brought up in a conservative family. I never heard anything else until I went to college. In college I was not interested in what was going on around me, I was only interested in what I was majoring in. Seeing the government work has made me more liberal. I didn't join the A.D.A., however. The old Republicanism was too intransigent. I object to a closed mind—both the A.D.A. and the Republicans make me mad."

Q28 and her husband discuss politics frequently and are interested in public affairs. Most of their friends have similar opinions, although there is some difference about civil rights. Most of them are "Southern in attitude."

Although she calls herself a Republican, *Q28* has preferred the Democratic candidate in each national election from 1948 to 1960. She explains this difference between her party preference and her candidate preference by saying, "I feel that the Republican party needs me, but I am ashamed to say I'm a Republican. The Republican party is rotten to the core. The Republicans in the House are 25 years behind. Dirksen, Bridges, and Halleck are awful. I am violently opposed to these kinds of Republicans."

She has been active in the League of Women Voters and on various civic committees. She has been an active "lobbyist" trying to get a change in the community government for 15 years. Her activities as a lobbyist have acquainted her with politics and politicians. Her major interests outside her family have been in the area of government. Her husband supports her activities and interests and has been an influence on her point of view.

Q28 is a woman who was not interested in politics or public affairs in college, but who has become very interested in them since marriage. Along with her increased interest and involvement in politics has come a decreased conservatism in outlook.

     ❖   ❖   ❖   ❖

G32 is another woman who came from a conservative family, remained conservative in college, and since college has become much less so. In her 1939 interview, G32 said that her family was "extremely conservative, especially my father. Father hates the New Deal. . . . I used to argue, now I give up—now I shut up." She went on to say, "I'm radical at home and conservative here [at Bennington]. I love to be perverse." She expressed the opinion in her 1961 interview that she didn't change much in college. She became interested in aspects of what was going on. "My family certainly was Republican and I was vaguely Republican."

She states that she has a more liberal attitude now than when in college. She says she has had a chance to work out a philosophy and she has been able to work out her ideas in regard to the existing parties. She considers herself more of a Democrat than a Republican, but the label of liberal Republican is acceptable to her, whereas that of conservative Democrat is not. She reports that her closest friends are reasonably similar in point of view. They are near enough so that there is some basis for free conversation.

Since 1948, G32 has preferred the Democratic candidates for president. In 1940 she voted for Willkie and she could not remember for whom she voted in 1944. Her husband has preferred the Democrats in every election. G32 has been active in the League of Women Voters and has collected money for the Democratic party. Her husband is a member of the American Civil Liberties Union, and she has done some work for disarmament groups. She mentioned the following magazines as ones which she reads regularly: *The New Yorker, The New Republic, The Reporter, Atlantic Monthly, Harpers,* and *Sunday New York Times.*

G32 became less conservative in her political opinions after marrying a man who was nonconservative. In college her attitudes had remained the same, although she had not given much thought to politics. Since college she has given much more thought to politics and has become more interested and less conservative.

Like *Q28*, *G32* married someone who was not conservative. Both of them became much more interested and involved in politics after leaving college. Along with growing interest and involvement in political matters they became less conservative.

Nonconservatives Who Became Conservative

One of the women who became more conservative after college was *M42*, who came from a liberal family, was nonconservative in college, and married someone who was more conservative than she.

In her 1939 interview, *M42* spoke of the experiences that influenced her point of view. Her parents were "radical and they discussed social issues constantly at home." During her four years at college, she felt she had become less extreme than she was as a freshman. Although she had been extremely pro-CIO and "uncritical," she felt she was becoming more critical, although still sympathetic to the union. She said that she was "trying to be more cautious . . . to be more scientific and to not overstate my case." In the same interview she also mentioned that her fiance came from a very conservative family, and that he was liberal chiefly because of her influence. She said she "could never marry an obstinate conservative—I couldn't stand it."

In her 1960 interview she recalled that as a student she was a Democrat. "The swing was to the left and everyone became Democrats." Since college she said that she has "become much more reactionary." She has become more reactionary because a "lot of economic inequalities have been balanced up. Labor unions have become so much stronger. It used to be that the National Association of Manufacturers was the big object of antagonism. Now they have mellowed. They are interested in the world situation. It is a matter of a balance of power. *No* group should dominate. Labor has to become more responsible."

She reports that she has a great variety of friends representing many points of view. Political attitudes run the extreme from right to left among her friends. However, four of the six people from Bennington whom she sees today scored above the median on conservatism.

M42 voted for Roosevelt in 1940 and 1944 and for the Republican candidates from 1948 to 1960. Her husband also preferred the Republican candidates since 1948, probably voting for Roosevelt in 1944 and for Willkie in 1940. She reports more conservative attitudes for her husband than for herself regarding public figures and public issues. It appears that her husband may have influenced her to become more conservative, although *M42* does not specifically mention her husband's attitudes as being an important influence on her opinions.

M42 describes herself as being the "perfect organization woman." Although she has been active in many groups and committees, very few of these activities have been related to politics. Among her activities have been the Junior League, the P.T.A., teaching Sunday School, charitable and welfare organizations, a writing club, and work for educational groups on the United Nations. She also mentions having done work for racial integration and civic improvement, although the type of work is not specified. She mentioned *The New Yorker, Time, Life, Newsweek, Sunday New York Times, National Geographic,* and *American Heritage* as the magazines which she reads regularly.

It is not clear from *M42*'s interview what have been the major influences for change in her point of view. Her husband is relatively conservative and is engaged in business where he has been confronted with labor-management problems. It appears that a key to *M42*'s change in viewpoint is a change in her attitude regarding labor, and in part this change may have come about from her husband's experiences. In any case, *M42* has become more conservative since graduation.

*   *   *   *

E12 came from a conservative family, became much less conservative in college, and married a Republican. She describes him as "a complete conservative."

When she was interviewed in 1939 and again when she was interviewed in 1961, *E12* described the change in her political attitudes in college as a rebellion against a very conservative family. However, in her senior interview she said that "if I had gone to a conservative college, I would have been conservative and would have rebelled in other ways." She had a tremendous desire to be accepted by her peers and probably would not have gone against the norms.

She describes the change which has taken place in her political attitudes since college in the following ways.

I have switched back after having been married to a complete conservative. . . . I am sneaking back to being a conservative. . . . My husband is not interested in politics at all and his friends aren't. Main contact with the world is conservative. My son has a radical point of view and we discuss it lots. I think it is a fine thing [son's radicalism].

(How would you describe your present political opinions?) That is difficult. In certain economic angles the Republicans have an edge—in certain thinking toward the future, the Democrats have an edge; I prefer them. I try to be independent. I don't know—I am getting . . . I think I'm basically a conservative.

E12 voted for Roosevelt in 1940, could not remember how she voted in 1944, voted for the Republicans in 1948, 1952, and 1956, and for Kennedy in 1960. She scored in the top third on the 1960 Political Conservatism Index, and reports her husband as being a good deal more conservative than she, according to the same index.

She has not been active in causes or committees related to political matters since college. She had withdrawn from most committee work by the time of the 1961 interview and was active in cultural groups. She felt that she had become less interested in public affairs since she left college, and did not discuss politics or public affairs with her friends very frequently.

From the interviews in 1939 and 1961, it appears that *E12* changed her political attitudes in college both because she needed to fit in with the group, and this was one way of accomplishing it, and also because she wanted to rebel against her family. When, after graduation, she married a conservative and moved into a conservative environment, she became more conservative again in her outlook. There were no influences on her to remain liberal, and a number of influences to return to conservatism.

✿   ✿   ✿   ✿

Not everyone who married someone more conservative than herself became more conservative after college, and *K42* is an interesting comparison to *E12*. After having become much less conservative in college, *K42* married a man who was more conservative than she. Although there are similar patterns in both of their lives, *K42* expressed liberal attitudes concerning public issues in 1961, in contrast to *E12* who had become moderately conservative about these same issues.

K42 had come from a conservative family, and changed a great deal while she was in college. She was aware of this change and of her relative nonconservatism. In an interview in 1939 she expressed the opinion that she was influenced by the people she respected— some seniors and some members of the faculty who were liberal. She also thought that if she had gone to a conservative college, she would have been conservative in her attitudes. She went on to say, "I could never be in a minority unless I felt very secure. I'm no rebel or non-conformist. I have never resented social pressure."

Her remarks about herself, and the changes that took place, give the impression of a person who is sensitive to social pressure, and if in the minority is very aware of her minority position. One would not expect *K42* to maintain her liberal political attitudes after graduation from Bennington if she were not associating with other like-minded people.

In her interview in 1961, she reports that soon after graduation she married a man who was a Republican, and she voted for Willkie in 1940, even though she preferred Roosevelt, because "it was important for my husband." She did not vote in 1944, and in 1948 she voted for Dewey, although she preferred Truman. In 1952 she voted for Stevenson, even though her husband voted for Eisenhower, and in 1956 and 1960 she voted for the Democratic candidates, whereas her husband continued to vote for the Republican candidates.

When asked whether she had changed her political opinions since graduation, *K42* replied that she did not think she had because she still believes the things she learned in college. She describes herself as a Democrat, a liberal, and emotional about politics. Almost all of her friends are Republicans and, in her own words, "they think of me as a traitor. They identify Republicanism with virtue."

On the basis of her 1961 interview, it appears that *K42* moved into a social environment after her graduation from Bennington that was more Republican and more conservative than her own point of view. Even though she and her husband preferred different candidates in each national election since 1940, there did not appear to be a great deal of difference between the point of view that *K42* expressed and the point of view which she reported for her husband. Sometimes she was unsure of what attitudes to report for her husband, but the only disagreements she reported between herself and her husband concerned the admission of Red China to the United Nations and their attitudes toward Truman and Reuther.

The attitudes she reported for her husband were about average in terms of the 1960 Political Conservatism Index, as compared with the Bennington respondents. Thus, although *K42* and her husband differed about politics, the differences did not appear to be very large.

Even so, on the basis of her own analysis of herself in her interview in 1939, one would have predicted that *K42* would not have maintained a political point of view that was in the minority, which is what she appears to have done. Even though, objectively, the difference in point of view between her husband and herself appears to be small, *K42* is very much aware of this difference and of her minority position in her community. She sees herself being viewed as a "traitor," which is a strong term to describe her dissent from community norms. Because her political attitudes have persisted for about 20 years or so, relatively unchanged, it appears that the point of view which she adopted in college was more than a response to the majority point of view, more than an act of conformity, but a relatively extensive change in her belief system and system of values. It seems unlikely that attitudes would have such permanence if they did not belong to an important system of beliefs.

There appears to be very little difference between the interests and activities of *K42* and *E12*, except that *K42* is still "emotionally involved" in politics, whereas *E12* has become much less interested in the topic since college. There is little in the 1939 interviews that would enable one to predict the relative nonconservatism of *K42* in 1961 and the relative conservatism of *E12* in 1961, given the fact that they both moved into conservative social environments.

✿   ✿   ✿   ✿

Two other cases are of interest, not because they are typical of the major trends in the study, but because they were discussed in great detail in the original study. These two women were friends in college and they were alike with respect to their prestige in the community, but they differed with regard to their relative conservatism. As a senior, *Q63* was described as being nonconservative, cooperative, and unaware of her relative nonconservatism, whereas *Q73* was described as conservative, non-negativistic, and aware of her conservatism. *Q63* was about average in conservatism when she entered Bennington and was somewhat below average in conservatism when she left. She was one of the students who followed the trend at Bennington and became less conservative. Her final PEP score was 23 points lower than the final PEP score of *Q73*. *Q73* hardly changed her position on the PEP scale over the four years at Bennington; she entered conservative and she left conservative.

At the time of her senior-year interview, *Q63* saw her class as "pretty liberal" and herself the same way, whereas *Q73* thought of herself as more conservative than a moderately liberal class. The two are described as follows:

> Here we have two individuals with many similarities. Both are enthusiastic, full of energy. Each has had her difficulties in making friendships. Each is anxious to hold college positions, and each has been more or less successful. Each admires and is very close to one parent of conservative opinions. Yet one of them has openly broken with that parent's opinions whereas the other has not. . . . *Q63* is willing to change her attitude responses in the direction of what she believes to be class conformity; *Q73* is not. . . . *Q63* is described both by herself and by faculty as lacking in self-confidence, until recently at least. *Q73* describes herself as self-confident, and faculty agree with her . . . (Newcomb, 1943, p. 94).

In college *Q63* and *Q73* were friends and they have remained friends during the years following graduation. When interviewed in 1961, the political attitudes of these two women were much more alike than they were in 1939. Both scored several points below the median of the interview sample on the 1960 Political Conservatism Index. *Q73* had become less conservative; *Q63* had remained about the same. Each had voted for the Republican candidate in every national election since 1940. The only issue on which they disagreed was the issue of the manner in which the U-2 incident was handled. *Q63* disapproved of the way in which it was handled; *Q73* approved.

They expressed much less agreement in their attitudes toward various public figures. They tended to disagree most about the men who were prominent in the 1930's and 1940's—their attitudes seemingly reflecting the points of view they held in college. Thus *Q63* was favorable to Roosevelt, Truman, and MacArthur, whereas *Q73* was unfavorable to them; *Q63* was unfavorable to Taft, of whom *Q73* approved. They tended to agree about the men who were prominent in the 1950's and 1960's. Both of the women were favorable to Eisenhower, Kennedy, Nixon, and Stevenson and very unfavorable to McCarthy.

Some of the interests and events in their lives which had affected their points of view may now be noted. *Q63*, who had left Bennington nonconservative, remarked when interviewed as a college senior that she was dependent on others, that her friends had a good deal to do with her political point of view, and that her chief ambition on first coming to Bennington was to make her way in a group and "not be a lemon." She was described by the interviewer in 1939 as "deeply aware of how her fate depends on others" (*ibid.*, p. 95).

When Q63 was interviewed in 1961, she expressed the feeling that the changes in political attitudes which had taken place in her and in many other girls in college were superficial changes, motivated by "vicarious emotional satisfaction." She felt that these changes did not last long and that most of the students went back to their original positions. To quote from this interview,

> I remember I would come home from the local labor union meeting and tell my family they were stuffy and then vote Republican anyway. . . . Girls came from conservative backgrounds to Bennington. They were fascinated by the idea of being radical, but then settled back to their original position. I think some of the girls who took politics very seriously were getting vicarious emotional satisfaction out of it. Others came from liberal backgrounds and were legitimate liberals.

In reply to a question about how she feels her political attitudes have changed since graduating from college, Q63 reported,

> I would say they haven't changed because I don't get terribly interested. I have always voted Republican . . . for very vague reasons. My fundamental notion is that if business is good the whole country is better. I certainly think of myself as a liberal as a result of going to Bennington College. Not extremely liberal and not extremely conservative. . . . Most of my friends voted for Kennedy and I didn't. . . . I regret it—much more impressed with Kennedy now than during the campaign—he is doing a swell job.

She sees her present friends as being more interested and informed about politics than she is, and states that she seldom talks about politics when she gets together with her friends. She also says that her husband is not interested at all in politics: "he votes, but we never discuss these things. Probably one reason I am not more involved." She and her husband have always voted for the same candidate, and her husband and her friends share her attitudes regarding the issues which were presented to her.

Q63 has not been very active in committees and organizations.

> I was very civic-minded when I lived in a small town and the children were in school. There was a complete reversal after the children left for boarding school. I was active in the P.T.A., art gallery, concerts, etc. I campaigned for Willkie in 1940.

Since college, Q63 has been involved in very few activities which would stimulate an interest in politics. She very seldom discusses politics either with her husband or with her friends. There is not much in her social environment which would stimulate an interest in public affairs. One of the impressions *Q63* gave in the interview in 1961 was that of a woman who thinks of herself as a liberal, who votes Republican out of habit, and who really does not care and is not informed about public affairs. There is no emotional commitment.

As to her Bennington College education and the effects it had on her later life, *Q63* said,

> Bennington was excellent for me. It opened up whole areas of interest and awareness that I never was aware of before. I received excellent training on how to organize ideas and material and put it down in writing. Bad feature of Bennington College is that it fosters a kind of aggressiveness. I don't think it makes women happy to be aggressive. One comes out with much too much self-inflation. I think one starts kicking around lots of ideas that one doesn't know anything about. Although one learns a certain thoroughness in one's field, the rest gives overconfidence with flimsy, undisciplined background. Although specializing has educational advantages, Bennington girls confuse college specialization with professional training. The two are very different things. The discipline of real professional training is not only necessary for job or work, but makes a much sounder person than the sort of half-baked specialist that comes out of Bennington College. (Any other dissatisfactions?) It is too hard to generalize—I meet many Vassar girls who are aggressive too! There is a great tendency to break down a girl's values and not substitute anything in their place. The education makes many Bennington College students dissatisfied with washing diapers, also.

Q63 also feels that the students at Bennington College are extremely sloppy—"that a self-indulgence system of education is related to self-indulgence and physical sloppiness." In spite of these criticisms she said that she was very satisfied with the education she received at Bennington.

When one compares the responses that *Q63* gave as a senior in 1939 with those of 1961, one gets the impression of a woman who as a college student was concerned about being accepted in the group and community and who was influenced by her friends. Because of the social environment she became more interested and informed about public affairs, and her attitudes about politics became less conservative. She married soon after graduation someone who was not at all interested in politics. In the intervening years her interests have been nonpolitical and there have been no strong forces or influences with regard to politics. The attitudes she expresses are those of a "New Deal" liberal, but not of one who has a strong commitment or an emotional involvement in the issues. She has not changed her political attitudes and neither has she participated enough in political discussions or activities to be exposed to influence or change. This appears to be a picture of political apathy.

The description of Q73's postcollege experience shows a different pattern of participation and involvement. As a student Q73 seemed to be very concerned about being independent—she described herself as independent and self-made. The faculty described her as self-confident. This still seems to be a primary concern for Q73; the theme of independence and self-reliance occurs over and over in her 1961 interview. In evaluating her Bennington College experience, Q73 said in 1961,

> It is the best thing that ever happened to me. Bennington has instilled in all of us that courage to read and think and form our own opinions and stand up and be counted—not to be afraid of being wrong and different. It is more than politics, this is true in behavior, dress, anything. We are not bound by conventions, not influenced by social pressures so much. One of the biggest shocks was to learn not to trust the printed word. This is not true of many other places I know. Bennington gave you a critical attitude toward many things—don't swallow things whole, or close self off from anything, regardless. It was a great eye-opener for many friends. Independence of thought.

Since graduation Q73 has become much more interested in public affairs and politics, largely through her interest in education. She also feels she has become better informed and more liberal. She sees her husband as being more conservative than she is in political matters. She describes the changes which have taken place since college as follows:

> I have been active in practically everything that has to do with education—P.T.A., member of the school board, youth groups. I resigned from the Junior League. . . . (Have you changed your political attitudes?) Indeed I have changed. I think that government help along certain lines is good, used to think it was more bad than good. I believe in a stronger central government than I used to; the public can't know about everything. I also approve of some federal aid to medicine, education, old age. The principal reason

for my change has been my one particular interest in education. I have done so much more reading in this area. There is such a close tie with so many things—apply to many areas. I am better informed about issues. Until recently I was a firm Republican. Now I think that Kennedy is terrific. The more I read, the more I am glad that Kennedy won. I say I am a Democrat in (*name of resort town*) but not really, just for the sake of discussion. I am about three-fourths of the way toward liberal.

$Q73$ is an example of a pattern which occurred fairly frequently of increased interest and involvement in political matters leading to a decrease in conservatism. The women who became involved in any one issue or cause became better better informed about other issues and better informed about ways of accomplishing changes in the community. This increased interest in politics led to more discussion of issues and often forced them to think through their political orientation more clearly.

Both $Q73$ and $Q63$ maintained their friendships with other Bennington alumnae, and each of them was mentioned frequently by other respondents in the study as friends. For the most part the friendships that they have maintained have been with people who also scored below the median on conservatism on the 1960 Political Conservatism Index.

The patterns of change in political attitudes on the part of $Q63$ and $Q73$ since they graduated from college are just the opposite of those that they experienced in college when $Q63$ became much less conservative and $Q73$ remained relatively unchanged. Since college, $Q63$ has remained relatively unchanged, whereas $Q73$ has become much less conservative. As a result of these changes, in 1960–1961 $Q63$ and $Q73$ were both relatively nonconservative as compared with their peers and very similar to each other. From the information in their interviews, it might be predicted that in the next few years $Q73$ will continue to become more liberal, whereas $Q63$ is likely, if anything, to become more conservative.

Overview

One of the important concerns of the follow-up study was the question: Under what conditions would individuals who had become less conservative during their college years remain relatively nonconservative 20-odd years later and under what conditions would they return to relatively conservative positions? From the data presented in earlier chapters it appears that one of the crucial factors in determining whether a person returned to a conservative political attitude after college was the attitudes of her husband or of her close friends.

Five women among the selected cases just presented had become much less conservative in college (*Q61, G32, E12, K42,* and *Q63*). Of these, only *E12* returned to her precollege conservative position in 1960–1961. She fits the pattern of becoming conservative again after having moved into a conservative social environment. However, *K42* also moved into a conservative environment and did not change back to a conservative outlook. The factors that enabled *K42* to maintain a nonconservative point of view are not provided by the information in the interview.

Another interesting variation of the general trend is provided by *G32*. Why did she marry a nonconservative and continue to become less conservative after college? It is true that her attitude scores on the PEP scale dropped considerably in college, but the change was from an extremely high score to a moderately high score. She still scored much above the median on conservativism when she graduated. Compared with her peers she was relatively conservative as a senior, yet in 1960–1961, compared to these same peers, she was relatively nonconservative. What kept her moving away from the conservative position? Nothing in her family or background supported this type of change.

Q61 and *Q63* vary somewhat from the trend described in the preceding chapters, although they were nonconservative when they graduated, married men with nonconservative attitudes, and were nonconservative in 1960–1961. Their postcollege experiences were not uniformly supportive of a nonconservative position. *Q61* had the support of her husband, but the opposition of her family, friends, and community, and she was much aware of this opposition. *Q63* had become disinterested in political matters and, although she reported no major opposition to her point of view, she also reported no support for it. Political matters or ideology were not subjects of discussion, so that her point of view remained the same for 20 years, mainly because it had not come up for review, apparently.

That *Q72* and *L91* maintained a position of relative nonconservatism over the years is not surprising because most of their experiences—precollege, college, and postcollege—supported a nonconservative position.

Similarly, *Q70* and *Q47* had maintained a conservative position in college in opposition to the majority trend, perhaps because of their precollege experiences, so that when they moved into a postcollege environment which supported a conservative outlook, they persisted in their conservative orientation over the years.

It is more difficult to understand why Q28 and Q73 became relatively nonconservative after college. Q28 is one of the few women who came to college conservative and, as measured by her attitude scores, left even more conservative. Because Q28 came from a conservative family and background and seemed to be unaffected by the nonconservative political climate at Bennington, one might have expected her to marry someone who was conservative and from the same background as she. However, she married someone who was nonconservative, who encouraged her to become active in political matters and who influenced her to become less conservative. One could not have predicted this outcome from Q28's precollege and college history.

Q73 does not fit any patterns derived from the total set of data. She came from a conservative background, remained conservative in college, married a conservative, lived in a conservative community, yet became relatively nonconservative after college. She explains this change as a result of her activities and interests in education which had forced her to become informed about many issues. She had been confronted with trying to induce change in her community and had become aware of the difficulties of producing change. The events which led to Q73's change in political philosophy are not predictable from her college and precollege history.

The case histories, viewed together, demonstrate that it is difficult to develop any single formula that will explain and describe the development of each person's political attitudes since she left college. The importance of public affairs to the individual, the degree to which her attitudes toward them are integrated with other values, the degree to which such attitudes were developed and set during college years—all of these factors are measured and known in imperfect fashion. In spite of error and the amount of critical information that is not known, the follow-up study shows clearly that the majority of graduates from Bennington in 1938, 1939, and 1940 have maintained attitudes until 1961 which are relatively the same as the positions they held as seniors in college. The critical influence for change on most of the women who changed their political orientation was the attitudes of their husbands. The exceptions to these findings are interesting, but occur in such small numbers that no generalizations about them can be made.

PART THREE

The College Community
in the Early 1960's

9. Community Norms, 1959–1962

The aim of this chapter is to explore the informal atmosphere or "student culture" found at Bennington College in the early 1960's.* The discussion will focus specifically upon what seemed to be the dominant social norms at that time, and will introduce data of various kinds to show the extent of consensus about these norms and the nature of the sanctions used to make them effective. In Chapter 10 we shall turn to the related question of how newcomers to the community adapt themselves to the existing norms.

The Setting

The student culture found on a campus at any given time is the product of many historical, geographical, ecological, and cultural forces, but certainly three of the most important are: (1) the history of the college and its formal traditions, (2) its current administrative policies, and (3) the background characteristics of the students who find themselves attracted to it. Such seems to be the case, at least, in the small student community found at Bennington College.

Like many "experimental" colleges, Bennington came into being with a sense of educational mission which it retains to this day, and which seems to leave its mark upon many of its graduates. Its original aim was not to be just another good small college, but rather to provide a viable alternative to the "traditional" liberal arts college through innovations in curricular as well as social policy. It was no accident that Bennington opened its doors in the early 1930's at a time when the progressive movement in education still enjoyed the verve of youth. Although John Dewey himself had no direct hand in the founding of the college, his influence was clearly present and

---

* An earlier version of this chapter and many of the findings reported in Chapter 10 were included in D. P. Warwick, *Socialization and Value Change in a College Community*, unpublished doctoral dissertation, University of Michigan, 1963.

even today his statue stands prominently in the entrance to the main classroom building. Also influential in the early history of Bennington was William H. Kilpatrick, a noted spokesman for the progressive education movement and long the chairman of the college's Board of Trustees.

Today Bennington is no longer considered a new experiment in education, but together with Sarah Lawrence College is still widely regarded as a prototype of the "experimental-artistic" college. Its reputation has now crystallized to the point where the stereotyped "Bennington girl" is the subject of cartoons in the *New Yorker*, with the result that the entering freshman of today probably has a better notion of what to expect from the college than did her counterpart of some 30 years ago. But in its formal aims, emphases, and educational policies Bennington has changed very little over the years, and this fact in itself lends the weight of tradition to some of the social norms found among the present generation of students.

The following statement taken from the Bennington College Catalogue for the years 1962–1963 summarizes the basic educational policies followed by the college since its foundation:

> The college encourages the students to engage voluntarily in learning, to acquire lasting interests and an objective understanding of the world in which they live. To this end, the student is encouraged to work at tasks which have meaning to her, to learn the inherent discipline of good work, and to take an active part in her own education. External discipline, such as compulsory courses, competitive grades, formal examinations, the numerical accumulation of credits, and other mechanical devices are avoided as seriously interfering with real incentives and active learning.

As we shall later show, these policies are more than a mere set of catalogue ideals; they are closely related to the norms of intellectuality and individualism in the student community.

There are three general ways in which the policies just cited are put into practice in the organization of activities at the college, all of them uncommon among colleges in the United States. First, following the lines set by its founders, Bennington takes positive steps to incorporate direct experience and active participation into the learning process. In the general curriculum of the college this policy is reflected in the fact that the creative and performing arts rank equally with the more traditional disciplines. Similarly, the college encourages direct experience in learning through small seminars whose success rests upon active student participation, and through individual projects and performances which are often coupled with tutorial sessions. Finally, the two-month nonresident winter term is an intrinsic part of the Bennington program, and is viewed as an effective means of helping the student to see the practical relevance of her studies by taking a job in a field related to her interests.

A second way in which Bennington College seeks to provide an atmosphere conducive to learning is by encouraging informality in faculty-student relations and by rejecting some of the most entrenched traditions of academia. Members of the faculty do not carry the usual academic ranks and titles, and students are not expected to address them as "Professor" or "Doctor." Grades are not used as the measure of a student's performance, nor are accumulated credit hours the primary criterion for graduation. Moreover, both students and faculty are members of an Educational Policies Committee which considers matters ranging from new courses to decisions about potential faculty members. Thus, although it would be unrealistic to say that faculty and students have an equal voice in policy decisions at Bennington, the gap that separates them is smaller than in most schools, and their interaction accordingly seems to be less stiff and constrained.

Third, Bennington continues to be distinctive in encouraging programs of study that are tailored to the individual interests and abilities of each student. The college does not rely upon the usual set of programmed courses leading to a "major," but rather leaves the arrangement of a schedule of study to the student and her counselor. To ensure that the original plan keeps pace with her interests and capacities, each student must prepare a summary and appraisal of her work at the end of her sophomore year. This analysis serves the double function of forcing the student to be clear about her goals and of preparing the way for the choice of a meaningful field of specialization.

Both through its administrative policies and through traditions that have accumulated over 30 years, Bennington College thus encourages the student to discover her interests and abilities and provides her with a maximum amount of freedom to develop them. Social rules, academic distinctions, and formal requirements are viewed as potential barriers to intellectual and social development, and are kept to a minimum. In these ways the college itself contributes to a distinctive social and intellectual atmosphere.

Another factor which undoubtedly reinforces the "unconventional" atmosphere of Bennington College is self-selection on the part of the students themselves. Bennington has now been in existence for more than 30 years, and has achieved a national reputation as one of the foremost "progressive-experimental" colleges. Moreover, there is a certain folklore about the college and its students that circulates on other campuses and has apparently reached many sections of the American public as well. Therefore it is probably a rare student indeed who comes to this campus thinking that it will be an alternative to Smith, Vassar, or Wellesley.

It is difficult to produce direct evidence of self-selection in the data collected for the present study, but there are several signs which point clearly in this direction. The first and most convincing is a set of data showing that entering students are aware of the distinctive characteristics of Bennington before they arrive on the campus, and that most of them preferred to come to Bennington rather than any other college.

The data under consideration were obtained from questionnaires administered to 110 entering freshmen in the summer of 1960, shortly before they arrived on the campus. The information on the students' awareness of the distinctive characteristics of Bennington College was drawn from responses to the following item:

Do you think that there is anything special or distinctive about students at Bennington College?
———Yes   ———No

(If yes) What are these special and distinctive characteristics?

Of the 110 respondents, 87% felt that there were special or distinctive characteristics, 11% felt that there were not, and 2% did not answer the question. The distinctive characteristics most frequently mentioned by the students who said "Yes" are shown in Table 9.1.

Responses closely related to individualism, unconventionality, and intellectuality account for 81% of the distinctive traits mentioned. Other data to be presented later in this chapter suggest that these perceptions are essentially correct, and that the distinctive characteristics of the student body coincide with the prevailing norms in the community.

The results of the same questionnaire given to prefreshmen show, further, that students entering Bennington are not only aware of the main characteristics of their future peers, but also prefer this college community to others. When asked, "What were your first three choices for college, in order of preference?" 78% of the 110 respondents listed Bennington as their first choice. It is also interesting to note that only 21% of this group mentioned one of the "Seven Sisters" as *any one* of their preferences. Thus it seems that a majority of the students entering Bennington have a fairly accurate image of the

Table 9.1   Distinctive Characteristics of Bennington College Students, as Mentioned by Prefreshmen, Summer of 1960 *

1. *Individualism, unconventionality:* independent, uninhibited, individualistic, self-aware, self-assured, noncomformist, introspective, etc.	41%
2. *Intellectuality, attitudes toward education:* intellectually involved, aware, esthetically interested, serious about work, dedicated to own field, creative, original, intelligent, etc.	40%
3. *Political-social attitudes:* liberal progressive, broadminded, unprejudiced, idealistic, concerned with others, etc.	10%
4. Other	6%
5. Don't know	3%
(*N* = 261 responses)	100%

* The data reported here were obtained by coding the first three characteristics mentioned by each respondent. A total of 261 responses were classified in this way, and the figures reported are percentages of this total.

college before they arrive on the campus, and choose this setting because they think that it will be compatible with their own attitudes, values, and beliefs. In this way a circle is begun in which the reputation of the college draws a certain type of student whose presence serves to reinforce the reputation and then attract others with similar views.

There are also two other, though less direct, indications that students entering Bennington are initially less conventional than those entering most other colleges. First, a comparative survey of attitudes and values on several campuses indicates that Bennington freshmen are more "unconventional" and "rebellious" than freshmen entering Vassar (Webster, Freedman, and Heist, 1962). The results of this survey were based upon several attitude scales drawn from the Omnibus Personality Inventory (Appendix L), and they suggest that Bennington students are more "flexible and uncompulsive; impunitive toward persons, but critical of institutional authority of family, state, or religion; nonconforming . . ." (p. 829).*

Second, students who enter Bennington seem to be less committed to formal religious institutions than their counterparts at most American colleges and universities. The results of the present study show that 60% of the freshman class in 1962 reported no attendance at

* The specific measure under discussion is the Developmental Status Scale, an index made up of attitude items that distinguish younger from older students.

religious services and only 7% reported regular attendance. These figures contrast with those obtained in a study of 11 major universities in which only 25% report no attendance and over half attend services at least once a month (Goldsen, Rosenberg, Suchman, and Williams, 1960, p. 157).

Certain background characteristics of the Bennington student body must also be noted. A relatively low proportion of students are Roman Catholics (4%) and a correspondingly high proportion are from Jewish families (39%). Also noteworthy is the geographic background of the students and their social class. In 1962 no less than 82% of sophomores, juniors, and seniors came from the eastern part of the United States, with nearly 50% from New York City or its environs. Within the same population, 81% reported themselves as coming from either the upper class (14%) or the upper-middle class (67%).

The political orientations of the present generation of entering freshmen are sharply different from those seen in 1936. In 1960 only 34% of the freshmen preferred the Republican candidate (Nixon) as compared with 62% who preferred Landon in 1936. This difference is even more striking in view of the facts that over 95% of the Bennington student body is non-Catholic and in 1960 60% of non-Catholic voters in the country preferred Nixon (see pp. 46–47). Evidently the college's image had undergone considerable change over the 24-year span.

An oversimplified but reasonably accurate picture of the typical student entering Bennington at the time of this study would be: Eastern, upper-middle class, Protestant or Jewish, but with little inclination toward formal worship, liberal in political beliefs, and more unconventional or rebellious in her attitudes than a freshman entering a more "traditional" college.

Consensus on Community Norms

We have been interested not just in describing the history and administrative policies of Bennington College and the backgrounds of its student body, but also in showing their influence upon contemporary student culture. It is hardly a secret that at many universities there is a wide gap between the formal ideals of education embodied in discourses by administrators and the standards observed in the student culture or subcultures. Similarly, the relationship between the characteristics of the entering freshmen and the dominant norms and values on the campus is not always self-evident. We shall present evidence to show that there is a rather close fit between the two factors mentioned and the broad lines of student culture at Bennington College.

We shall focus upon only one aspect of student culture—the prevailing social norms in the college community. For present purposes we may define norms as *standards on which there is acknowledged consensus within a group and to which sanctions are attached.* This definition immediately suggests two relevant questions: (1) Are there any standards on which a majority of Bennington students seem to be in agreement? and (2) Are there rewards for those who adhere to these standards, or punishments for those who do not?

Our evidence for consensus about a somewhat distinctive set of standards comes in two forms: direct statements from interviews with members of the student body, and statistical indicators such as the percentage of agreement on various adjectives describing the college. The interview material will be considered first, mainly because it conveys more of the flavor of life in the community.

The Words of the Students

One of the most fruitful sources of information about norms was a set of interviews with 101 students during 1961 and 1962. During these sessions the students were asked about a variety of topics relating to their experience at the college, including the ways in which they had changed, the major types of social pressures in the community, and the long-term effects of Bennington upon their lives.*
An analysis of their responses suggests the following as the most salient norms in the Bennington community: (1) individualism, (2) unconventionality, (3) intellectuality, and, somewhat less prominently, (4) tolerance of differences in others' behavior.

The two themes that seemed to generate the most ardent and lengthy discussions in the interviews were those dealing with individualism and unconventionality. Although there was some variation in the meaning attached to these terms, the following definitions would be accurate in most cases:

Individualism: a striving for self-awareness and self-expression and for a synthesis of values and beliefs that is unique to each person.

---

* For a complete list of the questions used in the interview see Appendix I. The procedures used to select the respondents to be interviewed are outlined in Chapter 10.

Unconventionality: a total or partial rejection of certain values, norms, and behavior patterns associated with the larger society, and especially the middle class and eastern "society."

We shall attempt to go beyond these terms to the pattern of expectations that they represent in the student community.

A close examination of the interview material suggests that both a striving for individualism and a rejection of conventional norms are expected at Bennington College, and are very closely related. In a sense they are two sides of the same coin, one positive and one negative. The negative side includes a widespread expectation that students who come to the community will seriously question their previous values and beliefs and will reject at least some forms of behavior that are considered conventional in the larger society. But the real point of this norm, according to the ideals expressed by many of the respondents, is to set the stage for a positive striving for self-discovery and self-expression or, in short, for individualism. Let us consider this process in the words of the students themselves.

Individualism

First, there are many indications that individualism, as reflected in self-awareness and self-expression, is a positive norm at the college, whereas there are only a few signs that unconventionality is valued in itself. Consider these statements indicating the salience of "being an individual."

> They expect you to be yourself, think for yourself. There is a premium on being yourself—don't conform.
>
> You should think individualistic, don't think like the rest . . . if you don't want to conform it's your own business.
>
> People expect you to maintain the Bennington idea of being an individual, of doing what you think.
>
> The principles of Bennington are nebulous . . . but things are based upon individual needs.
>
> You're forced to be yourself.

When questioned about the specific meaning of "being an individual," a number of the students pointed to a joint process of self-awareness and self-expression. The first step in this process is reported to be questioning oneself carefully and honestly about abilities, interests, problems, and aspirations, whereas the ultimate aim seems to be an ability to express oneself in various areas of life.

The following excerpts suggest that there are community pressures toward both self-awareness and self-expression:

There is a pressure to find out what you are. This is a completely new kind of thing—measured against what you should be.

There are many things here that expose you to yourself. This is a very egocentric school in some ways.

Thinking and self-expression—let them work inside you. Bennington propounds both.

It (Bennington) had an effect of making me more aware of myself . . . you're isolated up here and you have no contact with the outside world and there are certain academic and social pressures, and then you go immediately into a reverse situation (nonresident terms) where you have to do for yourself in a world where you aren't isolated and protected. It's a shock treatment in a way.

A specific source of pressures to discover oneself seems to be Bennington's emphasis upon independent study and the fulfillment of individual needs in academic work, as reflected in these remarks.

Since Bennington is set up to be an ivory-tower intellectual center, it almost forces you to think inwards.

Independent work is stressed so that you have to think of yourself a lot.

There is a certain involvement in work which requires you to look into yourself.

In the process of discovering who she is, the Bennington student must also discover who and what she is not, and this phase often involves a painstaking and sometimes painful reappraisal of earlier values and beliefs. Many of the students interviewed noted that an attitude of questioning and doubting one's initial values was not only encouraged in the community but also expected, especially in the earlier years.

Precedent is tabooed. Don't rest on your previous background.

Bennington is conducive to breaking away from values of your family.

If you have never questioned your values you are looked down upon. . . . You may throw away your old values, then come back to them.

The school has a tendency to break down the person and forces you to question everything. . . . It becomes intense. It takes about one year to put yourself together again.

Many freshmen want to negate home or church, but as juniors or seniors they no longer feel it is necessary to impose this on others. Freshmen who don't rebel in this way are looked down upon, and "who would associate with *them?*"

Unconventionality

The comments cited thus far point up the complex nature of the norm of individualism at Bennington College, and also suggest its close relationship with unconventionality. As the students themselves point out, the process of self-discovery often leads to doubts about earlier values and about conventional norms in general. From here it is only a short step to an outright rejection of conventions and to patterns of behavior widely regarded as unconventional. The following statements suggest that a good number of the students take this step at some point in their careers:

To be not conventional, to not conform, to do something bizarre is OK. To follow what is accepted on the outside is bad.

This college is delightful because it attracts people who don't think or act conventionally.

There is a freedom for eccentricity and variety.

There are two directions of unconventionality. One is negative: the idea of Bennington girls being loose and immoral—rich girls who can afford to be morally irresponsible. The other one is Bennington's education allowing girls a lot of freedom to work in the ways they feel most competent.

Perhaps the most commonly mentioned form of unconventionality at Bennington is in the area of dress and appearance, and the following remarks indicate that such unconventionality may be expected among some groups of students:

It seems that you're almost supposed to be a bit weird in dress just to say you're not bound by tradition or custom.

Conventional clothes, for one thing, aren't acceptable. As a sophomore, friends sat down and talked with me about my dress.

Now I can maintain a self without going to ridiculous extremes. This shows up in your hair and your lipstick. Some things are done only to be rebellious.

I don't care for the sloppiness at Bennington or the wild hair either.

But another way of manifesting one's unconventionality seems to lie in the rejection of certain groups considered by the students to embody "convention."

> There is a definitive feeling against Ivy League, preppy Smith College.
> But the frowned-upon thing is being too Smithy.
> (Pressures on) people who read *Life* magazine . . . and anything to do with Society or the Junior League or "coming out."

Finally, it is worth noting that the community norms regarding individualism and unconventionality are closely related to an expectation of tolerance among the students. Tolerance, in the sense in which it is used at Bennington, usually means an attitude of "live and let live," a willingness to let others discover themselves and engage in unconventional behaviors. The following statements suggest that this form of tolerance is also expected in the community:

> You have to be liberal about behavior. Don't impose your standards on someone else.
> A Bennington rule of thumb is: it doesn't matter what you do as long as you don't inconvenience someone. You can do whatever you like in private. . . . Most of my friends are very tolerant of each other.
> I think that I'm in such a liberal atmosphere and people are so liberal that I learn to mind my own business.
> You're free to do anything so long as it doesn't impinge on others around you.

Thus a search for self, a rejection of conventions, and a tolerance of unconventional behaviors all seem to form part of the same complex of norms at Bennington College. A summary of the specific expectations and some suggestions about their interrelationship are shown schematically in Figure 9.1.

Intellectuality

The second major cluster of norms found in the Bennington community is that of *intellectuality*—a commitment to intellectual pursuits in general and to the development of basic intellectual skills. In one sense it should not be surprising to find that students in a college community are dedicated to serious study and to the formation of

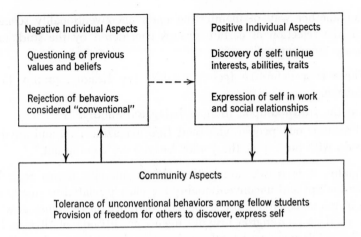

Figure 9.1 Community norms regarding individualism and unconventionality

the skills necessary to make them effective in their work. This is the stated aim of most colleges and universities. But it must also be admitted that there are wide differences in the extent to which this objective is reached, and that on some campuses the average level of intellectuality is reported to be low. Our argument, then, is not that Bennington is unique in possessing the qualities mentioned earlier, but that the entire area of intellectuality is more salient here than on many campuses, and that it is recognized as one of the major community norms.

The interview material is particularly clear in showing the extent of apparent intellectual involvement among the present generation of Bennington students. The remarks cited do not in themselves demonstrate the existence of a genuine commitment to learning, but they do point to strong community pressures in this direction. The following comments were typical:

There is a great emphasis upon intellectualism.

You have close friends who are academically excited about the same kinds of things.

One thing I've noticed when I go home and talk to my friends from Radcliffe and Smith is that I was the only one in the group who was excited about what we are doing academically. No damper is put on our enthusiasm.

I've never been with quite as much intellectual experience.

I came here in order not to be stifled. . . . Here so much energy is spent on intellectual things that there is not much left for staying out at night.

One of the specific ways in which the college contributes to intellectual involvement is by encouraging the development of an individualistic approach to study. Such an approach implies not only an understanding of material in the abstract, but an attempt to relate it to other fields and to one's own life. We have already seen that the college itself tries to foster this attitude in a formal way by its system of individual programs and counseling. The following remarks suggest that these efforts have been at least moderately successful:

I doubt that in any other college I could explore a field from my own viewpoint. Students from other colleges can spit back information, but they haven't thought things through as well. Bennington prepares you better for life.

Intellectually there is a tremendous emphasis upon your own response—pressure to use yourself and go into yourself. I've changed a great deal because of that.

You are allowed to think for yourself in the classroom. You can digest things for yourself. Teachers encourage you to find your own meaning.

(Bennington) has given me a new foundation for acquiring skills and knowledge. I may not know, but I know *how* to go about acquiring knowledge.

Another facet of intellectuality is the development of critical and analytic skills. Both students and faculty have noted the critical spirit that seems to emerge from the total experience at the college, an approach which is applied equally to assigned reading materials and to the norms of the larger society. The following comments illustrate this aspect of student culture:

It's a very critical atmosphere. Nothing comes up that isn't challenged.

It's a training period in how to evaluate things critically.

I've become much more critical of things in general.

A final aspect of intellectuality and perhaps the culmination of all the others is a commitment to learning and the arts after graduation.

Here, too, one might object that this is the aim of all colleges, but Bennington students more than many others seem to make a point of the long-term implications of their education. As the following students point out:

Bennington prepares you to keep a learning process going. It's so much centered about having you help yourself.

It gives you an incentive to go on with your education. I want to be able to read the books and go to concerts . . . that I haven't been able to do.

It has opened up an intellectual world for me. I will continue to be well informed and to know how to do it.

I'll have more of a desire to incorporate the arts in my life. This is a feeling more than a course.

Thus interviews with about one-third of the Bennington student body point to individualism-unconventionality and intellectuality as the most salient and perhaps most distinctive norms in the community. The themes that emerge from these interviews are quite different from those seen in the 1930's at Bennington when norms about public affairs were highly salient, and there were community pressures against political conservatism. Today's students, on the other hand, seem to encounter many pressures to discover themselves and to become involved in intellectual affairs, but not necessarily to change political views. In fact, some of the respondents openly admitted that they and many others at Bennington were fairly liberal in their political views, but also decidedly apathetic about the whole matter.

Supporting Data

The interview material considered thus far is not the only source of information about norms at Bennington College. Several other sets of data are available from the present study, and there are also independent observations made by other investigators.

Adjective Check List

One of the simplest and most direct indicators of consensus in the community consists of data obtained from an adjective check list given to the students in the fall of 1959. Respondents were asked to consider Bennington College students in general and then to check the

Table 9.2 Adjectives Reported to Be Distinctive of the Students at
Bennington College (*N* = 320)

Adjective	Percent of Students	Adjective	Percent of Students
Creative	95	Liberal	75
Independent	91	Serious	73
Individualistic	91	Unconventional	73
Original	83	Versatile	73
Progressive	83	Capable	72
Sensitive	77	Alert	71
Critical	76	Esthetic	70
Introspective	76	Interests wide	70
Resourceful	76	Outspoken	70

adjectives which distinguished them from women in other colleges.*
Table 9.2 shows those characteristics which were regarded as distinctive by at least 70% of the 320 students who completed the questionnaire.

Even a quick inspection of the findings in Table 9.2 shows that the adjectives form clusters which approximate the pattern of norms in the interviews. Without undue strain on the data it is possible to group these 18 adjectives under the headings used earlier, with the following result:

Individualism-unconventionality: creative, independent, individualistic, introspective, liberal, progressive, unconventional, outspoken.

Intellectuality: esthetic, alert, capable, critical, interests wide, original, resourceful, serious, versatile.

---

* The specific instructions were as follows:

There follows a list of adjectives, taken from a standard list developed at the University of California. You are to check those adjectives which apply, not to yourself or any other particular individual, but to Bennington College Students. Please read through the list quickly, and for each adjective insert a check mark if you consider it Somewhat Distinctive of a considerable number of persons listed at the top of the column. A check means Somewhat Distinctive of that group, not absolutely distinctive, since in any group individuals differ a good deal in most respects.

The column that provided the data reported here carried this heading: Bennington students in general, as compared with women in other colleges.

Although the fit between the characteristics and the categories is not perfect, the classification does underscore the salience of the themes of individualism-unconventionality and intellectuality in the Bennington culture. The principal weakness of these results for present purposes, however, is that they give no indication that the distinctive characteristics of the college are also *expected* among the students themselves. Considered in the context of the other findings reported here, however, they provide strong supporting evidence.

Definition of a "True Benningtonian"

A more striking source of data, but less susceptible to quantification, is the students' definitions of a "true Benningtonian." Perhaps because of the very norms of individualism and unconventionality which seem to be operative at the college, only one-half of the 184 persons questioned agreed that there was such a creature as a "true Benningtonian." The remainder either wrote that students at the college could not be classified, that the present generation no longer deserved the name, or that they did not know; or they left the space blank. Therefore the following statements are representative only of that segment of the student body which chose to answer the question with a positive response.

The principal inference to be drawn from these data is that some combination of individualism, unconventionality, and intellectuality is widely regarded as an ideal in the community. An analysis of the 92 definitions available shows that 33 of the responses (36%) reflect a combination of the major norms in the community. For example,

Intellectual, arty, somewhat eccentric, strong-minded.

Creative, sensitive, intellectual, individualistic.

Intent upon individual learning, intellectual, strong students, attractive in an individual way.

People who can think things through, are individual in what they say and how they act, are true to themselves.

Long hair, pale, very bright, very arty.

Open-minded, curious, bizarre, interesting.

Free-thinking, creative, off-beat, individual.

Mostly mature, interested, original, diverse backgrounds, sometimes creative, in general more than average intelligence. Interesting. Too wrapped up in themselves.

Creative as well as analytical, direct, open.

The definitions also include 26% that deal with individualism or unconventionality alone, 21% with intellectuality alone, and 17% with areas that are not related to these categories. Most of this last set were, however, consistent with the views expressed here about the culture at Bennington College. For example,

John Dewey disciple.

Confused, and so am I.

Dancers.

Those proud of the Bennington tradition.

A real swinger and member of the resistance. Also knows something about what she's resisting. Also new type hybridized with preppies.

Those who can last four years.

Only one of the 92 responses was inconsistent with the trends noted earlier, and that was a definition of the "true Benningtonian" as "middle-class."

Distinctive Characteristics of Students

Another set of data that is consonant with the hypothesis advanced in this chapter comes from an open question about the distinctive characteristics of Bennington students. Because the respondents were again left to their own resources in answering the question, there were many blank spaces, but nevertheless over half (55%) gave answers that fell into at least one of the following categories of individualism or unconventionality:

Individualistic, want to express themselves, be themselves, independent, free in thought or action, uninhibited, natural nonconformist, unconventional, rebellious, nongroup-minded, different.

Similarly, 35% singled out one or more of the following general intellectual attitudes as distinctive of their fellow students:

Intellectually involved, interested, intellectual, sophisticated, clear-thinking, esthetically oriented, interested in new ideas, inquisitive, curious.

Finally, 33% of the respondents noted that Bennington students showed at least one of the following attitudes toward education and their studies:

Interested in education for its own sake; academically oriented; serious about work, learning; dedicated to own field of study;

interested in pursuing own field of interests, developing their own talents.

The percentages reported here are not high in absolute terms, but they were the highest of any of the categories of "distinctive characteristics." * The specific phrases used by the students in responding to the question were often identical in wording or in content with responses that were made to the interview material. Thus the set of data as a whole provides one more indication that the dominant norms in the community center about the topics of individualism, unconventionality, and intellectuality, although it should be noted that these findings again do not show that the traits which are distinctive are also expected in the community.

Students' Descriptions of Themselves

The next set of findings is drawn not from statements about the community as such, but from students' descriptions of themselves as individuals. These findings are offered not to provide direct evidence of the existence of norms, but rather to show further the salience of the themes of individualism, unconventionality, and intellectuality at Bennington. Perhaps it is reasonable to assume that in a small, intimate community the students will place direct or indirect pressures upon their peers to adopt the traits most characteristic of themselves.

The self-descriptions under discussion are based upon a series of 19 items included in the final questionnaire given in 1962. The aim of these questions was to obtain more systematic information about certain traits commonly mentioned in the 40 interviews taken in 1961. The items were designed to include not only the characteristics most frequently noted in the interviews, such as "individualistic," but also others hardly mentioned at all, such as "committed to religious beliefs," and they were almost always phrased in the students' own words. The information used here was obtained by rating each of the 19 statements on a five-point scale ranging from "not at all characteristic of me" to "most characteristic of me." The complete set of items is shown in Table 9.3.

Table 9.3 shows that the four items most often reported as "most characteristic of me" deal precisely with the themes of individualism and intellectuality. These results show again that a significant proportion of the Bennington student body considers its main traits to be individualism and a long-term commitment to intellectuality,

---

* The total of the percentages mentioned exceeds 100% because more than one response was coded for this question.

Table 9.3   Proportion of Bennington Students Endorsing Items as "Most Characteristic of Me"

Items	Percent
Question things about myself	62
Individualistic—try to be myself	55
Able to continue the learning process after college	54
Express myself—what I think and feel	46
Approach and explore material from my own viewpoint	23
Willing to support my convictions with action	21
Absorbed in studies and academic work	20
Tolerant of behaviors that may violate my standards	19
Critical and analytic in my approach to material	17
Unconventional in opinions and beliefs	16
Committed to learning for its own sake	16
Question or doubt the beliefs or values I brought to college	10
Similar to my parents in values and beliefs	9
Disapprove of the style of life in Ivy League colleges	8
Conservative in political and economic views	7
Absorbed in social life and dating	6
Committed to religious beliefs	6
Bothered by ideas very different from my own	5
Self-centered—not concerned with the problems and needs of others	3

whereas very few check items such as "absorbed in social life and dating," "conservative in political and economic views," or other statements socially acceptable in other circles but contranormative here.

It is quite possible, of course, that the results would have been different if the list of traits had been expanded to include aspects of interpersonal relationships and personality in general, such as "kind," "warm," or "generous." But the present list did make it possible for nearly all students in the college to rank those characteristics singled out by individual members of the community as distinctive of the college, with results that lend support to other findings dealing more explicitly with the question of norms.

Other Studies

Perhaps because of its unusual history and its liberal policies, Bennington College has been included in a number of comparative studies of American colleges, several of which bear directly upon the question of norms. One of the most ambitious and elaborate of these comparative efforts is the series of investigations undertaken by Pace and Stern (Stern, 1962) with the College Characteristics Index and a related scale called the Activities Index. The principal aim of their research is to probe into the qualities and effects of various types of college environments by using the reports of students themselves. The questionnaires used to elicit this information are rather complicated, but deal basically with the reported needs of the student population and with the most prominent areas of social pressure ("college press").

Stern's analysis of the results obtained with these scales from a sample of Bennington students generally confirms the findings noted in the present study with regard to community norms.* The dominant themes running through his data on student needs and social pressures are approximately what we have termed individualism-unconventionality and intellectuality, although his terminology differs somewhat from our own. The following, for instance, are reported to be among the most notable forms of social pressures:

> *Intellectuality.* The marked intellectual needs and aspirations of these girls are very strongly supported by [pressures] at this school. . . . There are also especially strong facilities in the humanities, however, and the students express their interests in art, music, and the theater in many different ways. Long, serious intellectual discussions are common here. . . . Most courses are a real intellectual challenge, requiring intensive study and preparation out of class. . . . In class discusions, papers, and exams, the main emphasis is on breadth of understanding, perspective, and critical judgment.
>
> *Dependency needs.* Students are encouraged to be independent and individualistic, and there is a high degree of respect for nonconformity and intellectual freedom; students are encouraged in many ways to criticize administrative policies and teaching practices (Stern, 1962, pp. 720–721).

Thus, according to an independent report on the community, the over-all culture at Bennington College tends to spur the student in the directions of independence and individualism, intellectuality, and nonconformity, that is, the same areas of pressure suggested by our

---

* In the report cited here the author does not identify the community under study by name. However, subsequent correspondence with Professor Stern indicated that the school mentioned was Bennington College.

data. A more recent study by Stern (1963) lends further support to his thesis about the intellectuality of the college by showing that Bennington ranks with such colleges as Oberlin, Reed, and Swarthmore on an index of Intellectual Orientation.

Another source of comparative data lies in the studies conducted at the University of California with a series of measures collectively labeled Omnibus Personality Inventory. The principal findings relevant to the present discussion follow.

1. Bennington students scored significantly higher than Vassar students on three scales: (1) Developmental Status: an index of rebelliousness and independence, criticism of institutional authority, nonconformity, etc.; (2) Social Maturity: freedom from such characteristics as authoritarianism, rigidity, conventionality, and anti-intellectualism; and (3) Impulse Expression: readiness to express impulses, reflected in dominance, aggressiveness, and similar traits (findings summarized from Webster, Freedman, and Heist, 1962, p. 831).

2. Bennington freshmen obtained higher mean scores than freshmen at the University of California (Berkeley) and at San Francisco State College on scales called Agnosticism-Atheism, Developmental Status, Estheticism, and Originality. The differences between the scores for the colleges were statistically significant (Center for the Study of Higher Education, 1962, p. 61).

3. Bennington freshmen scored significantly higher on measures of Estheticism and Nonauthoritarianism than a sample of 259 female National Merit Scholars (Heist and Williams, 1957, p. 13).

Both the data collected in the present study and the results of other studies thus suggest that the prevailing norms at Bennington College center about the themes of individualism, unconventionality, intellectuality, and tolerance. Although much of the evidence regarding consensus on these themes is fragmentary, the aggregate of the material presented here indicates that expectations in these areas were part of the pattern of community life at Bennington College in the early 1960's. It remains now to show that there were sanctions attached to these expectations.

Sanctions and Community Norms

The specific sanctions used to enforce any set of community norms will depend upon the type of group involved and upon ecological factors such as size, isolation, and opportunities for members to interact and to monitor each other's behavior. In tightly controlled institutions such as armies, prisons, convents, and mental hospitals there is a marked tendency to rely upon sanctions deriving from prescribed rules and formal authority, and in a totalitarian society almost any sanction is used if it produces conformity. In the American college community, on the other hand, the really effective sanctions are usually not those meted out by the Dean of Students or other officials, but the subtle rewards and punishments administered informally by peers and faculty. At Bennington these informal sanctions are made especially powerful by the frequency and intimacy of student interaction, and by the relative absence of the usual formal rules governing conduct in the community.

In order to demonstrate that there are sanctions attached to the standards of individualism, unconventionality, intellectuality, and tolerance we shall present evidence showing that: (1) nonconformity with the prevailing standards is punished by isolation, ridicule, and other negative sanctions; and (2) rewards such as admiration and respect go to those individuals who reflect the dominant norms in their attitudes and behavior. We shall also show that the standard of political nonconservatism, a norm in the Bennington community of the 1930's, is now no longer directly related to sanctions in the community.

Negative Sanctions

It is a difficult task to obtain extensive and specific information about negative sanctions in a college community, for to do so would require a kind of participant observation that could readily be construed as spying. However, in the 101 interviews obtained in this study the students themselves gave at least some general indications of the types of negative sanctions used at Bennington, and of the types of behavior to which these were applied. An analysis of these interviews suggests that the measures taken differ considerably in their stringency, and range from direct steps such as harassment and face-to-face ridicule to indirect controls such as gossip and social ostracism. The most common types of negative sanctions are listed here, together with relevant statements from the interviews.

1. *Direct steps: harassment, face-to-face discussion of faults, etc.*
I have had no connection with my house. Lately they have been aroused and bother me. I don't want to play a game. The minute

they get in a group they have destructive tendencies. Individually they are fine. The names they would call me! A lot of people have this happen. Some don't care, some care and try to cope, some fight back. Harassment on many levels.

(Pressures at Bennington?) If they don't like what you think they'll tell you. May lead to arguments.

I was so disillusioned when I came here. I was scared of them. A few seniors laid it on the line to me.

On an intellectual basis they may reply to you, "That's ridiculous."

2. *Isolation from the community*

If a person was critical of Bennington College the students didn't talk to her, weren't friendly to her.

I think there is a lack of tolerance in a sense . . . girls a little more shy and not being able to really step up—they have been shoved into the background since other girls feel they don't have anything to offer. So you could go into a room and die and no one would know.

You may be ostracized socially—don't fit in.

3. *Gossip, denial of respect, other indirect measures*

I'm sort of tolerant. When people sit around and gossip and tear people apart I get angry. This is a good part of the life around here. I can't stand to see malicious gossip enlarge and grow. Meals are absolutely horrible for this. Also, whenever people get together.

People will talk about you, but it doesn't amount to anything. The community is small enough for people to notice what you do and condemn you for this.

People show their disapproval by talking critically with others who disapprove of it. It's never done face to face with the one who is being attacked.

One striking conclusion that emerges from a close analysis of the interview responses is that the negative sanctions are most frequently applied to behavior defined here as "conventional." The most common offenses seem to be identification with eastern Society and the Junior League, "collegiate" clothes, frequent dating, and a failure to question one's initial values and beliefs, as indicated in the following comments: *

---

* All of the statements quoted here were obtained in response to a question about standards and pressures at Bennington College. See Appendix I for the complete set of interview questions.

People who read *Life* magazine—you just don't do this. Precedent is tabooed—don't rest on your previous background. And anything to do with Society or the Junior League or "coming out." This is knocked and people are defensive about it. Real hostility . . . dating a lot is looked down upon, especially if you look the type (conventional).

Conventional clothes for one aren't acceptable. As a sophomore, friends sat down and talked with me about my dress. An awful lot of the girls wear muu-muus, etc.

Some kids go to church every Sunday and there are snickers around. To follow what is accepted on the outside is bad. In freshman year people talked to me about it.

The other behaviors which seem to merit sanctions such as isolation and backbiting include mainly a negative attitude toward Bennington and a failure to participate in the life of the community. Among the comments indicating this were the following:

The totally excluded girl would be introverted—the socially excluded girl is someone who is doing one thing too much.

I think there is a lack of tolerance in a sense . . . girls a little more shy and not being able to step up—they have been shoved into the background.

If a girl was critical of Bennington College the students didn't talk to her.

I had an anti-Bennington attitude, people reacted to this.

The interviews imply, then, that the tolerance often cited by the students as characteristic of Bennington is essentially a tolerance for behavior and attitudes which are considered unconventional in the society at large and not for infractions of norms within the community itself. Thus in order to gain at least minimal acceptance the entering freshman must divest herself of the more visible marks of conventionality, especially in her moral values, dress, and dating behavior, and must further show a tolerance for unconventional behavior on the part of others. Once she has made this adjustment she may or may not go on to win the admiration and respect of peers and faculty, but at least she will probably not be subjected to the more aggravating negative sanctions.

Positive Sanctions

Both the interviews and the questionnaires suggest that there are also positive sanctions at work in the Bennington community, and that the most potent of these are the respect and admiration of student peers. Here we will show that such sanctions are related to the prevailing norms in general, but that they are more closely related to the "ideal" norms of individualism and intellectuality than to the "minimal" norms of unconventionality and tolerance.

Our major source of evidence is a series of sociometric nominations in response to the following instructions:

Community Representative (Fall, 1959)

Suppose there was to be an important gathering of representative students from every type of American college during the coming winter. Each of the colleges selected is to be represented by three students who are to be chosen by their fellow students—not for ability to speak in public nor for any other special ability, but merely as worthy representatives of their institutions. . . . It is fair to assume that Bennington College will be judged, to a greater or less extent, by the students who represent it. List three students whom you consider most worthy to serve as such representatives.

Admiration (Fall, 1960)

Please enter below the names of at least two students (and no more than five) whom you *particularly admire,* no matter for what reasons.

With these two measures of respect and admiration it was possible to analyze the relationship between positive sanctions and standards.

Individualism. Three sets of statistical data indicate the extent to which the norm of individualism is supported with the sanctions of respect and admiration. In brief these are as follows:

1. Students frequently mentioned as *Creative Individualists* received more nominations as "Community Representative" and "Most Admired" than those listed as members of the *Social Group,* and these differences were statistically significant. In these comparisons the Creative Individualists were considered the embodiment of the ideal norms in the community, whereas the Social Group was portrayed as essentially conventional. The results showed that the Creative Individualists received an average of 3.9 nominations as Community Representative and 5.6 as Most Admired, whereas the corresponding

figures for the Social Group were 1.6 and 1.6; these differences are highly significant.*

2. Students with high scores on an index of individualism received more nominations as Community Representative than those with low scores, and the results were statistically significant $(p < .02)$. The measure of individualism was constructed by combining items measuring the perception of individualism as a distinctive feature of the college, scores on a six-item scale of Individual Orientation, and the ranking of "Opportunity to Be Creative and Original" as a career requirement. There was no significant relationship, however, between this index and nominations as Most Admired.

3. A statistically significant relationship $(r = .60)$ was found between nominations as Most Admired and as Creative and Original.† In this study creativity and originality are considered to be aspects of individualism and, more specifically, of self-expression. It is obvious, however, that these traits are also bound up with intellectuality.

---

* Nominations as *Creative Individualist* and as members of the *Social Group* were obtained from a panel of 40 students interviewed at that time. This panel included 10 members from each of the year levels at Bennington College. Each interviewee was presented with descriptions of six "types" of students and a list of students at her own year level or, in the case of the juniors and seniors, a list of students in both classes. They were then asked to select from the list the names of those students who fitted the description either partially or completely. In this way every student at the college was rated by at least 10 or 20 of her peers. (See Chapter 11 for further details.) The descriptions of Creative Individualists and members of the Social Group were as follows:

Creative Individualists. Girls who sincerely believe in certain principles and who stick by them though they are usually opposed by the society in general . . . people who feel they are superior intellectually and more sophisticated than other people . . . "intellectual snobs" according to some . . . seem very dedicated to creative pursuits . . . imaginative and free-thinking.

The Social Group. Very interested in their social life and talk about little else . . . do enough work to pass their courses, but main interest is in having as much fun as possible . . . concentrate on dating and meeting boys . . . because of interest in social life, may mask their intelligence . . . characterized as "preppy" by some . . . generally neat in appearance.

† The nominations as "Creative and Original" were obtained from a questionnaire administered in the fall of 1960 to all of the students but the freshmen. The specific item used was an open question which read as follows:

Please enter below the names of at least two students (and no more than five) whom you consider to be *unusually creative* or original.

Because of time differences in the several sociometric nominations it was not meaningful to relate nominations as Community Representative (1959) with those as Creative and Original (1960).

These results thus provide rather convincing evidence that individualism is related to the positive sanctions in the Bennington community. On all of the available measures, those who show many signs of individualistic attitudes or behavior receive more nominations as Community Representative and Most Admired than those who show few such signs; in almost every instance the differences are statistically significant.

Intellectuality. Similar kinds of data are available concerning the relationship between intellectuality and the positive sanctions of respect and admiration.

1. Estheticism and Theoretical Orientation, the two scales of the Omnibus Personality Inventory that most seemed to reflect intellectuality, were significantly related to the indices of positive sanctions. The Estheticism Scale was significantly related to both nominations as Community Representative ($p < .01$) and as Most Admired ($p < .05$). Theoretical Orientation, on the other hand, was significantly related to Community Representative ($p < .01$), but not to Most Admired.*

2. A measure of intellectuality was shown to be significantly related to nominations as Community Representative ($p < .05$), but not to Most Admired. This index of intellectuality consisted of a combination of the following items: ranking of estheticism as a value; frequency of nonassigned reading; number of books owned; extent of reading of "serious" magazines.

These findings suggest that intellectuality is associated with the positive sanctions of respect and admiration in the student community.

Unconventionality. The norm is more closely related to negative than to positive sanctions in the Bennington community. Although students who show signs of unconventionality do seem to receive more respect and admiration than those who do not, the relationship between unconventionality and these sanctions is generally weak.

Perhaps the best measure of unconventional attitudes available in this study is the Developmental Status Scale of the Omnibus Personality Inventory. This is an empirically developed scale which contains attitude items differentiating freshmen from seniors, and which seems to reflect a kind of "Rebellious Independence" (Webster and Heist, 1959). The scores on this scale were related to the number of nominations as Community Representative and Most Admired, in the

---

* The Omnibus Personality Inventory (OPI) will be discussed in greater detail in Appendix L.

expected direction, but neither of the comparisons was statistically significant.

Students who are repeatedly nominated as Creative Individualists also show significantly higher scores on the Developmental Status Scale than those classified as members of the Social Group. It was shown earlier that nominations as Creative Individualists are significantly related to respect and admiration (and negatively so for nominations as Social), whereas the present findings indicate that unconventionality as measured by the Developmental Status Scale is not significantly related to these sanctions. Those who enjoy a high degree of respect and admiration are above average in their unconventionality, but not everyone who is highly unconventional is rewarded with respect and admiration. Thus unconventionality appears to be a facilitating but not a sufficient condition for high prestige in the student community.

Sanctions and Political Norms

If a study of community norms were pushed to its logical limits it would have to show not only that certain sets of standards are related to sanctions in the community, but that other standards are not. Throughout the course of this study an effort was made to pursue both objectives, but it does not seem profitable here to list all of the possible attitudes, values, and behaviors that are *not* normative. There is one area, however, which cannot be omitted from this discussion, and that is the question of attitudes toward politics and public affairs.

The original study of the 1930's reported a consistent and significant relationship between nonconservative political attitudes and prestige in the college community. An index of reputed "identification with the college community" (plus scores), as opposed to "negative community attitude" (minus scores), yielded the following relationship to PEP scores (see Chapter 4) in 1939 (Newcomb, 1943, p. 71):

Identification scores	N	Mean PEP scores
+15 or above	15	54.4
+5 to +14	23	60.6
−4 to +4	63	65.3
−5 to −14	32	67.9
−15 or below	10	68.2

Because of the importance of politics and public affairs in the earlier study, many items in this general area were included in the present investigation—both to replicate the original work and to arrive at a better understanding of changes in the Bennington community during the past three decades.

The clear finding from the present study is that politics and public affairs are no longer burning issues in the community; attitudes in these areas are essentially unrelated to the respect and admiration of student peers. One of the scales used in this analysis, for instance, was a composite measure of political liberalism, similar in content to the progressivism scale used in the first study. Contrary to the findings of the 1930's, political attitudes are not closely related to respect and admiration in the community, although liberal students do receive more nominations as Community Representative and Most Admired than do those rated as conservative.

The information obtained during the interviews also supports the view that politics and public affairs are not major concerns among the present generation of students, and that political attitudes do not greatly affect one's standing in the community. These interviews leave little doubt that the prevailing atmosphere in the community is a liberal one, but it is an atmosphere that places little emphasis upon political involvement. A good number of students, in fact, simply described themselves as politically apathetic, and seemed to feel no regret about the matter. The correlation between nominations as Most Admired and Most Interested in Public Affairs was only .23, as contrasted with that of .60 between Most Admired and nominations as Creative Individualist.

The change in this respect over the intervening quarter-century can be indicated by the following excerpt from the original study of the 1930's. The "high-scoring" and "low-scoring" groups refer to the most and least conservative sixths, respectively (22 individuals in each group), of the seniors graduating in 1938, 1939, and 1940.

Half of the low-scoring group [11 individuals] are mentioned twice or more, and one-third of them [7 individuals] are mentioned five times or more as "most absorbed in national and international affairs," whereas only one individual among the high-scoring group is mentioned as often as twice [and none more often]. . . . The fact that a cross section of student judges mentioned so many individuals extremely low in PEP score and only one student extremely high . . . reveals what they thought the situation to be. Extreme interest in public affairs [as judged by peers] is associated with nonconservative attitude [as known by the investigator], whereas conservative attitude is associated with indifference (pp. 70–71).

A quarter of a century later there was virtually no such relationship; the majority of students, whether prestigious or not, tended to be nonconservative.

Although political attitudes are thus not irrelevant in determining a student's status at Bennington, they are viewed more along the dimension of conventionality-unconventionality than of liberalism-conservatism. A student with conservative attitudes will usually experience some pressures to question her stand, but more because an unquestioned conservatism is regarded as conventional than because these views in themselves are rejected. The community norm thus seems to deal more with the questioning of political values than with their content, although the "unquestioning" conservative is likely to be subjected to more pressures and negative sanctions than the "unquestioning" liberal.

Summary

Several distinctive norms appear in the student community at Bennington College; they center about the themes of individualism, unconventionality, intellectuality, and, to a lesser degree, tolerance. Evidence both from interviews with 101 students and from questionnaire responses by larger populations at different times indicates that there is a substantial degree of consensus on these standards, and that they are enforced with both positive and negative sanctions.

There also appear to be differences in the functions that these four norms serve in the community, differences which we have attempted to capture with the concepts of *ideal* and *minimal* norms. The minimal standards for acceptance in the student body at large include at least a modicum of unconventionality in one's attitudes and a tolerance for unconventional attitudes and behavior on the part of others. Students who do not comply with these standards are likely to be subjected to some of the more painful negative sanctions used at Bennington, especially direct criticism, isolation, and gossip. The ideal norms, on the other hand, lie in the areas of intellectuality and a striving for individualism, and these more than the others are rewarded with the positive sanctions of admiration and respect in the community.

Figure 9.2 summarizes the relationships that we have found between community norms, individuals' acceptance by their peers, and the nature of sanctions.

Norms accepted by student	Degree of acceptance by peers	Typical sanctions
Neither minimal nor ideal	None	*Strong negative:* isolation, harassment, direct criticism
Minimal, but not ideal	Low	*Mild negative:* gossip, denial of respect
Minimal, partial acceptance of ideal	Moderate	*Mild positive:* above-average respect and admiration
Minimal and ideal	High	*Strong positive:* high degree of respect and admiration

Figure 9.2   Norms and acceptance in the student community *

* This is intended to be an illustrative rather than a definitive model. It is possible, for instance, that there is a curvilinear relationship between individualism and respect, so that those who are extremely individualistic would receive less respect than those who show a lower degree of this characteristic.

10. Adapting to Community Norms

The study of group norms leads naturally to the question of the ways in which individuals adapt to these norms. This is an especially relevant question at Bennington College where two of the most prominent standards in the community, individualism and unconventionality, are essentially "anti-adaptive" in character. The aim of this chapter is to examine the most common reactions to the norms outlined earlier, both for the students in general and for specific groups within the college. The emphasis here will be upon individual adaptation through changes in attitudes, values, and beliefs, whereas in Chapter 11 we will consider various forms of social adaptation.

Perhaps the key proposition underlying the entire discussion which follows is that the student's reaction to community norms will depend upon the extent to which they have become a personal problem for her, and the type of problem that they present. There is little doubt that the whole issue of peer-group standards is a sensitive one for individuals at this stage in their lives, but there are also many factors which influence the extent to which these become a personal problem. In the Bennington setting, for instance, it is extremely important to consider the student's own views at the time of her entrance into college. Some appear on campus with attitudes that show great discrepancy with the prevailing norms, whereas others seem to have been thoroughly "prepped" for Bennington through high school experiences, conversations with alumnae, and reading. The first group is often profoundly shocked early in their stay, whereas the second makes the transition with little difficulty.

We should not forget, however, that even those who enter with "congruent" attitudes may experience their own brand of problems at Bennington. Their very congruence, for example, may free them from some of the usual pressures toward "unconventionality," but also make them more susceptible to pressures issuing from the "ideal" norms of individualism and intellectuality. Across the community there tend to be similarities as well as differences in student adaptations to the prevailing norms, and it is essential to consider both.

138

Data Concerning Directions of Change

There are two sources of information about the directions of change that we shall note: (1) interviews with a total of 101 students in 1961 and 1962, and (2) various questionnaires administered to almost the entire student body.* The interviews provide insights into many aspects of the process of change, but they suffer from a lack of structured questions that would provide adequate statistical information on change, and also from the sampling methods used. The questionnaires, on the other hand, yielded reasonably satisfactory statistical information on change, but lacked the depth and flavor of the interviews. Analyses of both types of data follow.

The Words of the Students

The most striking feature of the interview responses on change is that they strongly reflect the dominant norms discussed in Chapter 9. †
The findings presented in Table 10.1 show that the most prominent themes of change are identical with the most important norms: individualism and intellectuality. Almost three-fourths of the students interviewed (73%) report an increase on at least one of the specific dimensions of individualism or intellectuality, and many report change on more than one dimension.

---

* Interviews were held with 40 students in 1961 and with 61 in 1962, so that about one-third of the student body was included in this phase of the study. In 1961 the students were selected by one of the faculty members who was asked to choose 40 students who would be representative of the various houses, classes, and majors, and who would be willing to be interviewed. In 1962 the 61 students were selected on the basis of their scores on a set of attitude scales considered to reflect community norms, the Omnibus Personality Scale. An effort was made to choose a sample which would include those who showed high as well as low conformity to the dominant norms. The sampling, therefore, was not based upon random methods. The questions used during the interviews and the questionnaire measures of change are reproduced in Appendix I.

† The methods used in obtaining systematic data from the 101 interviews were fairly simple and direct. The first step involved the construction of a code based upon the data obtained rather than upon *a priori* categories. This was done by reviewing a large number of the statements on change found in the interviews, and then devising code categories that would cover the majority of these responses. The code was then applied to the entire set of interviews, and the results were tabulated along the lines indicated here.

Table 10.1   Major Directions of Change Observed in Interviews with
Bennington Students ($N = 101$)

Area of Change *		Percent
1. Individualism, any mention		73
(a) Increased self-awareness	49	
(b) Increased self-confidence, strength, independence	42	
(c) Increased self-expression	11	
2. Intellectuality, any mention		73
(a) Increased intellectual awareness, broadening	37	
(b) Development of basic intellectual skills	33	
(c) Increased intellectual involvement	31	
(d) Long-term intellectual commitment	13	
3. Tolerance, any mention		48
(a) Less irritation, annoyance with peers	16	
(b) Increased understanding, acceptance of differences	15	
(c) Development of relativistic viewpoint	5	
4. Unconventionality, any mention		24
(a) Cyclical change	14	
(b) Increased unconventionality	10	
5. Other, any mention		46
(a) Changes in interpersonal attitudes	17	
(b) Changes in psychological adjustment	14	
(c) Changes in political attitudes	8	
(d) Changes in religious commitment	5	
(e) Changes in social life and dating	5	
(f) Other	9	

* The main headings (Individualism, Intellectuality, etc.) include the percentage of students who mentioned *at least one* statement in the area under consideration. These categories include statements that fell under the more specific headings of individualism, for example, as well as certain general statements that could not be classified under these headings. It should also be noted that it was possible for any individual to give statements that fell into more than one of the subheadings. Therefore, the percentages for the general categories (for example, 73%) should not be interpreted as sums of the more specific figures.

Again tolerance occupies third place on the list, with a total of 48% reporting change in this area. The results also indicate that about one-fourth of the students interviewed (24%) either report more unconventionality during their stay at Bennington or note some type of cyclical change in unconventionality. These findings add further support to the hypothesis that unconventionality is a much less important norm in the student community than individualism. Finally, there are several minor areas of change that deserve mention, including changes in interpersonal attitudes (17%), psychological adjustment (14%), and political attitudes (8%). In the following, we present a number of excerpts from the interviews which deal with the more frequently mentioned themes indicated in Table 10.1. They are designed to provide concrete illustrations of the meaning of each of the areas noted, and will capture in the students' own words the subtleties and complexities of the processes of attitude and value change.

1. Individualism (73%)

One of the two most significant areas of change seen in the interviews is that of individualism—a striving for self-awareness and self-expression, and for a synthesis of values that is unique to each person. According to the report of the students the most basic aim of this striving is to develop an ability to express oneself in work or in other areas. But to develop this ability it is first necessary to be aware of who one is, one's principal strengths and limitations, the main influences upon one's values and previous experiences, and similar aspects of the self. When the student has become at least somewhat aware of who she is, what she is striving for, and what her main resources are, she is more likely than before to accept herself, to feel stronger, and to sense a greater independence of those around her. With this combination of self-knowledge and personal strength she is more ready and better able to express herself, whether it be in social relationships or in creative work. Illustrative excerpts follow.

1a. Self-awareness (49%)

A heightened sense of self-knowledge, self-awareness, and introspection is commonly mentioned. Processes of self-analysis are often touched off by the questioning or doubting of earlier values and beliefs or of abilities, personality traits, and other characteristics, as in the following examples:

Here you sort of shed your background. It has led me to question the values of my own environment and reassess them and come up with a synthesis.

(How changed?) * Just by being away from home and realizing that so many of my values were inherited and shaped by my home. I was entirely sure of myself and now I'm not sure of myself in many areas.

Besides the questioning and doubting of earlier values and personal characteristics, there are several types of social pressures that also converge to create pressures toward self-discovery. Among these are the small size of the college, the opportunities for frequent and relatively intense interactions with peers and faculty, and above all a high degree of consensus upon the desirability of examining the self in depth. The following statements suggest that these converging pressures ultimately influence the types of change which are seen at the college:

The most important thing Bennington has done is to make me aware of myself as an individual.

The main change is in becoming aware of yourself—this contains other things. This is a vacillating thing . . . always wondering and trying to find out . . . things must come from you. There is a stress on you as an individual to cope with these ideas. . . . There is a certain involvement in work which requires you to look into yourself.

Bennington has turned me to look inside myself. It might have been that another school would have concentrated on studies—outside myself.

Other parts of the interviews illustrate specific ways in which students increase their self-awareness and self-knowledge. Some noted, for instance, increased awareness of their intellectual capabilities and interests, whereas others pointed to increased objectivity about their own personality traits, including faults, reactions to others, moods, and defense mechanisms.

The interviews thus leave little doubt about the salience of self-awareness as an area of change, but they do reveal some disagreement over the long-range benefits of this change. Six of the respondents directly or indirectly suggested that the self-awareness developed at Bennington may be ultimately harmful to the individual in that it fosters an excessive concern with the self or destroys the person's

---

* Here and in the following pages the specific interview question used in obtaining a response will be mentioned if the response is not clear in itself. For a complete list of the questions, consult Appendix I.

ability to commit herself to a definite set of values. Although this viewpoint was clearly in the minority, the following excerpts indicate that excessive self-awareness has been a problem for some students:

> My first year and a half I fell into Bennington sickness. I became intensely involved with my own problems. You sit on a mountain top and all that's around you are your problems and your studies. (Effect of Bennington?) . . . destructive character. It undermines people's ability to be effective. A lot of my values have ceased to be absolute . . . can't just act on it.

1b. Increase of Self-confidence, Strength, and Independence (42%)

The emphasis in this category is less upon sheer knowledge and awareness of self than the more dynamic traits of acceptance, confidence, and strength. In the view of Erikson (1959) and other psychologists, one of the critical problems facing young adults (including college students) in American society is that of achieving a satisfactory *identity*—a sense of self that is adequately clear and consistent, and which is accepted by important "others." In the process of working toward this identity many students frequently flounder and are plagued with doubts about themselves, their capacities, and their future. But as they approach the end of their college years many seem to have a clearer notion of who they are and also are more willing to accept the self-definitions they have worked out during this period. The result is often an increase in feelings of self-confidence and a greater sense of personal strength— a strength that equips the individual to deal with a wide variety of persons and situations. So, too, at Bennington College, if the following excerpts are valid indicators of self-development:

> The biggest thing that I've got from this school is a tremendous amount of self-confidence. I've been especially influenced by the faculty here—many are superb. I have always done well at things. It's just that I never believed it.

> Bennington is very conducive to making one a strong person, someone more prepared to cope with an opposing view, to handle situations in which they may find themselves. . . . I've become more set . . . given a choice between two things I've asserted my own ideas.

> I have more strength as a person. . . . Being more aware of things, of the negative and positive things within yourself, I'm more stable even though I'm more confused.

I learned a great deal of self-discipline and independence. You're forced to turn to yourself—you have to because of the system.

I'm more dependent on self than on someone else. You tend to exist for yourself—you're forced to by the nature of the system.

Many or perhaps most of the types of changes in self-confidence and independence noted here would probably be expected among most students of this age, and it is thus difficult to know whether they are the result of distinctive experiences at Bennington College. Although only comparative studies of different college settings will answer this question, it seems likely that these changes stem at least in part from the freedom and encouragement to independence that are provided in this setting.

2. Intellectuality (73%)

The second major direction of change reflected in the interviews is that of *intellectuality*. Our findings indicate that changes in the general area of intellectuality rank equally with changes in individualism, and that these two are by far the most prominent themes in the interviews. As illustrated in the following, the intellectual changes reported are often striking, and seem to reflect the prevailing norms in the community.

2a. Increased Intellectual Awareness and Broadening (37%)

Over one-third of the respondents indicated that they had changed at Bennington by expanding their horizons of knowledge, becoming more aware of what there is to know, increasing their awareness in specific fields, etc. Among their statements were the following:

I feel I've changed enormously, first in awareness of what there is to know and what I don't know—literature, art, etc. . . . I can read philosophy and literature and begin to understand.

It has broadened me and broadened my outlook. . . . I broadened my views here.

A new world of intellectual ideas has opened up.

Of course, your horizons of knowledge expand.

I'm more aware politically and socially because of the people I've met. I've changed here—I've got more things to think about.

Thus changes in intellectual awarness may take many forms, ranging from a general broadening of one's outlook and perspective on life to a heightened awareness of society, politics, and fields of study, such as literature and the arts.

2b. *Development of Basic Intellectual Skills* (33%)

Another commonly mentioned effect of a Bennington education is the development of an ability to think more clearly, read with greater comprehension, approach materials more logically, be critical and analytic, or develop other intellectual skills. Some of these are undoubtedly changes that would be seen at any serious college or university, but others seem to be closely tied to the Bennington philosophy of education and the pressures arising from community norms. One such change which was specifically mentioned is the ability to approach material and to integrate different fields and points of view.

I learned to think here . . . to be able to look at material and know how to approach it.

My whole outlook on life has been broadened. You are allowed to think for yourself in the classroom. You can digest things for yourself. Teachers encourage you to find your own meaning. . . . I have learned to look more deeply.

My major interests have not changed, but my way of approaching things has. . . . I now approach things on the whole. . . . I try to analyze things now.

Last semester I saw courses fit together as a whole . . . not separate parts which could be made into something. . . . I was amazed at my development—much higher now.

Eleven of the students also pointed to an increase in the ability to be critical and analytic as an important form of change during their college years; several of these students again related this development to specific pressures within the community.

Bennington has made me a lot more critical. It has sharpened my mind in the direction of becoming more analytic.

(Effect of Bennington?) It has given me the tools for an analytic and critical interest and capacity.

The quality of my work is better. I had to become more analytic and precise.

The community pressures to develop critical and analytic skills are further illustrated in two dissenting opinions on the value of "the Bennington approach."

> Here the nonessential things are emphasized. The techniques, the methodology are more important than the meaning. There should be a seriousness of purpose, a passionate belief in one thing or another rather than a rather blasé blah-blah. . . . Professors teach methods of approaching things.

> My intellectual development has changed. It started with writing a paper to tear down things, come up with your own theory. . . . Girls talk off the top of their heads, girls don't know things. The patterns of criticism are the same—learn how to criticize. You hear the same comments. You can just about predict the comments on the oral reports.

Thus both those who praise and those who damn the Bennington system agree on the types of skills which it seems to impart—methods of approaching materials, integration of different viewpoints, and critical and analytic skills.

2c. Intellectual Involvement (31%)

The interviews also indicate that a good number of students change not only by broadening their range of knowledge and intellectual skills, but also by deepening their involvement in study and other intellectual efforts. The excerpts which follow point up the importance of such changes.

> I am more excited intellectually.

> I've developed an intellectual and social curiosity. I'm very interested in mores and I've had a realization of systems out there in the social world.

> I have now become genuinely interested in studying for its own sake and not just because I am supposed to.

> My intellectual interests have been intensified and clarified.

These and similar statements all suggest an increase in the student's general attraction to study and other intellectual pursuits that is reflected in an increased interest in study for its own sake, excitement about one's work, concern about intellectual issues, and love or enjoyment of the arts.

2d. *Long-term Intellectual Commitment* (13%)

Several of this group of students, together with a few others, indicated that their intellectual commitment would continue beyond their years at Bennington. Some spoke of "keeping the learning process going," others of "always being a thinking person" or "going on with my education," but in each case there was the clear implication that the effects of Bennington would endure. For example,

> The change here is not one you feel right away. They allow you to go on after four years. You have to—you can't stop. It provides the soil for growth. The development is mostly in the area of possibilities.
>
> . . . I've learned to think for myself and to really learn for the sake of learning, rather than for some arbitrary system of points. I've learned to know just because I want to know. This will make me a more curious member, and a more active one, of the society. It will definitely make a difference in my career.

3. Tolerance (48%)

Apart from individualism and intellectuality there was only one other type of change which involved a sizeable proportion of the student body (48%), and this was in the area of tolerance. Changes in this area are not surprising, for Bennington attracts a large number of students with attitudes and values that differ from those expected in the community, and these students must often develop tolerant attitudes in order to gain the acceptance of their peers. It is clear from the next statements quoted that one of the areas in which tolerance is most likely to develop is that of differences in moral codes, especially those dealing with sexual behavior. But it often extends to the intellectual sphere as well, and is reflected in a greater openness to all sides of a question.

> I learned to grow more tolerant of lots of kinds of people. When I first came I was shocked to find people not having the same reference points as I have. I learned to be friends even though we are not alike. In high school everyone had to feel one way about religion, politics, and certain moral standards. . . . It was a shock to find atheists and people who could sleep with someone even though

not married to him. You don't categorize people by the way they act or the way they look, I've learned.

I think I've become more tolerant, more accepting of new ideas, less dogmatic. Here it was personal relationships more than anything else. You're exposed to new things.

I am more tolerant of their social and sexual mores. I got to know people intimately as time went on. As a freshman, I was quite taken aback by some of the things I heard about people.

The interviews further suggest that there are several different ways in which tolerance can develop during the college years, especially the following: (1) less irritation and annoyance with differences; (2) increased acceptance and understanding of differences; and (3) a relativistic approach to differences. These three types illustrate the varied reference points that tolerance can take, and deserve additional documentation.

3a. Less Irritation and Annoyance with Differences (16%)

The reference point here is the student's own reactions to differences rather than, for instance, the viewpoint of the person who happens to hold other views. For example,

I was surprised and shocked at girls carrying on with so many different people at once. I wouldn't want it for myself, but it doesn't bother me any more. . . . I was very surprised in my freshman year.

I am less critical of people. . . . Even though I can't understand why they act the way they do, I'm not so annoyed as I was.

I came prudish and shocked over things. I changed in that I cannot judge because it is not my place. I still don't think that they are right.

These statements illustrate different patterns of change in tolerance, but they have in common the tendency of the student to react to differences by becoming less bothered, less annoyed, less willing to judge.

3b. Acceptance and Understanding of Differences (15%)

The emphasis in this category is not so much upon one's own feelings as upon "taking the role of the other" in order to understand, accept, appreciate, and perhaps even enjoy his ideas. Fifteen of the students interviewed gave responses indicating change in this direction, including the following:

I have grown appreciably in being able to benefit from others' points of view. . . . I am more liberal, more sympathetic, more tolerant, can see the other side of the picture.

I am more ready to accept different kinds of people. Bennington aided me in understanding people more. My prejudices have been completely destroyed.

I've noticed great differences in moral codes, what's considered right. This doesn't bother me—this is the way she feels. There can be an appreciation of each other's view.

These excerpts emphasize the development of understanding and respect for opposing views. One byproduct of this change may be less shock and irritation with others, but it also involves some attempt to appreciate the point of view of those who differ in moral codes, beliefs, or behavior.

3c. Relativistic Approach to Differences (7%)

Increased tolerance may be based upon the assumption that the validity of beliefs is relative, in that it depends upon the individual who holds them. This implies not only that the individual is less bothered or more understanding, but also that the rightness or wrongness of others' positions depends upon their value to the individual. The following responses were among those classified under the heading of "relativistic" tolerance.

Here you are forced to live with people who think differently. I had to see that what they are doing is right for them—it forces you to be less rigid about other people's standards. Previously I condemned others who did not have the same standards in dating and drinking. I came to realize that my standards are mine and that others have theirs and that they are right for them.

I notice quite a difference in morals. . . . Understanding things from a different point of view changes your ideas. At first I condemned people, couldn't help feeling it was wrong. Now I am more tolerant; I see that their ideas are better for them.

Bennington does open your eyes to the fact that there are different ways of doing things here. . . . Now I have come to accept the differences. If they think they are right, O.K.

4. Unconventionality (24%)

The process of questioning and doubting may bring with it either a relatively permanent increase in unconventional attitudes, or a temporary rebellion against older values and beliefs followed by some degree of return toward the earlier positions.

4a. Cyclical Change (14%)

The 14 statements dealing with cyclical change provide some of the most insightful and colorful passages found in the interviews. They underscore an aspect of attitude and value change which is often recognized in armchair discussions (witness the concept of "sophomore slump"), but which is rarely considered in more serious research in the field.

My change has been cyclical—have some of the ideas I had before and I have gone away and come back to them. I have them for different reasons. I have become much more convinced of a certain conservatism. Do a job well and don't worry about others. I have learned the importance of responsibility, mainly through its absence at the college. . . . Spontaneity is fine, but it is important to have responsibility. The idea of the individual being important so that one forgets that we live in an interpersonal world—there is no responsibility for others. I have seen the effects of total self-absorption and of art without responsibility to people and to a feeling of living on a community. . . . But you have to have a sense of other people here.

When I came I was in a social set-up—prep school, etc. Changed from this, now have come back a bit. I have grown, but my friends will be similar to what they would have been five years ago. . . . For a while, I was against money, WASP, etc., very narrow. Now I have combined all points of view, I went through a cycle. Now I feel that money is fine, socialism has problems.

. . . I've come almost full circle from the beliefs I had when I was in high school. I had a period of flux, then came back to the same beliefs and codes, but in a more adult way. . . . I went to extremes in rejecting middle-class values—hitchhiked a hundred miles. . . . Also, in my sophomore year I went through a period of wondering why I was here. I found a reason, a holding point. Now I have an underlying structure for what I am doing. . . . It was almost that if you think a thought then immediately, by god, you should act on it. Middle-class morality is ridiculous, cast it aside. But it just doesn't work that way—it's much deeper.

These remarks plainly suggest the need for studies of change in which questions are asked at several points in time, including the period before the student enters college. Several of these respondents indicated, for example, that their own rebellion took place before they came to Bennington, and that the cycle of change was completed in their freshman or sophomore year.

4b. Reduced Conventionality (10%)

Another group of ten students gave evidence that they had become less conventional or "conservative" during their years at Bennington, but showed no signs of cyclical change. The term "conventionality" was generally used to cover the norms and patterns of morality typical of the middle classes, and also the style of life of eastern Society, as in the following cases.

I was very conscious of society and society rules, and if you go against society you hurt yourself. Now I have decided that it is a lousy thing—no room for exceptions in standards. I think it stinks and is unfair. They aren't giving the individual a chance to breathe —they condemn the nonconformity bit.

Now I don't want the PTA, the woman's club, and teas. I'm much more aware of middle-class smallness. . . . Here you are accepted as an individual, outside you are classified.

My school had conventional morality. I've changed, but probably would have anyway. When I first came here I was shocked. These things were outside my realm of experience—I went out very little in high school, had no idea. . . . Some say the atmosphere of Bennington is infectious and does impose new views of sexual morality on people. I don't think this is true of Bennington any more than anywhere else.

It is entirely possible, of course, that the students who made statements such as these were reporting change as it occurred during one part of a cycle, and that their responses would be different at a later date. Whether this is true or not, it does appear that change in unconventionality occurs for some students during their stay at Bennington, but much less frequently than changes in individualism or intellectualism.

5. Other Directions of Change (46%)

The previous four categories cover by far the majority of changes in attitudes, values, beliefs, and behavior reported by the students who were interviewed. As one might expect, however, there were a number of other miscellaneous types of change which did not fit any of these categories, including a few comments which were inconsistent with the major trends, such as "less tolerant" and "less self-confident." There follows a brief review of these less common types of change.

1. Interpersonal attitudes (17%). Not surprisingly, several of the students reported changes in their attitudes toward others in general or toward their fellow students. Some found that Bennington had a positive influence upon their ability to relate with their peers, others indicated that their experiences had led to an increased cynicism and made them less trusting and open. Similarly, a few found that they had changed by developing negative attitudes toward their peers in the student community.

2. Psychological adjustment (14%). The remarks in this category were about equally divided between those who found that their problems of adjustment and emotional balance had increased during their stay at Bennington, and those who felt more stable, outgoing, happy, and secure. One of the major sources of psychological difficulties for some was the considerable amount of freedom and independence encouraged by the Bennington system of education.

3. Political attitudes (8%). No clear pattern emerges from the reports on change in political attitudes. One student noted that she had become more conservative, another more liberal, and a third more apathetic. Others spoke of changes in the level of their commitment to political action, the sureness of their views, and the awareness of the complexity of the art of politics.

4. Religion (5%). Four of the five students who made reference to changes in religious attitudes reported that they had moved away from a belief in God or organized religion.

5. Social life and dating (5%). Four of these five students indicated that their earlier interest in dating gradually wore off, and that their need for extensive social life was replaced by other interests.

These are the minor currents seen in the interviews. Other changes reported fall into no pattern, being either consistent with the major directions of change or simply irrelevant to these dimensions. The interviews strongly suggest that changes occurred mainly in relation to the dominant norms in the student community: individualism, intellectualism, tolerance, and, to a lesser extent, unconventionality.

Questionnaire Data and Directions of Change

The results of the first set of 40 interviews (in 1961) were so clear in suggesting directions of change that they were used as the basis of a series of items in the 1962 questionnaire. The aim here was to structure the items in the students' own words to the extent possible, and then obtain responses in more uniform ways about these areas of change from the entire student body. We tried to include not only those changes mentioned by a majority of the students, such as "more individualistic," but also those mentioned only occasionally, such as "committed to religious beliefs." The complete list of items is shown in Table 10.2; the students evaluated each of their changes on the following scale:

Very much *less* this way now	Less now	*No change* in college	More now	*Very much* *more* this way now
L_____I	I	I	I	I_____I

The analyses of the data in Table 10.2 are based upon percentages of students who checked either the first two positions on the scale ("less" or "very much less this way now") or the last two positions ("more" or "very much more this way now"). We are thus considering the more *significant* changes reported by the students on the items under consideration rather than just any change.

The patterns of change emerging from these responses and from the interview data are very similar. The predominating themes again are individualism, intellectuality, and tolerance.

The "minor" areas of change receive relatively greater attention in the questionnaires than in the interviews. Thus in the questionnaires about 20% of the respondents report that they have become less committed to religious beliefs, less conservative in their political and economic views, and less absorbed in social life and dating, whereas in the interviews the corresponding figures were between 5 and 7%. In the questionnaire, students were asked directly about their changes in each of the areas, and thus were almost forced to give a response, but in the interviews they were asked only general questions about change and given considerable freedom to comment upon the areas most salient for them. It is not surprising, then, that the rates of

Table 10.2 Proportion of Bennington Students Reporting Significant Change on Selected Characteristics (N = 309)

Items	"Much more this way now"	Inter-mediate	"Much less this way now"
I. Individualism			
Question things about myself	51%	47%	2% *
Express myself—what I think and feel	46	52	2
Approach and explore material from my own viewpoint	44	54	2
Individualistic—try to be myself	43	55	2
II. Intellectuality			
Able to continue the learning process after college	59	40	1
Absorbed in studies and academic work	58	37	5
Critical and analytic in my approach to material	50	49	1
Committed to learning for its own sake	38	54	8
III. Tolerance			
Tolerant of behaviors that may violate my standards	43	52	5
Bothered by ideas very different from my own	4	63	33
IV. Unconventionality			
Unconventional in opinions and beliefs	28	68	4
Disapprove of the style of life in Ivy League colleges	20	69	11
V. Other			
Willing to support my convictions with action	32	66	2
Absorbed in social life and dating	12	70	18
Question or doubt the beliefs and values I brought to college	11	62	27
Similar to my parents in values and beliefs	11	63	26
Self-centered: not concerned with others' problems and needs	9	69	22
Committed to religious beliefs	6	74	20
Conservative in political and economic views	4	77	19

* Each row totals to 100%.

response for the "minor" areas are generally higher in the questionnaires.

It is the similarities between the two sets of data, however, that are most striking. In particular, both sets of data indicate that the main directions of attitude and value change are approximately the same as the prevailing norms in the Bennington College community.

Variations in the Patterns of Change

The discussion thus far has emphasized the similarities in the patterns of change among Bennington students, but there are notable differences as well. The problems facing one student on entering the college are not always the same as those facing another, nor are their responses to these problems the same. Some, for instance, enter with attitudes, values, and beliefs which show a sharp discrepancy with the dominant norms in the community, then pass through a period of intense questioning, doubting, and searching, and change mainly by becoming more tolerant of ideas which differ from their own. At the other extreme are those who come to Bennington with views that are basically consistent with the community norms, experience few pressures from their peers to change, and yet report major developments in individualism or intellectuality. We shall show that there are individual differences in the observed patterns of change, and that these differences are related both to the initial characteristics of the students themselves, and to their experiences while in college.

The Initial Characteristics of the Student

We have shown that one crucial stimulus to change for many students is a painful discrepancy between her initial views and those expected in the community. Sometimes at Bennington this discrepancy is between the "conventional" views of the entering student and the "unconventional" expectations of her peers, but not always. There are instances in which unconventional values at the time of entry created problems of adaptation, especially when the student later developed friendships with "conventional" peers. In attempting to understand the process of attitude and value change it is important to search out the problems that stimulate change, and one of the key sources of problems is the student's initial characteristics.

We shall examine certain patterns of initial characteristics in terms of *congruence*. A student's attitudes are considered congruent if they are generally consistent with the principal norms in the student community—individualism-unconventionality, intellectuality, and tolerance. They are called incongruent when they are inconsistent with these norms. Students entering with congruent attitudes are often nominated as "creative individualists" in sociometric rankings, whereas those with incongruent views are frequently dubbed "conventional," "preppy," or "social."

Through the use of this concept it is possible to test two hypotheses:

1. Increases in tolerance and unconventionality will be more frequent among those initially incongruent in their attitudes, values, and beliefs than among those initially congruent.

2. Increases in individualism and intellectualism will be more frequent among students initially congruent in their views than among those initially incongruent.

Hypothesis 1 is based upon the assumption that the principal problem facing the incongruent group is that of winning the acceptance of their peers and social support for their values, beliefs, and self-definitions. In order to gain this acceptance and support they will ordinarily find it necessary to change at least some of their conventional beliefs and behaviors, for these serve as an obvious sign of their incongruity. Similarly, they will be placed under pressure to develop an attitude of tolerance toward views that differ from their own as a further sign of their assimilation into the community. Even those who do not change any of their fundamental religious, moral, political, or social values will often find it necessary to become more tolerant, usually because this attitude is necessary for maintaining cordial relations with peers in the majority group. In one sense, then, the principal problem confronting students with incongruent values is that of meeting the "minimal" norms for acceptance in a community which include unconventionality and tolerance toward those with opposing views.

Hypothesis 2 follows from the notion that the congruent group will be less concerned than others with meeting the "minimal" standards for acceptance, and will thus be freer to work toward the ideal norms of individualism and intellectualism. Students in this group will thus have to spend less of their energy trying to win the acceptance and support of their peers, and will have greater freedom to become aware of themselves, consolidate their values, achieve a greater sense of self-confidence, and pursue their intellectual interests. They may experience some difficulty in relating to members of the minority group who hold to strongly conventional views, but this will not be a great problem for them since they approach such relationships from a position of strength.

The index of congruence that seemed most appropriate was the student's score on the first administration of the Developmental Status Scale. This scale, administered shortly after the students arrived on campus, seemed to be a good measure of initial attitudes. According to its authors (Webster and Heist, 1959) it seems to be tapping a general factor of "rebellious independence" which corresponds quite closely to the concept of "unconventionality" used in this study. We have therefore considered the 49 students who fell into the top third of the distribution of scores on the first administration of this scale as congruent, and the 55 in the lowest third as incongruent.

The data relevant to our hypotheses came from two sources: (1) questionnaires administered to the entire group of 104 students classified as congruent or incongruent; and (2) statements from the 46 members of this group who also were in the interview sample. In the case of the interviews, information on changes in attitudes and values was coded according to the categories described earlier in this chapter, and the responses of the congruent and incongruent students were then compared.

Hypothesis 1: Changes in tolerance and unconventionality. The findings in Table 10.3 are based upon interview statements showing changes in tolerance among 19 students classified as congruent and 27 classified as incongruent. These results support the hypothesis that an increase in tolerance will be more frequent among students who are initially incongruent than among those initially congruent.

Table 10.3 Change in Tolerance according to Initial Congruence: Interview Data

	Increase in Tolerance Reported	No Increase in Tolerance Reported	N
Students initially incongruent	14	5	19
Students initially congruent	10	17	27
N	24	22	46

$X^2 = 4.62; p < .05$

Table 10.4   Change in Tolerance according to Initial Congruence:
Questionnaire Data

| | "Tolerant of behaviors that may violate my standards" | | |
	"Much more this way now"	Lesser Degree of Change	N
Students initially incongruent	26	28	54
Students initially congruent	17	32	49
	43	60	103

X^2 = NS

Of the 19 incongruent respondents, 14 report an increase in tolerance of views that differ from their own, whereas only 10 of the 27 listed as congruent report such a change. Additional support for this hypothesis is also found in the self-report data on change from questionnaires administered to over 90% of the members of the student body. Congruent and incongruent groups were compared with respect to

Table 10.5   Change in Unconventionality according to Initial Continuity
in Attitudes

	55 Students Initially Incongruent	49 Students Initially Congruent
1. Mean change on two administrations of the Developmental Status Scale $t = 4.68; \; p < .001$	+4.73	+0.65 *
2. Questionnaire item: "Unconventional in opinions and beliefs"		
Much more this way now	18	9
Lesser degree of change	37	40
	55	49

X^2 = NS

* It is possible that the differences observed here may be the result of a "ceiling effect" for the continuous group. This would mean that the lesser change by this group could be explained by the fact that its initially congruent scores leave little room for change toward further congruence. For further discussion of this and related problems see Appendix K.

reports of significant change on the characteristic "tolerant of behaviors that may violate my standards."

Table 10.4 indicates that 26 of the 54 initially incongruent students (48%) report a significant change in tolerance as compared with 17 of the 49 initially congruent students (35%). Although these differences are not statistically significant, the direction of the findings does tend to support the first hypothesis.

It was also predicted in the first hypothesis that the incongruent group would show more change in unconventionality than the congruent group; the data presented in Table 10.5 also tend to confirm this observation. The findings in the first part of the table deal with the changes observed in two administrations of the Developmental Status Scale, the measure used here as an index of unconventionality. Again, students who enter the college with incongruent attitudes show significantly more change toward unconventionality than those who enter with congruent attitudes.

The second half of Table 10.5 shows the extent of reported change in unconventionality for the two groups under consideration. Although the direction of these findings is as expected, the differences are not statistically significant. As we suggested earlier, perhaps these changes in tolerance and unconventionality serve as a kind of admission pass for students who enter with incongruent attitudes and wish to be accepted by the majority group of peers in the Bennington community.

Hypothesis 2: Changes in individualism and intellectualism. According to this hypothesis, there should be a similar relationship between congruence and change in individualism and intellectualism. Table 10.6 provides clear support for this hypothesis. The two groups differ

Table 10.6   Changes in Individualism and Intellectualism according to Initial Congruence of Attitudes

	Reported Increase in Both Individualism and Intellectualism		
	Yes	No	N
Students initially incongruent	2	17	19
Students initially congruent	19	8	27
N	21	25	46

$X^2 = 13.77; \ p < .001$

significantly in change toward community norms in respect to *both* individualism and intellectualism.

The statistical data presented here indicate that there are important differences in the patterns of change followed by students who are initially congruent and incongruent in their attitudes. Although students in the two categories seem to share certain types of change toward community norms, those classified as incongruent show a stronger movement toward tolerance and unconventionality. Those considered congruent, on the other hand, give evidence of greater change in the directions considered particularly "ideal" in the community: individualism and intellectuality.*

Experience during the College Years

There are undoubtedly many experiences on and off the campus which can have a significant impact upon the student's views, most notably interactions with family, student peers, faculty members, and other "reference groups"; periods of questioning, doubting, and emotional upsets; academic successes and failures; various types of reading; work experiences during vacations or nonresident terms; and participation in programs such as those sponsored by Civil Rights or Peace groups. There are two among these which seem to be especially important in accounting for change: (1) the questioning and doubting of attitudes, values, and beliefs; and (2) relationships with reference groups, especially family and student peers.

1. Questioning and Doubting

There are probably few students who pass through college without questioning or doubting some of their initial views, but the effects of this questioning differ greatly from student to student. Some seem to reject their original views almost completely, at least for a time; others change them slightly, and still others do not change at all or change mainly by becoming more sure of the rational bases for their

---

* Apparently we must reject the interpretation that these changes result from "regressive" effects, that is, the probability that individuals initially extreme in score will tend to respond less extremely at a later time. The fact is that those initially at the incongruent extreme showed far more change than individuals equally extreme at the other end of the scale, whereas sheerly regressive effects should be the same at both ends. Further discussion of this problem appears in Appendix K.

initial positions. It seems, then, that the questioning and doubting of values is an important condition for change, but that changes will also depend upon other factors such as the initial congruence of the student's attitudes and her interactions with reference groups.

It was possible to test two hypotheses dealing with the relationship between questioning of values and changes in attitudes:

1. In general, change in the direction of community norms will be greater among students who question their values than among those who do not.

2. The relationship between questioning and change toward community norms will be closer for students initially incongruent in their views than for those initially congruent.

In the second hypothesis, our assumption is that when a student enters with incongruent views, and later questions these attitudes, the road to change is clearly marked should she be prepared to take it. If she questions her original attitudes it is often because she finds that those attitudes are not accepted by peers in the student community whom she admires and whose approval she desires. Actual changes, in her case, are often the means of winning the support of student peers, and will ordinarily be in the direction of the norms held by these peers. In the Bennington community these norms are reasonably clear and well defined, and therefore we should expect that the initially incongruent student will ordinarily move toward the dominant norms.

The situation is somewhat different, on the other hand, for the student who enters with congruent attitudes and later questions her initial positions. For her there is no clearly marked path to change, mainly because she already possesses enough of the valued attitudes to be accepted by the majority group. She is, in a sense, freer—free to move toward the dominant norms of intellectualism, free to become less individualistic and unconventional if she feels that she has gone too far in these directions, or free to change in other ways. Hence, although both groups may change when they question their attitudes, values, and beliefs, the change for the incongruent group should be more predictable.

Table 10.7 tends to support both of the hypotheses about questioning and doubting of values. Change in the direction of community norms, in this instance toward unconventionality, is greater among those who question their values and beliefs than among those who do not or who do so only slightly. The data on mean change indicate that change in Developmental Status increases with the amount of

Table 10.7   Questioning of Moral Standards and Change in Developmental Status

	Mean Change in Developmental Status			
Degree of Questioning Moral Standards	Students Initially Incongruent	N	Students Initially Congruent	N
Low questioning *	+3.61	33	−0.11	28
High Questioning	+6.41	22	+1.67	21
		55		49
	$t = 2.20$		$t = 1.56$	
	$p < .05$		$p = $ NS	

* The category listed as "low questioning" includes those students who reported no questioning, slight questioning, or moderate questioning. The category of "high questioning" includes students reporting "intense questioning" of moral standards.

questioning reported. Table 10.7 also indicates that there is a closer relationship between questioning and change for students who were initially incongruent in their attitudes than among those initially congruent.*

The correlation between questioning and change among those initially incongruent is .36 (statistically significant), whereas for the congruent group it is an insignificant .13. The questioning and doubting of values during the college years is thus an important concomitant of attitude and value change; and the effects of such questioning and doubting are different for those who are initially congruent than for those initially incongruent in their views.

2. Relationships with Reference Groups

One of the most important factors in attitude change is the individual's relationships with "reference groups," which have been defined as follows:

---

* Initial congruence and incongruence are defined as described earlier in the chapter: those in the upper third of the scores on the first administration of the Developmental Scale, and those in the bottom third, respectively.

A group functions as a normative reference group for a person to the extent that its evaluations of him are based upon the degree of his conformity to certain standards of behavior or attitudes, and to the extent that the delivery of rewards and punishments is conditional upon these evaluations (H. H. Kelley, 1952).

For the college student two of the most important reference groups seem to be the family and campus peers, especially friends. Even though students may be placed under heavy pressures to adopt the norms and values of their peers while at college, it is also true that the family often remains an important standard of self-evaluation. The typical freshman, for instance, may feel strongly attracted to her new-found friends on the campus, and may also feel that the views of her family are at least mildly antiquated, but she is not likely to be completely unresponsive to the opinions and attitudes of her parents. Information concerning the shifting of reference group attachments that occur during the college years, especially attachments to parents and college friends, is therefore important in a study like this one. (See also Newcomb, 1952.)

One way in which we were able to ascertain the degree to which college friends served as reference groups, with respect to unconventionality, was a questionnaire item which asked the students to provide ratings of the conventionality of their Bennington friends.* Our assumption was simply that persons considered as friends would probably also serve as reference groups.

The specific hypotheses tested with such data were the following:

1. Change in the direction of unconventionality will be directly related to the reported unconventionality of Bennington friends.

2. The relationship between change in unconventionality and reported unconventionality of Bennington friends will be closer for those initially incongruent in their views than for those initially congruent.

As these hypotheses imply, we expected to find that most students who became more unconventional would have unconventional friends, and that this change would be more apparent in the case of those who entered with conventional attitudes.

---

* The specific item rated was as follows:

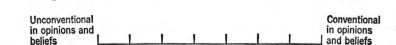

Table 10.8 supports both of these hypotheses. First, it is clear from both the means and the correlation coefficients that change in un-conventionality, as measured by the Developmental Status Scale, is directly related to the unconventionality of the student's friends. But, as predicted by the second hypothesis, the relationship is closer when students enter with incongruent (conventional) attitudes than when they enter with congruent attitudes. It is also interesting to note that those who enter with congruent attitudes and then associate with conventional friends (low and medium unconventionality in Table 10.8) show an average decrease in Developmental Status, whereas the remaining groups register an increase. It is likely, then, that the student's college friends serve as key reference groups for change in attitudes and values, particularly in areas that are related to the dominant norms of the college community.

Indices of attachment to parents as reference groups were not successfully developed. One of the difficulties was that we could not assume, as we did in the case of friends, that the student's parents would ordinarily serve as positive reference groups for changes in values; after all, they could not choose their parents. We also found from the interviews that there were wide differences in the types of expectations held out by parents for their daughters. We can only say that, typically, parents served as positive reference groups in respect to unconventionality less frequently than did college friends, with whom parents were often contrasted.

Table 10.8   Reported Unconventionality of Bennington Friends and Change in Developmental Status

	Mean Change in Developmental Status			
Reported Unconventionality of Bennington Friends	Students Initially Incongruent	N	Students Initially Congruent	N
Low unconventionality	+3.50	10	−0.50	4
Medium unconventionality	+4.32	31	−0.14	21
High unconventionality	+6.50	14	+1.54	24
Total	+4.75	55	+0.65	49

$X^2 = 6.75$, $p < .05$ (2 df)
product-moment correlation
(unconventionality and change)   .30 $(p < .05)$ .19 (NS)

Summary

We have attempted to show both similarities and differences in the patterns of change followed by a recent generation of Bennington students. The similarities are well defined, and seem to be essentially adaptations to the community norms described in the previous chapter. Both interviews with 101 students and questionnaire data from almost the entire student body suggest that the main directions of change are toward increased individualism, intellectuality, tolerance, and, to a lesser extent, unconventionality. The most common forms of change in individualism are in the areas of self-awareness, feelings of self-confidence, strength, or independence, and self-expression. Similarly, changes in intellectuality are reflected in various ways, especially increased intellectual awareness and broadening, the development of basic intellectual skills, heightened intellectual involvement, and long-term intellectual commitment. The interviews also suggest that the development of tolerance can take different forms, most notably less irritation and annoyance with differences, increased understanding and acceptance of differences, or a relativistic approach to differences. The major directions of change seem to represent adaptations to the community norms.

Equally important are the findings showing variations in the patterns of change followed by these students. Our data indicate that change in the direction of community norms depends upon at least two factors: (1) the initial characteristics of the student, in this case the degree of congruence of her initial attitudes with those expected in the community; and (2) experiences during the college years, especially questioning and doubting of values and beliefs and interactions with reference groups. It was found that students entering with initially incongruent attitudes show a greater tendency to change in tolerance and unconventionality than in individualism and intellectuality, whereas the pattern is reversed for those entering with congruent attitudes. Similarly, it was shown that change in the direction of unconventionality is greater when students question their values and beliefs than when they do not, and that the effects of such questioning are more apparent for students entering with incongruent attitudes. Finally, there were indications that the attitudes of the student's friends, presumably serving as a "reference group," were also related to the extent of her change toward community norms.

11. Student Types, Subgroups, and Subcultures *

As of the 1930's the student culture at Bennington was found to be quite homogeneous in certain ways. There were, of course, students who did not follow the collegewide pattern of increasing nonconservativism, but most of these "deviants" tended to be isolated and relatively uninvolved in the life of the college.

It was therefore our expectation that the student culture of the early 1960's would be similarly homogeneous. This expectation was reinforced by the fact that the student body is a very small and highly select one—slightly more than 300 girls who come from rather similar family backgrounds, geographic regions, and precollege experiences. We did not anticipate the kind of heterogeneous, pluralistic atmosphere found at most larger colleges and universities.

The results of our first data collection, in the fall of 1959, seemed to support this expectation fairly well. Responses to adjective check list and other data (see Chapter 9) seemed to suggest a fairly general consensus at the college concerning the distinctive and normative characteristics of the student body. One of our first indications that this might not be the full story came when we examined the results of the spring, 1960, questionnaire, the second one we administered. This questionnaire included the query, "Is there anything characteristic about the students who live in the various houses on campus?" The students were asked to comment briefly on each of the 12 houses.

A great many adjectives were used by the students to describe the various houses, but it became clear that certain houses were perceived rather distinctively and uniformly by a large number of the students. The most striking finding was that many students characterized at least two of the houses in ways that did not seem to be consistent with the "intellectual" and "individualistic" norms which prevailed in

---

* A fuller version of this report appears in Richard Flacks, *Adaptations of Deviants in a College Community*, unpublished doctoral dissertation, University of Michigan, 1962.

166

the student culture. Of the 320 students who answered the questionnaire, 150 characterized one of the houses (which we shall call "Taylor") in at least one of the following ways:

Preppy, social, socialite, socially minded, date-happy, collegiate, superficial party-house, sorority-like, playgirls, society, Smithy, tweedy, debs, Williams, boy-crazy, circle-pin crowd, the skiers, concerned with respectability, high society, gung-ho, rock and roll, Ivy League, cheerleaders, fashion conscious, conventional, snobbish, not intellectual, camel hair coats.

Nearly as many (112) students characterized "Cabot" house in similar ways. Whereas one-third to almost one-half of the respondents used these terms to characterize these two houses, no other house received such descriptions from more than 32 respondents, and seven houses were characterized in this fashion by fewer than 13 respondents out of 320.

The terms just listed seemed to differ from the dominant student norms in that they implied an interest in social activities rather than intellectual activity, and an acceptance of conventional social attitudes and standards. The students in these houses were seen as having a different appearance from the Bennington norm ("tweedy, circle pin, camel hair coat"). The students at Taylor House were described by a resident as follows:

Normal—in the sense that for the most part they are nonconformers to the conforming nonconformity at Bennington.

Both Taylor and Cabot were frequently described as "not Benningtonian."

Other stereotypes with an entirely different content were applied to some of the other houses. "Ellington House," for example, was frequently characterized as "intellectual, arty, bohemian, beat, nonconformist, unconventional, free-thinking." Several other houses, particularly "Astor" and "Irving," received similar characterizations from a large number of students.

The existence of these stereotypes—accompanied by a rich, and to some extent indigenous, vocabulary—was a matter of great interest to us. In the first place, if we could find a way to identify students who tended to fit these stereotypes we would have an excellent way to validate and enrich our paper-and-pencil measures of norm acceptance. If students who were typed in an "Ellington House" way were high scorers on the OPI scales (see Appendix L) and those who fitted the "Taylor House" pattern were low on these scales, then we would have additional support for assuming that these scales were related to norm acceptance at the college, and also have more confidence in our description of the content of these norms. These conclusions would receive further support if the two types of students were markedly different in status at the college.

The existence of these stereotypes pointed, too, to the possibility that there had been a change since the 1930's in the process of socialization at Bennington. For if the types were real—in the sense that actual students could be said to fit them—and if these students tended to interact with each other, than our anticipations about a homogeneous student culture at Bennington would not be valid. Instead, we might find that, alongside the dominant student culture, there had grown up one or more subcultures with different sets of norms counterposed to those which were dominant. If so, perhaps we were observing a change in the ways in which students who arrive on campus with nonconforming attitudes attempt to cope with their nonconformity. In the thirties, such students either tended to move toward conformity, or they tended to withdraw into relative isolation. The observation of nonconforming *houses* in the sixties suggested to us that a new, *subcultural,* mechanism had emerged at Bennington which enabled students who experienced strain between their own attitudes and the dominant atmosphere on the campus to cope with the fact of their nonconformity in a *collective* fashion.

In order to test these suppositions, however, a series of operational steps was required. It was necessary to establish a typology which could be used to identify particular students. Such a typology, to be useful, would have to be based on the perception and language of the students, rather than imposed by the investigators. Second, a way had to be found to use this typology to identify actual students. Third, the criteria used to fit students to the types had to be tested against independent criteria of similar attributes. Finally, we were interested in seeing if students who fitted the types tended to form actual groups, or whether the typology simply described characteristics of discrete individuals who did not necessarily associate with one another.

Building a Typology of Students

Our first task was to see if there was a stable pattern within the variety of adjectives that students used to describe the various houses.

In the fall, 1960, questionnaire we included an item, to be answered by sophomores, juniors, and seniors only, which was intended to

Cluster I *	Cluster II *
Collegiate	Arty
Preppy	Free-thinking
Smithy	Boho
Social	Eccentric
Socialites	Benningtonian
Debs	Beat
Tweedy	Wild
Ann Carter	Intellectual
American girl-type	
All-around	
Gung-ho	

Figure 11.1 Clusters derived from students "sorting" of stereotypes.

determine whether such a patterning was commonly perceived by students who had been at the college for at least a year. We listed 28 adjectives which had been most frequently used by students in the spring to describe the various houses. These adjectives were

. . . all-around, American girl-type, Ann Carter, arty, beat, Benningtonian, boho, collegiate, community-minded, conscientious, conservative, debs, eccentric, folksy, free-thinkers, gung-ho, horsey, intellectual, 'old Bennington'-type, preppy, Smithy, social, socialites, social-science-types, swinging, tweedy, wild, woodsy.

We asked the students to group the terms which had similar meanings or which could be used to describe the same type of person. Clusters of these adjectives were constructed by the following criterion: an adjective was included in a cluster if 50 or more students grouped it with at least two other adjectives in the cluster (50 was approximately one-third of those who responded to this question). Two clusters were isolated by this technique; these are listed in Figure 11.1.

These two clusters were quite distinct from each other; no adjective in either group was paired more than five times with an adjective in the other cluster. No other clusters were at all discernible; the adjectives remaining were either associated slightly with the two clusters or

---

* Adjectives are listed in order of the number of other adjectives in the cluster with which they are associated. Thus, for example, "collegiate" was associated with all the other adjectives in Cluster I, and "gung-ho" with only three other adjectives, by 50 or more students.

not paired with other adjectives by any substantial number of students.

The two clusters, furthermore, seem to represent the two poles alluded to earlier as represented by Ellington House vs. Taylor House. Cluster I includes terms referring to students who are neither "intellectual" nor "individualistic," but rather socially oriented, and conventional in the "collegiate" sense. Cluster II refers to students who are "individualistic" (free-thinking, boho, eccentric, beat, wild) and, to a certain extent, "intellectual." It is interesting that "Benningtonian" clearly falls within this cluster.

This analysis supported our expectation that the students' characterizations of the various houses were patterned, rather than haphazard. The analysis suggests, in fact, that some rather stable, widely shared stereotypes exist in the Bennington student culture about various kinds of students at the college.

Also in the fall of 1960 we asked our respondents to describe the kinds of subgroups they had observed at Bennington, that is, "sets of people who share certain interests, attitudes, or values." The purpose of this question was to get as exhaustive and systematic a listing as possible of the types and groupings of students perceived to exist on the campus.

A very large number of descriptions were, of course, elicited by this question. One basis of differentiation that was prominently mentioned had to do with such relatively obvious and formal categories as groups of students who majored in particular areas or who shared common academic interests. Our primary concern, however, was to construct a typology based on attitudinal differentiation rather than more formal categories. Fortunately, the students supplied us with rich and detailed descriptions of informal social groupings at the college.

Our intention was to use these descriptions to derive a typology of Bennington students which could then be employed to classify as many students as possible. Such a typology would, in effect, constitute a hypothesis about the major bases of differentiation with respect to attitudes and values in the student body. Once the typology was developed, and students were categorized with respect to it, we could then test the validity of the typology by comparing, in various ways, the students who had been classified according to its criteria.

Thus, initially, the typology we developed was based in large measure on intuition and impression, rather than being a rigorous attempt to code all of the descriptions of subgroups we had in hand. We decided to see whether the subgroups listed by the students could

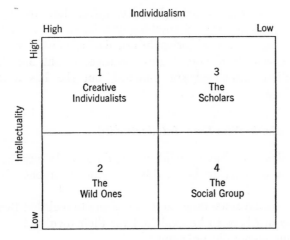

Figure 11.2 A hypothetical typology of norm acceptance—individualism.

be ordered in the following way. We assumed that the two clusters of norms we had isolated, "individualism" and "intellectualism," were independent dimensions, each constituting a fundamental basis of differentiation and association among the students. If so, some students would be high on both dimensions, some low on both, and some high on one, but not the other (see Figure 11.2 above). We then went back to the students' questionnaire responses, to see if the subgroup descriptions they offered could be fitted reasonably into this four-fold scheme. The following are some representative descriptions culled from these responses and the categories to which they were assigned by a process of independent coding:

1. High Individualism-High Intellectuality

Arty—girls who sincerely believe in certain principles and who stick by them, although they are usually opposed by society in general.

Intellectual snobs—the type of people who feel they are superior intellectually and more sophisticated than other people. Frequently students majoring in drama, art, literature.

Those who believe they are liberal and free-thinking.

Intellectual snobs—to me these people are all mind and no emotion; they are cynical and ridicule anything nonacademic.

Artistic—witty, imaginative girls, wild, sometimes appear in a dream world, fun at social gatherings.

Dionysians who are irrational and creative; they are mystics who await revelations and regard anything of a factual or verifiable nature as sacrilegious, usually majoring in art, dance, music, or creative lit.

Bohemian—she is usually highly creative, bright and individual. She is neither anti-social nor immoral, but she has a dislike for irrational fetters.

2. High Individualism-Low Intellectuality

Degenerates—love having wild orgies, do as little work as possible.

Beat—girls who try to be as different from everyone else as they can.

Wild ones—who since they came here seem to feel that Bennington's liberal rules are here to be exploited for their own ends.

Bohemians—generally unkempt.

Uninhibited (loose regarding morals).

Weird ones—"misunderstood," strange outfits, unclean, no direction, think everyone hates them.

Beatniks—affected dress and ideas characterize this group, who model themselves on the Village or San Francisco contingents. It is all very unnatural.

Wild, free, bizarre girls caring little about work and a lot about excitement.

3. Low Individualism-High Intellectuality

Those who seem to concentrate only on their work.

Girls who have an especial interest in learning and furthering their education.

Come-out-for-air group—they lurk within the library or in the removed suites of their houses. . . . Together they have nothing much to say to each other after the topic of work is exhausted.

Grinds—they don't get much out of school either, because they miss the friends and companionship.

Grinds—those who seem to see how long they can spend in library each day.

Bookworms—girls who are rarely seen except at the most secluded corner of the library and at meals.

Apollonians—are rational and critical. They are bookworms who await the *New York Times* daily and regard anything of an inspirational nature as they would a mirage.

4. Low Individualism-Low Intellectuality

So-called social group—very interested in their social life, and hold petty conversations on this subject.

Socialites—more interested in dating than in doing good work.

Those who do just enough work to pass their courses and spend most of their time discussing boys.

Social girls whose main interests are in attracting as many boys as possible.

Those interested in having as much fun as possible and doing as little work as they can manage. They take advantage of Bennington's system.

Social bugs—main interest is in dating and meeting boys.

Conservatives—those who refuse to be changed by Bennington and can band together to refrain from doing so.

Very interested in social life and the popular manner, usually to the point of masking their intelligence.

The foregoing responses are representative of a much larger number of descriptions which could be fitted under each of the categories we have indicated. Those which could not be so classified were either descriptions based on particular majors (for example, dancers, music majors, social-science majors were all said to form subgroups), or were characterizations based entirely on personal attributes, rather than membership in a larger group of students (for example, "neurotics," "gossipers," "average, normal, friendly girls"). Occasionally it was mentioned that there were groups of students who were active in student government, as well as "political activists" who engaged themselves in various social movements. We were particularly interested in these types, even though they were rarely mentioned—first, because they provided a link to the thirties when community participation and political activism were dominating norms on the campus; and, second, because we were interested to see what kinds of students held power and rank in the formal structure of student organization at Bennington, and how this structure related to informal patterns of influence and status.

Thus we emerged with six types of students who seemed to be fairly prevalent at the college. Four of the types were those most frequently mentioned by the students, and we hypothesized that they were derived from differences in orientation to the dominant norms of the student culture. Two others, not frequently mentioned, were deemed to be worthwhile foci for study, and we also anticipated that these two would not necessarily be independent of the four principal types.

Our next task was to construct brief descriptions of each of these types so that these could be "fed back" to the students in order to enable us to classify particular students with respect to these categories.

The descriptions which we used for this purpose were developed according to the following criteria:

1. The description should reflect the hypothesized source of the type, for example, the description of a "high individualism-high intellectuality" type should clearly suggest both dimensions to those exposed to it.

2. Each description should use direct quotes from the students' questionnaire responses.

3. All descriptions should be as nearly equivalent as possible in "social desirability."

With these requisites in mind, we formulated the following descriptions taken mainly from students' own phrasing (see Figure 11.2).

1. High Individualism-High Intellectuality

Creative Individualists—girls who sincerely believe in certain principles and who stick by those though they are usually opposed by society in general . . . people who feel they are superior intellectually and more sophisticated than other people . . . intellectual snobs according to some . . . seem very dedicated to creative pursuits . . . imaginative and free-thinking.

2. High Individualism-Low Intellectuality

Wild Ones—wild, free, bizarre girls caring little about work and a lot about excitement . . . uninhibited, generally unkempt . . . try to be as different from everyone else as they can . . . love having wild parties . . . may feel they are misunderstood.

3. Low Individualism-High Intellectuality

Scholars—those who seem to concentrate only on their work . . . seem to do little but study . . . come-out-for-air group . . . definite scholars . . . sublimate social interests . . . seem to spend most of their time in the library.

4. *Low Individualism-Low Intellectuality*

The Social Group—very interested in their social life and talk about little else . . . do enough work to pass their courses, but main interest is in having as much fun as possible . . . concentrate on dating and meeting boys . . . because of interest in social life, may mask their intelligence . . . characterized as "preppy" by some . . . generally neat in appearance.

And, in addition, student government and political activist types were described as follows.

5. *Leaders*—particularly interested in Bennington College government . . . organize committees or groups . . . may be characterized by friendliness among major part of the student body.

6. *Political Activists*—people interested in public affairs, interested in civil rights, sane nuclear policy—circulate petitions . . . civic-minded reformists either of campus politics or of social conditions in the country as a whole.

Using the Typology to Classify Students

In the spring of 1961 the foregoing descriptions were given to each of the 40 students who were interviewed at that time. Each interviewee was presented with descriptions of each of the six types and a list of names of students at her own year level (juniors and seniors were given the names of students at both year levels). Instructions were to indicate, for each type, the names of those students who fitted, to some degree, part or all of the description. Thus each student at the college was rated by at least ten (and in the case of juniors and seniors, 20) panelists. The panel members could put the same person in more than one category. They were not expected to categorize every person on the list, nor were they expected to use categories which they felt did not apply to anyone. In addition, each panelist was asked to suggest changes in the typology, and to describe other important groupings which might exist, which we had not included. None of the 40 interviewees suggested additional types or groups that we had not included. Moreover, although many questioned specific details of the descriptions, the panel members were virtually unanimous in feeling that the types were "real," that actual persons at the college belonged in these categories; however, several juniors and seniors felt that no upperclassmen were "social" or "wild."

In addition to the foregoing procedure, all students at the college were provided with the descriptions of the six types. They were asked to rank the six groups according to the degree to which they would prefer to be identified as a member of each group. This procedure, it was hoped, would provide some indication of the validity of our panel's judgments, and, more importantly, it would provide information about how these groups were stratified at the college.

As noted earlier, each student theoretically had at least ten chances to be placed in each category, assuming that each panel member knew every person on her list and that all panelists agreed completely on the defining characteristics of each category. Because these conditions did not actually hold, the true probabilities of placement were much lower, and unknown. Consequently, some rather arbitrary cutting points were used. Since not every student who was nominated deserved to be included, some minimum number of nominations was decided upon for each category. The number which was chosen was the highest number in each category which would provide a usable N for that category (the minimum acceptable N was 25). Table 11.1 lists the cutting points and resultant N's for each category; for example, in line 1, each of 46 different individuals was named by four or more panelists.

Our first question concerned the distinctiveness of these categories.

Table 11.1   Number of Nominations and Number of Cases in Each Category

Category	Minimum Number of Nominations	N
Creative individualists	4	46
Scholars	3	25
Wild ones	2	35
Social group	3	45
Leaders	3	30
Political activists	2	42

Table 11.2   Percent of Students Assigned to Each Category Who Were
Also Assigned to Other Categories *

Category	Percent Also Assigned to						
	Creative	Scholar	Wild	Social	Leader	Pol. Act.	N
Creative	—	22	15	4	20	26	46
Scholar	40	—	8	0	32	44	25
Wild	20	6	—	14	0	14	35
Social	4	0	13	—	9	7	45
Leader	30	27	0	13	—	60	30
Pol. act.	29	26	12	7	43	—	42

* Rounded to nearest integer.

To what degree were the same persons assigned to more than one category by our procedure? Table 11.2 shows the percentages of persons in each category who were also assigned by one or more judges to each of the other categories.

Obviously, there is overlap among these groups. It should be noted, however, that this overlap is almost entirely among the groups *adjacent* to each other on our normative dimensions—individualism and intellectuality. Thus the categories with highest overlap (excluding Leaders and Political Activists, who were not expected to be completely distinctive) are Creative Individualists and Scholars. These groups were hypothesized to be similar with respect to "intellectuality" and were expected to differ with respect to "individualism." The second greatest overlap within the first four categories is between Creative Individualists and Wild Ones, expected to be similar with respect to "individualism." Finally, there is some overlap between Wild Ones and the Social Group, who were expected to be similar with respect to "intellectuality" (both low).

Little overlap exists between the Creative Individualists and the Social Group or between the Scholars and the Wild Ones. These pairs were expected to be least similar in their attributes. As we had initially suspected, the Leaders and Political Activists categories tend to cut across some of the others (particularly Creative Individualist and Scholar) and also overlap each other to a high degree. Finally, it is of interest to note that no students received nominations as both "Social" and "Scholar," nor was there any overlap between the Leaders and the Wild Ones.

Differences among the Types with Respect to Norm Acceptance

The students assigned to the various categories were compared on a wide variety of indices relating to norm acceptance. We expected that these comparisons would show the Creative Individualists to be highest in norm acceptance, since they were hypothesized to be high in both individualism and intellectualism, and that the Social Group would be lowest, since they were hypothesized to be low on both dimensions. The Scholars and the Wild Ones were expected to fall between these categories, with Scholars relatively high on intellectualism and low on individualism, and the Wild Ones high on individualism and low on intellectualism.

In general, the results bore out these predictions. The most striking and most consistent findings had to do with differences between the Creative Individualists and the Social Group, and it is these data that we shall present here in tabular form. Findings with respect to the other types will be reported more briefly. (A more detailed analysis is available in Flacks, 1962.)

The most important measure of norm acceptance was the Omnibus Personality Inventory (see Appendix M for a discussion of the validity of the OPI as a measure of norm acceptance). Table 11.3 presents data concerning the means of the Creative Individualists and the Social Group on all scales of the OPI, as well as the means for the total college. The obtained differences between the two groups are all in the predicted direction, and statistically significant ($p < .01$) for all scales except nonauthoritarianism.

Table 11.3   Mean OPI Scores for "Creative Individualists" and "Social Group"

Type	OPI Scale *							
	AA	DS	Es	Li	NA	OR	TO	N †
Creative individualists	39.4	48.6	38.0	62.7	14.4	69.2	41.1	36–38
Social group	34.2	40.1	32.4	53.4	13.0	61.4	34.4	38–39
Total college	35.3	44.0	34.9	58.5	13.8	65.0	37.4	266–279

* See Appendix L for identification of these scales.

† Differences in *N* reflect differences in the numbers who completed the several scales.

Table 11.4 Mean Self-Ratings of "Creative Individualists" and "Social Group" on Selected Traits

	Total College (N = 297)	Creative (N = 37)	Social (N = 40)	Sig. Level *
Traits related to individualism				
Conventional in dress or appearance	3.8	3.0	4.8	.01
Conventional in opinion or belief	3.1	2.3	3.7	.01
Conservative	3.1	2.2	3.5	.01
Compliant	3.9	3.3	4.0	NS
Absorbed in social life and dating	4.0	3.1	5.4	.01
Traits related to intellectualism				
Intellectual	5.6	6.1	5.5	NS
Absorbed in studies and academic work	5.9	6.5	6.2	NS
Interested in national and international affairs	5.6	5.8	5.6	NS
Traits unrelated to norms				
Tenseness	5.0	4.8	5.1	NS
Impulsiveness	4.8	4.6	5.1	NS
Interested in religion	4.2	3.4	4.8	.01
Dedicated to a special field	5.6	6.3	5.7	NS

* Significance determined by t-test between means for Creative Individualist and Social Group; probabilities above .05 are regarded as not significant (NS). The higher the score, the closer the respondent to the pole indicated by the phrase at the left.

As for the other groups, the Wild Ones, the Political Activists, and the Scholars tended to be closer to the Creative Individualists than to the total college on all scales, whereas the Leaders did not differ significantly from the total college on any of the scales. The OPI failed to discriminate clearly between the Scholars and the Wild Ones, but our expectations concerning the Creative Individualists and the Social Group were clearly borne out by the OPI data.

Table 11.4 presents the means of self-ratings by the Creative Individualists and the Social Group on each of 12 seven-point rating scales. The grouping of the traits, in this table, is based on a factor analysis of the self-ratings of the entire college sample. Traits listed under "individualism" were all loaded heavily on a rotated first factor. Creative Individualists and the Social Group differ in the expected direction with regard to all four of them and, except for "compliance," the differences are statistically significant. Traits listed under "intellectualism" were all loaded on a second factor; here the differences are all in the expected direction, but they did not reach statistical significance.

Four traits are listed which did not load on either factor, the only significant difference between the two types being that Creative Individualists rated themselves as less interested in religion than did the Social Group. Clearly, there are important differences in the "self-images" of these two groups, particularly in what we have called "individualism": those nominated for membership in the Social Group saw themselves as much more conservative, conventional, and date-conscious than did the Creative Individualists.

Results for the groups other than Creative Individualists and the Social Group were as follows:

The Wild Ones were particularly high in such traits as unconventionality in dress and appearance, and opinions and beliefs, intellectualism, tenseness, impulsiveness, and interest in social life, and were the lowest group in self-rating of "absorption in academic life and studies."

The Scholars did not present a picture of high intellectualism, but tended to be low in "absorbed in social life" and in "critical of rules."

The Leaders' self-ratings were very close to those of the Social Group, except that they saw themselves as highly "critical of rules."

The Political Activists presented no major differences from the college average, except that they were uniquely high in "interest in international and national affairs," and uniquely low in "compliance."

In general, then, the results of these self-ratings tend to conform to the images of these people which others held of them: the Creative Individualists saw themselves as high in all traits connected with the norms of the college, and the Social Group saw themselves as relatively low in most of these traits. As with the OPI, not all of the expected traits of the Wild Ones and the Scholars were reflected in their scores, although the former did see themselves as both highly unconventional and highly social, whereas the latter tended to regard themselves as somewhat aloof from social life. As expected, Political Activists were high in traits reflecting their political interest and noncompliant, activist behavior. It is interesting, and not expected, that the Leaders should tend to see themselves as somewhat divergent from the Bennington norms on many traits.

Table 11.5 provides some further data on differences between Creative Individualists and the Social Group on indices of norm acceptance. The "index of conventionality" is a scale based on the list of Bennington stereotypes mentioned earlier (see Figure 11.1). The index represents the average number of adjectives from Cluster I (for example, collegiate, preppy, Smithy, social, etc.) which the respondent checked as "favorable." The Social Group clearly so regarded many of these, whereas hardly any of the adjectives were selected as favorable by the Creative Individualists.

The other indices are intended to be measures of "intellectualism." The "small-talk" index is based on the amount of time the respondent reported that she spent in conversations having to do with social life, personal problems, gossip, and so on. The "serious conversation" index represents the reported amount of time the respondent spent in discussing the arts, public affairs, philosophical issues, and other intellectual matters. "Number of weekends on campus" refers to the mean number of weekends the respondents said they had remained at Bennington (this gives some indication of the amount of dating and off-campus interests that the respondent engaged in). On all of these variables, with the exception of the "serious conversation" index, the Creative Individualists were significantly more "intellectual" than the Social Group ($p < .05$ for differences between means).

If Bennington's norms are indeed concerned with what we have called "individualism" and "intellectuality," then our data rather clearly suggest the existence of categories of students who differ in the degree to which they accept these norms. At one extreme are the Creative

Table 11.5 Scores of "Creative Individualists" and "Social Group" on Miscellaneous Indices of Norm Acceptance

	Creative Individualists		Social Group	
	Mean	N	Mean	N
Index of conventionality *	0.2	23	4.2	26
"Small talk" index	4.2	30	5.9	36
"Serious conversation" index	4.8	30	4.2	36
Number of weekends on campus	16.0	34	12.5	41

* This item was not given to freshmen.

Individualists who tend to score at or near the top of the population on all indices related to these norms. In their self-descriptions, their attitudes, and their reported activities the students reputed to fall into this category seem to embody the dominant norms of the college. At the other extreme is the Social Group, whose self-images, attitudes, and activities consistently run counter to the prevailing norms of the student body. These students, to a surprising degree, seemed to respond to our questionnaire in ways that fitted the stereotype which others have of them. Between these extremes there are apparently pockets of students who, reputedly, accept only partially the norms embodied by the Creative Individualists.

The Scholars and the Wild Ones, however, in terms of our measures, failed to present fully coherent pictures; they failed to fit their stereotypes to the same degree as the Creative Individualists and the Social Group fitted theirs. Perhaps the clearest thing that emerges about these types is that, although both the Scholars and the Wild Ones are at or above the college average in norm acceptance, they differ from the norms in this respect: the Scholars are below average in their social interest, whereas the Wild Ones are substantially above average in their participation in social life.

The two remaining types, the Leaders and the Political Activists, are even less consistent in their orientation to the norms. The Political Activists tend generally to be high in norm acceptance, but, true to their reputation, are above average in political interest. More interesting is the fact that students reputed to be community Leaders (in the sense that they are most active in student government) tend to emerge as more conventional, more socially minded, and less intellectual than the college average.

Other Comparisons of the Types

The members of these categories were compared on a number of variables in addition to those measuring norm acceptance. The findings may be summarized as follows (see Flacks, 1962, for more detailed analysis).

Political interest and attitudes. The dimension of political interest and attitudes, so crucial for differentiating Bennington students in the thirties, is not an important basis for differentiating our present categories. Self-reports of political interest did not discriminate among our types, except that those nominated as Leaders and Political

Table 11.6   Party Preference by Type

Type	Republican	Other *	Total	N
Creative individualists	32%	68%	100%	38
Scholars	36	64	100	25
Wild ones	20	80	100	30
Social group	42	58	100	41
Leaders	41	59	100	29
Political activists	22	78	100	41

* Includes Democratic, Independent Democratic, Liberal, Socialist, independent, indifferent.

Activists did tend to report greater interest in political activity. Measures of political attitude were somewhat more likely to be discriminating. The Political Activists, of course, scored significantly higher than other types on measures of "radicalism" and a "welfare-civil-liberties" index, and there was a tendency for the Social Group nominees to score lowest on these scales.

Table 11.6, showing political party preference by type, represents a reasonable summary of the relationship between political attitude and our typology. This table indicates that the majority of students in all categories do not favor the Republican party (and, in fact, favor the Democratic or other liberal parties). Although the differences between the most Republican categories (Social and Leaders) and least Republican categories (Wild Ones and Political Activists) are statistically significant, from one-fifth to two-fifths of all groups are Republican. Thus political liberals and conservatives can be found in all our categories.

Community participation. In the thirties, participation in activities related to the government of the Bennington community was an important student norm. Our present data suggest that, as in the thirties, participation in community government and other extra-curricular activity was, on the whole, related to norm acceptance. By far the lowest participators in student government were the Wild Ones (three-quarters of whom never held a student government office, whereas the majority of students in all other categories had held at least one office). Student government activists were recruited, for the most part, from the Leader Group, followed closely by the Creative Individualists, Political Activists, and Scholars. The Social

Group tended to be evenly divided between participators and non-participators (as measured by election to office, participation in activities, and expressed interests).

Some data on background and interests. Interpretation of the nature of our types would be facilitated if significant differences in background were apparent. These differences ought to be sharp enough so that we might infer that girls of similar background tend to seek each other out and hence come to share common orientations. On the other hand, the differences ought not to be so great as to account for all the variance in attitudes and behavior among the types.

Our data on socio-economic status were relatively sparse. However, two indices of status provided results which are interesting and representative. Somewhat more than half of the Bennington student body had attended public school; about 40% had attended private high school for at least one year. A suggestive finding with respect to our types is that more than half of the students in all categories except the Social Group had attended *only* public school. Sixty-two percent of the Social Group, however, had attended private school at least for some part of their secondary school career. By contrast, 63% of the Creative Individualists had attended only public school (a difference which is significant with a p value of less than .05).

Similarly, the Social Group had the highest proportion of fathers with business occupations (57%, as compared with a college average of 45%). Professional, government, artistic, and lower-status occupations were under-represented among the fathers of the Social Group.

The Social Group was differentiated from the other types with respect to career interests as well. Social Group members were heavily recruited from social-science majors; such majors as literature, dance, and drama were quite under-represented in this category. Similarly, more than half of the Social Group nominees expressed an interest in careers classified as "service, general cultural (education, social work, journalism, college teaching), and business"—this compared with a strong tendency for members of other categories, particularly Creative Individualists, to orient toward careers in the arts.

It is also important to note the distribution of our types by year level. Table 11.7 suggests that the Creative Individualists and Leaders are predominantly juniors and seniors, whereas the Wild Ones and the Social Group are mainly composed of freshmen and sophomores. These findings are fully consistent with our depiction of the Creative Individualists as representative of the dominant community norms.

Table 11.7 Percentages Belonging to Categories, by Year Level *

	51 Freshmen	62 Sophomores	58 Juniors	52 Seniors	Total	N
Creative individualists	17	17	30	35	99%	46
Scholars	16	36	32	16	100	25
Wild ones	40	34	14	11	99	35
Social group	27	33	27	13	100	45
Leaders	0	27	37	36	100	30
Political activists	31	24	21	24	100	42

* Rounded to nearest integer.

They suggest that students tend to perceive seniors as more likely to be Creative Individualists and freshmen as more likely to be Social. They also reflect a related finding indicating that the Social Group has a significantly higher drop-out rate than any other category. For example, 11 (24%) of the 45 students in the Social Group dropped out after the spring semester in 1961. This was 2½ times the college average (10%). No other group exceeded the college average in drop-out rate.

The Typology and Social Structure

The data just reviewed demonstrate that students identified by other students as belonging in various stereotyped categories differed substantially in their orientation to the norms of the student culture. But such evidence is not sufficient to establish that a student subculture existed. The categories we had isolated might consist simply of sets of students with similar attitudes whose orientations and actions are independent of one another. We might regard these as *types* of students, but a *subculture* implies more than a collection of people holding similar attitudes; it implies, too, that they are mutually attracted to one another, and that they are aware of their common orientation. The data collected in the spring of 1961 provided some initial clues about which of the various types we had isolated had subcultural attributes.

Table 11.8 reports data on the extent to which the friendship choices of the students within each category were accorded to others

Table 11.8   Within-Group Friendship Choices by Types

| | Within-Group Choices as Percent of Total Choices | | |
	N	Expected	Obtained
Creative individualists	46	15%	35%
Scholars	25	7	26
Wild ones	35	10	5
Social group	45	14	45
Leaders	30	9	28
Political activists	42	12	28

in that category. The actual number of within-group choices divided by the total number of choices made by the group members is compared with the expected proportion of within-group choices. The expected proportion of within-group choices is equal to the size of the category relative to the total N of the student body.

Table 11.8 indicates that there is a substantial degree of within-group choice among persons named as Creative Individualists and as Social, and that Scholars, Leaders, and Political Activists show some degree of intragroup attraction. The Wild Ones, on the other hand, do not seem to be a subcultural group; the degree of intragroup attraction was approximately at the chance level. Thus, as with our previously reported findings on attitudinal differences, the most clearly defined groups were the Creative Individualists and the Social Group.

There was some interesting evidence that the members of each category tended to identify themselves with that category. More precisely, those who were nominated by others as belonging to a particular category tended to rank that category higher than it was ranked by those in the other categories or by the total college. These data are shown in Table 11.9, which presents the mean ranking of each category by the student body as a whole and by the members of each category. An inspection of this table shows that, although all groups generally followed a similar pattern of rank-ordering, with the exception of Political Activists, the members of a particular category gave a higher rank to the category in which they had been assigned than others had given to the category.

Table 11.9 further indicates that the status order of the college as a whole rather neatly fitted our expectations. The Creative Individualists were ranked first, the Social Group received the lowest rank.

Table 11.9 Rank Order of the Types

Preferences Expressed by	N	Mean Preferences for					
		Creative Individualists	Scholars	Leaders	Political Activists	Wild Ones	Social Group
Total college	291	1.8	3.0	3.2	3.4	4.8	4.9
Creative individualists	35	1.5(1) *	2.5(2)	3.7(4)	3.1(3)	4.9(5)	5.5(6)
Scholars	24	1.8(1)	2.4(2)	3.7(4)	3.1(3)	4.6(5)	5.4(6)
Leaders	27	2.5(2)	2.9(3)	2.2(1)	3.0(4)	5.4(6)	5.0(5)
Political activists	36	2.1(1)	2.7(2)	3.1(3)	2.9(4)	4.9(5)	5.4(6)
Wild ones	32	1.4(1)	3.5(3)	4.0(5)	2.4(2)	3.6(4)	4.2(6)
Social group	39	2.3(1)	3.7(4)	2.6(2)	3.5(3)	4.7(6)	4.0(5)

* Numbers in parentheses indicate rank orders of preference expressed by the type described at the left.

The entire rank order was: Creative Individualists, Scholars, Leaders, Political Activists, Wild Ones, and Social Group. This rank ordering fits the hypothesis that a group will be ranked according to its degree of acceptance of the norms of the community.

Similar results concerning status are obtained when measures of individual status are used. Table 11.10 compares the Creative Individualists and the Social Group on several indices of status. "Community representative" is the mean number of nominations received as a worthy representative of the student body at a national gathering of college students. "Most admired" represents the mean number of nominations received as a "student you particularly admire." "Most creative" represents the mean number of nominations received as a "student you regard as unusually creative or original in her work." On each of these measures, the Creative Individualists scored much higher than the Social Group, the latter scoring somewhat below the college mean on the three variables.

When all six types are compared on the three measures of status, the following picture emerges.

Creative Individualists always receive the highest status of the six.

The Leaders are close to the Creative Individualists on the Community Representative and Most Admired indices, but have a mean score of only 1.0 on the Most Creative index.

The Wild Ones are close to the Social Group on the Community Representative and Most Admired indices, both being below all other groups, but the former have a higher mean score on the Most Creative index.

The Scholars had relatively high status as measured by the Most

Table 11.10 "Creative Individualists" and "Social Group" on Three Measures of Status

	Community Representative		Most Admired		Most Creative	
	Mn	N	Mn	N	Mn	N
Creative individualist	3.9	37	5.6	37	5.3	37
Social group	1.6	32	1.6	32	0.8	32
Total college	1.8	223	2.2	227	1.8	214

Admired index, but did not differ from the college average on the other two indices.

Political Activists were similar in status to the Leaders.

Thus measures of individual status provided a status order similar to that derived from the rank-orderings of the types. Creative Individualists were highest in status, Social Group and the Wild Ones were lowest, and the Leaders, Scholars, and Political Activists ranged in between these extremes.

Summary

The data summarized in this chapter constitute an exploration of the possibility that divergent subcultures existed at Bennington in the early sixties. The exploration began when we noticed that certain student houses were described in ways which did not seem to fit the pattern of norms we believed to have been dominant at that time. The terms used to describe these houses were subsequently found to be perceived by the students as corresponding to a coherent pattern. We constructed a preliminary model of the social structure of the student body, a model which said that subgroups would tend to form among those who had common orientations to the prevailing norms. We developed "ideal types," descriptions of students who differed in their orientation to the norms, and used the language of the students in developing the descriptions of these types. We then found that students could identify actual girls who fitted each of these types. And, finally, we found certain marked, even striking, differences among the girls so identified.

Particularly striking and coherent were the differences between the Creative Individualists (those hypothesized to be high on the normative patterns of "individualism" and "intellectualism") and the Social Group (those who, in our model, were expected to be low with respect to the same norms). These two groups differed widely in their degree of norm acceptance, and in the expected directions. They differed markedly in the amount of prestige accorded them by the rest of the college, again in the directions one would expect. Finally, unlike the other categories we developed, there was a strong tendency for those identified in each of these ways to interact with one another and to choose each other as friends, thus suggesting that their similar orientations were not fortuitous, but shared.

12. Subcultures and Deviant Adaptations

Our findings with respect to the emergence of divergent subcultures at Bennington were somewhat unexpected. The original study (1943) indicated that most Bennington students shared a common set of attitudes, and that nonconforming students tended to be isolated, "negativistic," or peripheral individuals. Moreover, the small and highly selected character of the student body had led us to expect that the social structure and interaction processes in the 1960's would not be very different from those observed 25 years earlier. What we found, however, was that students who did not accept the prevailing norms at the college no longer appeared to be isolated and uninvolved; instead, a large proportion of such students had clustered together to create an identifiable "subculture."

This change, though unanticipated, is readily intelligible when viewed from the perspective of sociological and social-psychological theory about "deviant behavior" and nonconformity. Considerable prior research and theoretical formulation with respect to nonconformity tends to converge with respect to the following generalizations.

First, when attitudes become normative in a group or organization, participants who do not, at the outset, share the dominant attitudes are likely to experience considerable psychological "strain."

Second, this stress occurs for at least two reasons. On the one hand, any discrepancy between one's own attitudes and the attitudes of people with whom one regularly interacts and finds attractive is likely to produce discomfort or "cognitive imbalance" (Heider, 1958; Newcomb, 1961). In addition, insofar as the nonconformist becomes visible as such, other group members are likely to communicate disapproval and accord him low status. A good demonstration of the latter is the isolated position of many conservative students at Bennington in the 1930's.

Third, there are several ways in which the deviant member can cope with this situation. One way is to reduce his participation or withdraw entirely from the group. This was a typical response of the deviants at Bennington in the 1930's; as we noted in the previous chapter, "dropping out" was quite prevalent among "Social" types in the 1960's. But other responses are possible as well. In particular, nonconformists can seek the support of like-minded individuals. Such a process of group formation among deviants can reduce the degree of psychological stress arising from attitudinal discrepancy. In addition, the developing deviant subgroup is likely to place high value on the kinds of behavior which the deviants *can* enact, standards which they *are* capable of achieving, and attitudes which they *can* accept. Thus those who are status-deprived in the larger system can achieve approval within the subgroup (Cohen, 1955, 1959).

Our decision to try to interpret the "Social Group" as a "deviant subculture" led us to a number of hypotheses about the consequences of the group for its members. The most important hypothesis was that the Social Group served to insulate participants from pressures to change toward the dominant norms of "individualism" and "intellectuality." Another function that participation performed, we hypothesized, was to provide opportunities for friendship, acceptance, and prestige which would not otherwise be available to the participants. Furthermore, despite the finding that a large proportion of Social Group members dropped out, we speculated that the rate of departure would have been even higher for girls with initially deviant attitudes had they not had the opportunity to participate in the subculture. The function of the subculture was thus to enable relatively conventional and unintellectual Bennington students to remain at the college while successfully avoiding substantial disruption of their basic values and style of life.

In these terms, the Social Group at Bennington was seen as not very different from "collegiate" subcultures found in studies of a number of other campuses (for example, Trow, 1959, 1960; Coleman, 1961; Goldsen et al., 1960; Bushnell, 1962; Freedman, 1956). In all such studies, the "collegiate-Greek-social" subculture is seen as composed of students relatively indifferent to intellectual concerns, effectively insulating such students from pressures toward academic seriousness emanating from the faculty.

An apparent difference, however, between the situation at Bennington and other well-studied schools (Vassar, for instance) is that at Bennington the "collegiate" subculture is deviant rather than dominant. At Vassar, the collegiate type is said to dominate; intellectuals and nonconformists tend to drop out or form closely knit subgroups (Freedman, 1956, p. 20). At Bennington, the situation is exactly reversed. This striking contrast between Bennington and Vassar suggests that the adaptation of students cannot be understood on the basis of individual predispositions only; rather, we need to place such dispositions in the context of the larger student culture and social structure. The relationship between individual attitudes and the dominant normative structure is a key to understanding both inter-personal relations on the campus and the ways in which students respond to the college and the values it transmits.

It became apparent that the Bennington situation provided an opportunity to observe the outcomes of a "natural experiment." Our interpretation of the "collegiate" subculture, namely, as a principal mechanism which students who enter the college with deviant pre-dispositions use to cope with their deviance, would be reinforced if theoretical expectations concerning deviant subcultures could be supported by observations of the consequences of participation in the Social Group. If deviants who participated in the subculture could be compared with a control group of deviants who did *not* participate, then we would have conditions approximating an experi-mental test of our hypotheses. We now turn to this problem.

Classifying Students as Deviants

In order to establish experimental and control groups of deviants, we needed first to establish criteria for classifying entering students as initially "deviant" with respect to the attitudes that were normative at Bennington. The best available instrument in our battery for measuring initial attitudes and change over time was the Omnibus Personality Inventory.

We had strong reasons for believing that the OPI was a reasonably adequate instrument for quantitatively ascertaining agreement with the norms of the Bennington student culture. The basis for this assessment is detailed in Appendix M. As suggested there, we were less interested in whether the OPI scales measured what they purported to measure (for example, "originality," "liberalism," or "estheticism") than in whether they were strongly related to in-dependent measures of norm acceptance at the college. In particular, we needed to be sure that the test as a whole adequately discriminated between those who accepted and those who did not accept the dominant norms at Bennington. The data presented in Appendix L suggest that, in fact, this purpose was fulfilled by the scales.

Therefore, we assume that those who were initially low on the

OPI scales were "deviant" when they entered Bennington. More specifically, those whose scores fell below the median on Developmental Status, Estheticism, Liberalism, Originality, and Theoretical Orientation on the first administration of the test are defined as "deviant." (See Chapter 9, where one of these scales is used as an index of initial "congruence.") Our sample of deviants was limited only to those who received *both* administrations of the test, since those who took the test only once cannot be measured for change. A total of 157 students completed both administrations of the OPI; of these, 37 fell below the median, on the first administration, of *all five* of the scales just mentioned. These 37 constitute our sample of "deviants." * These 37 students constitute the sample on which most of our hypotheses will be tested. There were 16 of the 37 who subsequently participated in the collegiate subculture (according to our criteria of participation, to be defined). The remaining 21 did not meet our criteria for classification as "collegiate," and hence constitute our control group.

Our hypotheses concerning the effects of participation in a deviant subculture and the structure of that subculture were tested primarily by comparing these two groups of deviants, although in some cases our findings were verified by drawing additional matched samples of collegiate and noncollegiate students whose initial scores were less deviant.

Thus our two groups are equivalent in initial scores on the OPI. This is especially important if attitude change is to be measured, since initial position on a scale is strongly related to the direction and amount of subsequent change. This is because of "regression" effects, that is, tendencies for persons in extreme positions to move toward the mean of the scale, and because of "ceiling" effects, that is, tendencies for persons who score extremely high initially to increase their scores less than those who score low. It is thus

---

* The OPI was first administered to the entire college in the fall of 1959, and to all entering freshmen in the fall of 1960. On these first administrations, 109 students fell below the median on all five scales. Of these 109, there were 69 who graduated or for other reasons left school before the second administration in the spring of 1962; and our sample does not include three students who were initially deviant and who could have completed the second administration of the OPI, but did not. In addition, there were two students (not included in the 109) who did not take the OPI on the first opportunity, but did take it in the spring of 1962 and fell below the median on all five scales. Thus of the potential "deviants" who could have been in our sample, that is, who remained at the college long enough for us to observe their behavior over time, 88% were actually included.

Table 12.1   OPI Scores in 1959 or 1960 for Two Groups of Initial
Deviants and Total College

	DS *	Es	Li	OR	TO	N
Collegiate deviants	22.7	27.4	37.0	48.2	25.3	16
Noncollegiate deviants	26.6	29.6	40.0	47.2	24.2	21
Total college †	31.1	35.7	47.1	54.8	30.3	548

* Here and elsewhere, the scale abbreviations stand for, in the order of
appearance, Developmental Status, Estheticism, Liberalism, Originality, and
Theoretical Orientation.

† Represents all students who ever completed the OPI at least once.

important to control on initial position when comparing for amount
of attitude change (see Appendix K).

Table 12.1 gives the mean scores on the OPI scales for our two
groups of deviants, collegiate and noncollegiate, and for the total
college. None of the differences between the two groups of deviants
approaches statistical significance (p is greater than .20 in all cases),
whereas both groups differ significantly from the mean of the total
college in all cases ($p < .01$).

Classifying Students as "Collegiate"

In addition to developing an operational definition of "deviance,"
it was necessary to develop a valid technique for classifying deviant
students as participants or nonparticipants in the "collegiate" subculture. The procedure used was as follows.

In the spring of 1962, as in 1961, we interviewed a sample of
students. As before, the interview schedule included items asking
students to identify others who belonged to certain categories. The
original list of six types was for this purpose reduced to two, Creative
Individualists and Social Group. In addition, our interviewees were
asked to list the names of students who formed cliques, or "hung
around together a great deal." The information gathered in these
ways was used as the basis for delimiting the "collegiate" subculture
at Bennington and identifying its members.

The question concerning cliques posed some difficulty. Altogether,
a very large number of students were mentioned in response to the
question. Some groups of two, three, four, and five or more were

mentioned quite frequently by our respondents, but rarely were exactly the same people always listed as belonging with each other. It thus became necessary to establish criteria for reliably assigning students to particular cliques, and for limiting the size and extent of the cliques. The criterion established was as follows: a student was to be included in a clique if she was mentioned at least twice as associating with two or more other members of the clique. Thus the minimum number of persons in a clique was three, and the existence of this group had to be noted by at least two respondents.

Altogether, twenty-one groups of three or more students were isolated in this way. Of the twenty-one, the ten largest had six or more members (the largest included fifteen); the remaining eleven were triads, and because of their smallness were not regarded as crucial for defining the social structure of the student body. Some of the cliques were highly concentrated within particular houses, and others were composed of students majoring in particular fields, but the principal distinguishing characteristic of each clique tended to be whether Creative Individualists or Social Group members predominated within it. The sharp differences among the cliques in this respect are illustrated in Table 12.2, which shows the proportion of members of each of the ten main cliques who received one or more nominations either as Creative Individualists or as Social. Except for cliques 3 and 7, it is clear from this table that each clique has a

Table 12.2   Proportion of "Creative Individualists" and "Social" Types in Ten Cliques

| Clique | Proportion Receiving at Least One Nomination as | | |
	Creative	Social	N
1	93.3%	6.7%	15
2	66.7	13.3	15
3	72.7	100.0	11
4	85.7	21.4	14
5	83.3	0.0	6
6	83.3	33.3	6
7	53.3	46.7	15
8	30.0	70.0	10
9	28.6	71.5	7
10	62.5	0.0	8

heavy preponderance of people nominated for one or the other of these categories.

Cliques 1, 2, 4, 5, 6, and 10 are heavily composed of Creative Individualists. Although not as clearly differentiated as these, cliques 3, 8, and 9 are preponderantly Social—50% or more of their members received at least three nominations as Social, and probably the reason why a relatively high proportion of their members also received one or more nominations as Creative Individualists is that the latter category is more diffuse than the Social category. A given individual was more likely to receive a nomination as a Creative Individualist simply by virtue of being a senior, or highly popular or well known. However, the apparent unreliability of this category disappears when three or more nominations are used as a basis for classification. Thus, of the 28 members of the preponderantly Social cliques, only one received three or more nominations as Creative Individualist, whereas 37.5% of the members of the remaining cliques were nominated three or more times as Creative Individualists.

Based on these considerations, we defined membership in the Social or collegiate subculture (we shall use these labels interchangeably) according to the following criteria:

First, a girl was included in the subculture if she received at least three nominations as a member of the Social Group.

Second, a girl was included in the subculture if she was part of a clique in which at least 50% of the other members had been nominated as Social.

The second criterion was added in order to include those who were seen as interacting with Social Group members even if they themselves were not reputed to be Social. In part, this was deemed desirable because girls who belonged to a particular group should reflect the influence process in that group; also, this decision was based on the possibility that, for one reason or another, many Social— oriented students would not be directly visible as such.

Thus, designation as Social was based entirely on "objective" criteria, that is, on the *reputation* of the person, rather than self-report. It is clear that if we are dealing with traits that are "deviant," many students would not readily admit to possessing them. The technique we used, similar to those used in studies of social stratification in small-town communities, seemed to constitute a reasonable approximation of objective observational procedures.

This operational definition does not, of course, establish that the girls so selected do, in fact, constitute a subculture, that is, a set of persons who share a common orientation to the norms of the larger culture and who form an interacting group. Whether or not the procedures outlined previously did isolate a subculture is a matter for empirical test. We are, however, at least reasonably assured that the students selected in this way were *seen by others* as having a common orientation to the norms and as interacting with each other.

Testing the Hypothesis of a Deviant Subculture

If the collegiate group did, in fact, constitute a deviant subculture, then the members of the group should be characterized by such patterns as the following:

1. They should tend to have collegiate friends, whereas noncollegiate students should not.

2. They should tend to have friends whose attitudes will resemble their own; this tendency should be less marked for noncollegiate students.

3. They should tend to be concentrated in particular houses, noncollegiate deviants being located randomly with respect to housing.

4. They should be more readily identifiable by other students as deviant than are noncollegiate deviants.

5. They should be more likely to identify themselves as deviant than do noncollegiate deviants.

6. Students accorded high status by the collegiate deviants should tend to have different characteristics than students accorded high status by noncollegiate deviants.

A second set of predictions has to do with patterns of attitude change, status conferral, and participation which would be expected if the collegiate group were, in fact, serving the function of insulation, social support, and integration; these, we hypothesized, are central to understanding the development of deviant subcultures. Therefore, the following predictions about collegiate deviants were also tested:

7. They should tend to change their attitudes less than noncollegiate deviants do.

8. Nondeviants should accord less status to them than to noncollegiate deviants.

9. They should tend to accord higher status to one another than they accord to noncollegiate deviants.

10. They should show a lower rate of drop-outs than noncollegiate deviants; both types of deviants should be more likely than non-deviants to drop out.

Findings Concerning Patterns of Association

1. Do collegiate deviants tend to have collegiate friends, and non-collegiate deviants noncollegiate friends? In the spring of 1962 we asked the students to list at least two and not more than five other students whom they considered to be particularly good friends of theirs. These friends were then classified according to the same criteria that we applied to our sample of deviants (see p. 196), that is, a student was classified as collegiate if she had received at least three nominations as a member of the Social Group or had been listed as a member of a clique in which at least 50% of the members had been so nominated at least three times. Table 12.3 shows the number of friends of each type of deviant who were classified as collegiate and noncollegiate.

This table clearly supports our expectation that collegiate students would tend to choose collegiate friends. Even more striking is the fact that very few of the 21 noncollegiate deviants had any collegiate friends. They named only six collegiate friends, altogether.

2. Are the friends of collegiate deviants more deviant in their attitudes than the friends of noncollegiate deviants? As previously noted, we defined a deviant as a student who fell below the median on all five scales of the OPI. The extent to which a student deviated from the norms, then, could conveniently be measured by the number

Table 12.3 Numbers of Friends Classified as Collegiate and Noncollegiate for Two Types of Deviants

Deviants Are	Friends Are		
	Collegiate	Noncollegiate	Total
Collegiate	37	22	59
Noncollegiate	6	56	62 *
Total	43	78	121

$X^2 = 37.9$; $p < .001$ (1 df)

* Data not available for one friend.

Table 12.4 Numbers of Friends with Low and High
Deviance Scores for Two Types of Deviants

	Deviance Score of Friends		
Deviants Are	Low (0–2)	High (3–5)	Total
Collegiate	22	34	56 *
Noncollegiate	36	27	63
Total	58	61	119

$X^2 = 3.82$; $p < .05$ (1 df)

* Data were unavailable for three friends.

of scales on which she fell below the median. A Deviance score of 0
would mean that the student scored above the median on all scales,
and a Deviance score of 3 that she scored below the median on
three of the five scales. Each friend of every deviant of both types
was scored in this way for Deviance, and Table 12.4 indicates the
proportion of friends of each type who had Deviance scores of 0 to 2
and 3 to 5.

As the table shows, there was a significant tendency for collegiate
deviants to choose friends who had high Deviance scores, and for
noncollegiate deviants to choose friends who had low Deviance scores.
This tendency is even more markedly revealed in Table 12.5, which
compares the extent to which each type of deviant chose friends who
were high in norm acceptance (that is, had Deviance scores of 0)
as against friends who were relatively lower (that is, fell below the
median on one or more scales of the OPI). Although both groups

Table 12.5 Numbers of High-Scoring vs. Low-
Scoring Friends for Two Types of Deviants

	Deviance Score of Friends		
Deviants Are	0	1–5	Total
Collegiate	6	50	56
Noncollegiate	19	44	63
Total	25	94	119

$X^2 = 6.7$; $p < .01$ (1 df)

Table 12.6   Distribution in Houses for Two Types of
Deviants

	Number Living in		Total
	Four Social Houses	Eight Other Houses	
Collegiate	11	5	16
Noncollegiate	6	15	21
Total	17	20	37

$X^2 = 4.3$; $p < .05$ (1 df)

tended to choose low rather than high scorers as friends, there was a significant tendency for noncollegiate deviants to choose high scorers more than the collegiate deviants did.

3. *Were collegiate deviants concentrated in particular houses?* Thirty-seven students altogether met our criteria for inclusion in the collegiate subculture (of these 37, 16 were deviant in terms of their OPI scores). If these students had been randomly distributed as to house, there would have been approximately three in each of the 12 houses on campus. Actually, 30 of the 37 lived in five houses, the other seven being distributed among the remaining seven houses. Each of the five houses, Taylor, Cabot, Endicott, Evans, and Adams, had either five, six, or seven collegiate students, which meant that in each of these houses, members of the collegiate subculture made up about 20% of those living there. (The discrepancy between the obtained distribution and the expected distribution of collegiate students with respect to house, incidentally, yielded a chi-square of 26.8 which, with 11 degrees of freedom, has a *p* value of .005.)

Clearly the collegiate students did tend to concentrate in particular houses. This, moreover, was nothing new in 1962; in 1959—three years before these data were collected, when the composition of the houses was rather different, and when the students who figured in the foregoing analysis were all freshmen and sophomores—two of the houses in which collegiate types were concentrated in 1962, Taylor and Cabot had earlier been regarded as "collegiate-social-preppy" houses (see Chapter 11). The other three were also mentioned occasionally in these terms, but with a much lower frequency.

When collegiate deviants are compared with noncollegiate deviants it becomes clear that the former are concentrated in four of the five social houses (Endicott had only one collegiate deviant), whereas the noncollegiate deviants are more randomly distributed, with some tendency for them *not* to live in these same houses. This finding appears in Table 12.6.

Findings Concerning Visibility and Awareness

1. Were collegiate deviants more likely to be seen as deviant by others than noncollegiate deviants? One item on the spring questionnaire of 1961 asked students to rate themselves on a series of seven-point rating scales, most of which were designed to be related to the dominant norms of the student culture. Immediately after this, the students were asked to name three others who would be "most similar" and "least similar" to them in their self-ratings. The number of times a student was mentioned as *"least similar"* seems a reasonably good index of her *visibility as a deviant*. We predicted that collegiate deviants would be more visible—more likely to be named as "least similar"—than noncollegiate deviants. Table 12.7 indicates that whereas 75% of collegiate deviants received two or more mentions as "least similar," only 40% of the noncollegiate deviants were mentioned at least twice.

2. Did collegiate deviants tend to see themselves as more deviant than did noncollegiate deviants? If collegiate deviants are more visible than noncollegiate deviants, we might expect them to see themselves

Table 12.7 Visibility as a Deviant for Two
Types of Deviants

	Number of Mentions as "Least Similar"		
	0–1	Two or More	Total
Collegiate	4	12	16
Noncollegiate	12	8	20 *
Total	16	20	36

$X^2 = 3.8$; $p < .05$ (1 df)

* One student was not on campus during this semester.

Table 12.8   Perceived Similarity to Norms for Two Types
of Deviants

	Perceived Similarity to Norms		
	Low (0–2)	Moderate to High (Three or More)	Total
Collegiate	11	3	14
Noncollegiate	1	17	18
Total	12	20	32 *

$X^2 = 14.9$; $p < .001$ (1 df)

* Complete data were not available for five students.

as more distant from the norms in response to the definition of themselves that they receive from others.

The rating scales provide a simple way of measuring perceived
distance from the norms. The students' responses in the spring of 1961
included self-ratings on these scales, and also ratings of a number of
groups of other people, among them "most seniors at Bennington."
This procedure was repeated in the spring of 1962 except that "someone admired by most Bennington students" was substituted for "most
Bennington seniors" as an object to be rated. The number of cor-
respondences between a student's self-rating and the ratings she
assigned to the presumably normative groups, divided by two, was
used as an index of perceived similarity to the norms. If data were
missing from either of these two administrations, the respondent was
left out of the analysis. We had substantial data to show that the
category "most Bennington seniors" was consistently rated highest of
any stimulus object on norm-related scales by most students; similar
results were obtained with "someone admired by most Bennington
students," which is why these two categories were chosen to compare
with self-ratings. The number of scales on which such comparisons
were made was nine in both cases.

Table 12.8 shows the number of collegiate and noncollegiate
deviants who were high and low in perceived similarity to the norms.
Of 18 noncollegiate deviants for whom complete data were available,
only one had a perceived similarity score of 2 or less, whereas 11 of
the 14 collegiate deviants had scores this low—a clear indication of
a tendency for collegiate deviants to see themselves as relatively
distant from the norms (or, perhaps more precisely, from types of

persons generally defined as embodying the norms). Just as they had been defined by others as deviant, so, too, did the collegiate types tend to define themselves as deviant.

Findings Concerning Attitude Change

1. Did noncollegiate deviants change their attitudes more than collegiate deviants? Our measure of attitude change is based on a comparison of a student's score on the first and second administrations of the OPI scales. The first score on each scale (the ones used were Developmental Status, Estheticism, Liberalism, Originality, and Theoretical Orientation) was subtracted from the second score (obtained two to three years later). The differences thus obtained were summed algebraically, and divided by 5 (the number of separate scales used). The resulting score represents the Attitude Change Score for the individual student. Because low scorers on the first administration tended, in general, to change more than those who scored high initially, it is important to remember that the initial scores for collegiate and noncollegiate deviants were similar. Hence the comparisons made here are between two groups, neither of which, so to speak, had an initial advantage.

Table 12.9 shows that noncollegiate deviants had a mean attitude change score of 4.8, compared with a mean of 1.3 for collegiate deviants. This difference in means was significant with a probability level of less than .01.

To check this finding we drew a sample of what might be called "quasi-deviants," that is, students who scored below the median on three or four scales of the OPI. Again we separated these into collegiate and noncollegiate groups, using the same criteria we had

Table 12.9   Mean Attitude Change for Two Types
of Deviants

	Collegiate Deviants	Noncollegiate Deviants
Mean change on OPI	1.3	4.8
Variance	20.4	13.2
N	16	21

$t = 2.5$; $p < .01$

Table 12.10   Mean Attitude Change for Two Groups of
"Quasi-Deviants"

| | Students with Deviance Score of 3–4 Who Were | |
	Collegiate	Noncollegiate
Mean attitude change	0.8	1.9
Variance	13.9	8.6
N	26	11

$t = 3.7;\ p < .005$

originally established. As shown in Table 12.10, these two groups exhibited the same pattern of attitude change—the collegiate changing much less than the noncollegiate, although the amount of change for both groups was considerably less. The greater change for the lower-scoring deviants (in Table 12.9) is undoubtedly due, at least in part, to regression effects, illustrating the necessity for comparing groups matched for initial score.

Thus it seems possible to make the generalization that students who participated in the collegiate subculture were less likely to change in the direction of the norms than students with initially similar attitudes who did not participate in the subculture. Our expectation about the central function of the subculture—to facilitate resistance to influence—is supported by these findings.

Findings Concerning Status

1. *Did collegiate deviants receive lower status ratings from non-deviants than noncollegiate deviants?* In the spring of 1962 we asked the students to name at least two and not more than five students who would be worthy representatives of the college at a gathering of students from many colleges. This measure, both in the 1930's and in preliminary stages of the present study, turned out to be a reasonably good index of status at the college. Most students received one nomination or none for "community representative," and a small number received very many nominations. Data cited in Chapter 11 showed, for example, that Creative Individualists tend to gather the most nominations.

Table 12.11   Mean Nominations for Community Representative
for Two Types of Deviants

	Collegiate	Noncollegiate
Mean nominations from nondeviants	3.3	2.5
SD	4.5	4.3
N	16	21
	NS	

One of our important assumptions was that participation in a deviant subculture entailed loss of status for the participant. Thus we predicted that collegiate deviants would have lower status than noncollegiate deviants among nondeviant students, that is, they would receive fewer nominations for "community representative" from students with Deviance scores of less than 5 than would noncollegiate deviants. As Table 12.11 indicates, this prediction was not supported by our data. In fact, the mean number of nominations received by noncollegiate deviants was lower than the mean for collegiate deviants, although this difference was not significant.

Because, in this analysis, we had included among the "nondeviants" those collegiate students who had Deviance scores of less than 5, we decided to make a more precise analysis. We hypothesized that collegiate deviants had "inflated" status due to the nominations they received from other members of the collegiate group. Perhaps if these two sources of status were distinguished, then our predictions about the status of collegiate and noncollegiate students in the larger culture would tend to be supported. These data are presented in Table 12.12,

Table 12.12   Number of Nominations from "Collegiate" and
"Noncollegiate" Sources for Two Types of Deviants

Type of Deviant	Source of Nominations			Mean per Nominee
	Collegiate	Noncollegiate	Total	
Collegiate ($n = 16$)	27	38	65	4.06
Noncollegiate ($n = 21$)	8	58	66	3.14
Total	35	96	131	

$X^2 = 8.3$; $p < .005$ (1 df)

from which it is clear that, on the average, collegiate deviants receive more nominations than noncollegiate deviants; but the latters' nominations come almost entirely from other noncollegiate students, whereas a very large proportion of the collegiate deviants' nominations come from other collegiate students. If the collegiate "vote" is ignored, then noncollegiate deviants have a slightly higher mean number of nominations, but this difference would not be statistically significant.

Our prediction that collegiate deviants would suffer in status in the larger community, as compared with noncollegiate deviants, is not supported. But our expectation that participants in a deviant subculture do gain in status because of the prestige received from other members of their own subculture is supported by the data.

2. Do the criteria for status of collegiate deviants differ from those of noncollegiate deviants? We have shown that girls who participate in the collegiate subculture tend to give prestige to and receive prestige from other members of that subculture. This fact is an important defining characteristic of any subculture. Data now to be summarized indicate that noncollegiate deviants tend to give highest status to girls who have high status in the college as a whole, whereas collegiate deviants tend to give highest status to students who are visibly collegiate.

Whereas our previous findings were based on mean numbers of nominations for community representative for total groups of persons, it is also desirable to examine the attributes of students who are particularly high in the number of nominations they receive. We therefore examined the nominations that each of our two groups made for community representative. Selecting the five students who received the most nominations from each group, we found the following.

The five students considered most prestigious by noncollegiate deviants received no nominations as collegiate from our panel of interviewees, whereas the five considered most prestigious by collegiate deviants received an average of six such nominations each.

Furthermore, those considered most prestigious by collegiate students received virtually no nominations as Creative Individualists, whereas the noncollegiate deviants accorded high status to students who had been mentioned as Creative Individualists about six times each, on the average.

Thus the noncollegiate deviants tended to resemble the student body as a whole in according highest status to students reputed to be Creative Individualists. The collegiate deviants, on the other hand, accorded prestige to other collegiate students, although failing to "vote" for Creative Individualists.

Our final set of data concerning differences between collegiate and noncollegiate criteria for status is based on a task assigned to the students in the spring of 1961—rank-ordering the six Bennington types in terms of their desire to be identified as a member of each of the six groups. (It will be recalled that the groups were: Creative Individualist, Scholar, Wild Ones, Social Group, Political Activists, and Leaders.) As noted in Chapter 10, the overwhelming preponderance of students preferred to be known as Creative Individualists. We compared our two groups of deviants in terms of the proportion within each group who ranked Creative Individualists first. The results of this comparison appear in Table 12.13.

Table 12.13 indicates that only two out of fifteen collegiate students wanted to be identified as a Creative Individualist (in fact, most preferred to be known as a member of the Social Group or as a Leader). Sixty percent (12) of the noncollegiate deviants, on the other hand, wished to be known as Creative Individualists (in fact, only one wished to be a member of the Social Group, and seven had other choices). It is clear that the collegiate deviants' view of the dominant culture, and the referents which such deviants have at Bennington, differ quite radically from those of both the noncollegiate deviants and the student body as a whole.

3. Were deviants more likely to drop out than nondeviants? On the assumption that leaving college before graduation is one way deviant students can cope with the fact of their deviance, we examined the proportion of deviants who dropped out in comparison with the drop-out rate for nondeviants.

Table 12.13 First Choices of "Collegiate" and "Noncollegiate" Deviants among Six Bennington Types

	Number Giving First Choice to		
	Creative Individualist	Other	Total
Collegiate *	2	13	15
Noncollegiate *	12	8	20
Total	14	21	35

$X^2 = 5.95$; $p < .02$ (1 df)

* One student did not complete this item.

Of the students who were attending Bennington in the fall of 1959 and who took the OPI then, or entered in the fall of 1960 and completed the test in that year, 109 scored below the median on all five scales and hence are classifiable as deviant. Nondeviants numbered 276.

Of the 109 deviants, 44 subsequently dropped out, a proportion of 40.4%.

Of the 276 nondeviants, 81 subsequently dropped out, a proportion of 29.3%.

The critical ratio for the difference between these two percentages is 2.00, which has a probability of less than .05.

Thus, significantly more deviants, as we have defined them, left Bennington during the years of our study.

4. Were noncollegiate deviants more likely to drop out than collegiate deviants? We predicted that noncollegiate deviants would show a higher drop-out rate than collegiate deviants, on the assumption that the former would receive less support for their deviant position, and experience more strain as a result of it. Unfortunately, there were not enough drop-outs from our sample of deviants to permit direct comparison between our two types. However, we did have data on deviants who had dropped out in 1960 and 1961, but who had been present when the first attempt to identify collegiate students was made in 1960. We also knew the number of nominations that these drop-outs had received from our panel of interviewees. We classified these students as collegiate if they had received at least three such nominations, and noncollegiate if they had received less than three nominations. We did not have, for this earlier group, indications of membership in collegiate cliques, so that for this prediction our index of collegiate participation is less refined than the one we have been using so far. A more serious difficulty is that 19 of the 44 deviant drop-outs had left school during the first year of our study, and so we had no information about collegiate participation for them; consequently, our usable sample of drop-outs was greatly reduced.

Our prediction that a larger proportion of noncollegiate than of collegiate deviants would drop out was only partially supported. Of 53 deviants who had received two or less nominations as collegiate, 19, or 36%, dropped out. Of 26 deviants who had received at least three nominations as "collegiate," only six, or 23%, dropped out. This difference is in the predicted direction, but it is not statistically significant. It is unfortunate that so many of our drop-outs were "lost" before we could acquire more complete data concerning them; we have no way of knowing how they might have affected the differences in drop-out rates between our two groups.

Summary of the Findings

The data reported in this chapter provide strong support for the notion that those we had identified as collegiate students at Bennington did constitute a deviant subculture—an intensively interacting group of students sharing norms which diverge from the dominant student culture and thus serve to insulate its members from the influences of the larger culture. That these students did associate with each other was indicated by the fact that they chose each other as friends and tended to concentrate in particular houses. The insulating function of the subculture was revealed by comparing participants with deviants who did not participate in it. The latter chose nondeviants as friends, whereas the former tended to prefer those who shared their initial attitudes rather than those who did not. Noncollegiate deviants tended to change their attitudes in the direction of the collegewide norms, whereas collegiate students did not exhibit such change.

Collegiate deviants clearly gain in interpersonal rewards, as compared with noncollegiate deviants. This was demonstrated by the fact that, although the two types did not differ in the amount of status received from nondeviant students, the collegiate students also received status from their own subculture. As compared with noncollegiate deviants, collegiate deviants did not suffer the predicted deficit in status in the larger community. On the other hand, it is clear that participants in the collegiate subculture were not likely to receive very high status in the larger community; those who were prestigeful within the deviant subculture did not tend to receive high status outside it.

Differences in standards between the collegiate subculture and the dominant student culture were demonstrated by comparing those who received high status in each of the two cultures. Collegiate students "voted" for other collegiate students but not for Creative Individualists, whereas noncollegiate students showed precisely the opposite pattern. This difference was also illustrated when preferences among various Bennington reference groups were compared. Collegiate deviants preferred to be identified as Leaders or as Social, but not as Creative Individualists, whereas noncollegiate deviants preferred the latter type above all others.

Finally, as predicted, we found that deviants do, in fact, "leave the field"; this may be a means for coping with their deviant position. However, we failed to find a statistically significant difference in drop-out rates between the relatively few "collegiate" and the "noncollegiate" deviants. We were therefore not able to demonstrate conclusively that participation in a deviant subculture and "leaving the field" represent *alternative solutions* to problems of adaptation which deviants face.

Some Problems of Interpretation

Our data have shown some clear differences between our two groups of deviants, especially with respect to the kinds of persons they chose as friends and as worthy of admiration, and with respect to attitude change. We have tended to assume a "causal" relationship between these two facts; that is, we have asserted that the greater attitude change on the part of noncollegiate deviants was related to the fact that they tended to associate with nondeviants, whereas the minimal amounts of change shown by collegiate deviants was related to their interaction with other deviants and their participation in the collegiate subculture.

These assumptions are valid only to the extent that one further assumes the following: any differences that existed between the two groups initially could not simultaneously account for differences in sociometric patterns and differences in attitude change. It is, however, important to realize that such initial predispositions *could* have existed, so that, for example, students who later were identified as collegiate were predisposed to choose like-minded students as friends and were also predisposed to resist the norms, whereas noncollegiate deviants were predisposed to avoid friendships with collegiate students and also to accept the norms. The crucial fact here is that the only basis on which these two groups were "matched" was with respect to their OPI scores, and similarity with respect to these scores could be masking important differences between the two groups.

It seems quite likely that these two groups were not identical before their arrival on the Bennington campus, and differences between them did affect their subsequent behavior in various ways. However, it is possible to show that the extent of friendship with like-minded students was related to attitude change independently of the "collegiate-noncollegiate" dimension. There was sufficient variance within each of these two categories with respect to these variables to permit us to test directly the hypothesis that the extent of attitude change by a deviant is related to the extent of her friendship with nondeviants.

Table 12.14 presents data relevant to this hypothesis. Deviants having two or more friends with deviance scores of 3 or higher are compared with deviants whose friends did not meet this criterion (the higher the deviance score, the more deviant the friend). Deviants who tended to have nondeviant friends showed significantly more attitude change, on the average, than deviants whose friends tended to be deviant.

Table 12.14 suggests that, regardless of whether a deviant was categorized as collegiate or noncollegiate, attitude change was, in fact, related to the degree to which she associated with nondeviants.

Patently, similarity between one's own attitudes and those of one's friends is not the only determining influence in attitude change. But the foregoing finding does provide support for our assumption that these variables are related to each other; the differences between collegiate and noncollegiate deviants, however much they may reflect predispositional differences between the two types, are supported by experiences in college.

Perhaps the best interpretation to be given to our data is that, in fact, there were important differences between students destined to become collegiate and those who did not later participate in that subculture. It is likely that collegiate students were, for one reason or another, more strongly predisposed to resist the norms than non-

Table 12.14 Attitude Change by Deviance of Friends

	Deviance of Friends	
	High	Low
Mean change on OPI	2.0	4.8
Variance	18.5	15.3
N	19 *	18 †

$t = 2.0$; $p < .05$ (35 df)

* Includes 10 collegiate and 9 noncollegiate deviants.

† Includes 6 collegiate and 12 noncollegiate deviants.

collegiate students. But the crucial point seems to be that *without participation in the deviant subculture,* such resistance to the norms would have been much more difficult, if not impossible, had the student continued at Bennington.

Our study has left open the important question of just what were the factors which predisposed particular students to resist the norms. Deviants are likely to resist conformity when such conformity would entail substantial cost to them; when imposed norms present *specific problems of adaptation* for individuals, then deviant subcultures tend to arise. Our study has failed to specify in concrete terms the particular problem(s) of adjustment which led students at Bennington to participate in the collegiate subculture—problems which non-collegiate deviants apparently did not face to the same degree. In part, participation in the subculture may have been due to ecological factors—deviants who were placed in collegiate houses may have been more likely to participate in the subculture, for example. But such factors could not account entirely for the variance; some collegiate students did not live in collegiate houses, and some noncollegiate deviants did live in such houses.

This issue—that of what determines the decisions of students to participate in particular campus subcultures—is an important next step in research on student peer culture. For it is now clear, as further documented by this study, that such cultures have an important determining influence on student responses to higher education.

One important source of hypotheses concerning the roots of the collegiate subculture, and the kinds of adaptive problems which collegiate-oriented students face, is the highly popular *The Feminine Mystique,* by Betty Friedan (1963). Mrs. Friedan's speculations concerning the feminine role in contemporary American society seem highly relevant to Bennington College. Her chief hypothesis is that there is an increasing and highly organized tendency to define the feminine role as one of domesticity and housewifery, and to define as deviant those women who seek independent identity, a career, and personal autonomy.

Mrs. Friedan suggests that what we have defined as the collegiate subculture, particularly as it manifests itself in colleges such as Vassar, is but a reflection of the feminine mystique. That is, women students' tendency to define their role in college primarily in social terms and specifically to reject involvement in intellectual affairs represents, for Betty Friedan, preliminary socialization for the role of housewife-and-mother.

Carrying these speculations one step further, it is interesting to note that Bennington has consciously avoided the path traveled by some other women's colleges. Bennington's norms remain rather militantly antihousewifery, and very markedly in favor of "the experiences, the testing, the failures, and successes in various spheres of activity that are necessary for a person to achieve full maturity, individual identity" (Friedan, 1963, p. 180).

Thus students who have been strongly inculcated with the ideology of the feminine mystique may be highly threatened by Bennington's norms. We may hypothesize—and suggest for further research—that the concrete problem which results in the development of the collegiate subculture is the conflict between the norms symbolized by the feminine mystique and those promulgated at an institution such as Bennington.

This hypothesis needs qualification at the outset, however. For the collegiate subculture is not restricted to women; in fact, its historical origins seem to lie in the fraternities of state universities, rather than the houses of eastern women's colleges. And, as Trow (1959) has pointed out, the problem of anti-intellectualism and provincialism in American higher education is neither as recent nor as simple as Mrs. Friedan's discussion of the feminine mystique would suggest. A full program of research on the sources of student peer cultures would entail consideration of identity problems among American adolescents; the functions of higher education for different social strata in our society; problems of decision-making and alienation with respect to occupational choice; ethnic, regional and ecological subcultures in the larger society; and so on. Such a program would inevitably be complex, but if, as seems apparent, the student peer culture is a major agent of socialization for members of the American middle and upper classes, then such a program is well worth undertaking.

PART FOUR

Then and Now

13. The Early and the More Recent College Community: A Comparison

The formal structure of Bennington College, its educational policies, and its physical plant remained almost the same from 1939 to 1960. Student enrollment increased from about 265 students to 350 students. The size of the faculty remained at about 50. Though the college community had many similar characteristics in, say, 1935 and 1960, in some important ways it was different. The students of the later period came from somewhat different backgrounds, and they apparently had selected Bennington on the basis of its reputation for liberalism, its emphasis on the arts, and its educational policies. In many instances, the later students already shared the norms and values of the majority of students at the college, on arrival.

The backgrounds of the students reflect some of the differences between the two student bodies. At the time of the presidential election of 1960, a much higher proportion of the students reported that their parents were Democratic than had been the case in 1936. Table 13.1 shows the political party preferences of the parents of

Table 13.1 Political Party Preferences of Parents, in Percentages

Party Preference	1936 (N = 101)		1960 (N = 288)	
	Father	Mother	Father	Mother
Republican	72%	64%	44%	36%
Democratic	23	26	52	61
Other	5	10	4	3
Total	100%	100%	100%	100%

Table 13.2   Religious Preferences of Bennington Students

	1930's ($N = 139$)		1960's ($N = 301$)	
	N	Percent	N	Percent
Protestant	100	72	105	35
Jewish	9	6	71	24
Roman Catholic	7	5	7	2
Other	—	—	13	4
None	19	14	105	35
Not ascertained	4	3	—	—
Total	139	100	301	100

Bennington students at these times, as reported by presumably representative samples of students. Considering only the two major parties, both fathers and mothers were reported as less frequently having Republican preferences at the later time, by highly significant differences ($p < .001$).

There were also differences in religious backgrounds. In the late 1930's most of Bennington's students were Protestants; in the 1960's the student body was about equally divided among Protestants, Jews, and those with no religious preference. As shown in Table 13.2, at the later time a larger percentage of the students had no religious preference, a larger percentage were Jewish, and a smaller percentage Protestants.

Not only is there evidence that the two student bodies differed, but, as we have shown, there were also differences in community norms. At the earlier time these had emphasized the rejection of political conservatism, and a concern with public affairs. More recently they came to embody the qualities of intellectuality, individualism, and unconventionality.

Earlier, there was also more agreement among the students regarding the "prestigeful" members of the community. In the 1930's and again in 1960 the students were asked to list those members of the community whom they would wish to represent Bennington College at a national conference. In 1938 and 1939, the person who received the most nominations was mentioned by 89 and 90 students, respectively, nearly 40% of all respondents. In 1959 and again in 1962, the most popular individual received 37 "votes," just slightly more than 10%. In 1939, 15 students (6%) received more than 20 "votes," whereas in 1962 only 7 students (2%) received as many as 20, and in

1959 only 2 students received that many nominations. In the 1960's, no one student, or group of students, stood out as the obvious leaders of the community, nominations being spread among many different people.

Judging either from reports appearing in *Personality and Social Change* or from the recollections of the respondents, the college community was more homogeneous and "monolithic" in the 1930's than in 1960.

A Comparison of Bennington College Alumnae and Students in 1960

A number of the questions which were asked of the students at Bennington College between 1959 and 1962 were also included in the interview of the alumnae in 1960–1961, so that the two generations could be compared on a number of issues. Information about voting preferences in 1960 was collected from the students in late October, 1960, and from the alumnae in the months between October, 1960, and October, 1961. Table 13.3 shows the proportions of students and of alumnae who preferred each of the two major candidates.

There is a greater proportion, barely significant ($p < .05$), of alumnae than students who preferred Nixon in 1960. When the student

Table 13.3   A Comparison of Student and Alumnae Preferences in the Election of 1960

	Nixon	Kennedy	Other	Not Ascertained	Total	N
Freshmen (before coming to college, 1960)	34%	58%	8%	—	100%	110
Freshmen (Oct. '60)	25	65	8	2%	100	102
Sophomores (Oct. '60)	26	65	9	—	100	102
Juniors (Oct. '60)	21	65	10	4	100	48
Seniors (Oct. '60)	27	67	6	—	100	55
Total students (Oct. '60)	26	65	8	1	100	307
Alumnae (classes of '38, '39, '40)	38	60	2	—	100	138

population is divided into each of the four classes, the alumnae have a significantly greater proportion of people preferring Nixon than have the freshman, sophomore, or junior classes, singly.

On most of the specific items related to liberalism or to political issues there is no significant difference between the responses of the alumnae and students. Comparing the responses of the alumnae and seniors at Bennington in 1960 to the 20-item Liberalism scale, we find no over-all difference, but on an item-by-item analysis, seven statements are answered quite differently by the two groups. These seven items are listed in Table 13.4.

The differences which do exist between the responses of the seniors and the alumnae group are not consistent indicators of the relative liberalism of the two groups. There is some evidence in the foregoing responses that the alumnae group may be more active and interested in politics and public affairs than the seniors. Some of the differences, moreover, may be typical of their respective age groups. However, the differences between the alumnae and students on issues and political attitudes are small, judging from the data we have available. The majority of both groups appear to be moderately left of center.

The 20-item Nonauthoritarianism Scale was given to both the students and the alumnae group; somewhat unexpectedly, the average

Table 13.4   Percentages of Alumnae and Seniors Agreeing to Statements from the Liberalism Scale of the OPI

Statements	Alumnae ($N = 106$)	Seniors ($N = 43$)
I discuss the causes and possible solutions of social, political, economic, or international problems.	93%	76%
I believe I can influence my congressman if I want to.	77	40
I will probably belong to more than one political party in my lifetime.	61	76
I would enjoy showing foreigners around my town or state.	92	76
You can change human nature.	72	42
Communism is the most hateful thing in the world today.	27	13
I would be ashamed not to use my privilege of voting.	91	67

Table 13.5   Mean Nonauthoritarianism Scores for
Students and Alumnae *

	N	Mean NA	Standard Deviation
Freshmen	110	13.4	2.6
Sophomores	69	13.8	2.4
Juniors	47	13.8	2.3
Seniors	43	13.9	2.9
Alumnae	106	14.9	2.8

* The differences in mean score between the alumnae and freshmen and between alumnae and sophomores are significant; $p < .01$. The differences between the alumnae and juniors, and the alumnae and seniors are also signifiant; $p < .05$.

scores of the two groups are significantly different. Although the differences are not very large, the probability is small that they could have occurred by chance. Table 13.5 shows the mean scores on the NA scale for the alumnae and students. The lesser authoritarianism of the alumnae may, again, be partly attributable to sheer differences in age.

Although the alumnae as a group are somewhat less authoritarian than the students in terms of their responses to the NA scale, both the students and the alumnae tend to reject the authoritarian responses to the items. Ninety percent of 2,390 American college freshmen, according to the Center for the Study of Higher Education (1962), score below the mean of the alumnae; 84% score below the means of the Bennington sophomores, juniors, and seniors; and 72% score below the mean of the Bennington College freshmen. Relative to many other college freshmen, Bennington students are very low on authoritarianism.

The impression gained from interviewing students and alumnae is that the two groups are similar in political attitudes and liberalism, the alumnae being more concerned about and interested in political matters. The students seemed to be characterized more by their interest in esthetic and individualistic intellectual values. Although the alumnae also expressed much interest in esthetic values, estheticism did not appear to play as prominent a role in their lives as in the lives of the students. Some support for these impressions is found in the questionnaire responses.

Both the students and the alumnae were asked to rank-order the six Spranger values (theoretical, economic, esthetic, social, political, and religious) in terms of their importance to themselves. A total of 320 students and 121 alumnae performed this task; 28% of the students as compared with 8% of the alumnae ranked the esthetic value first. This difference in proportions is statistically significant. None of the other five values showed significant differences.

The full Estheticism Scale from the OPI was not given to the alumnae group, but five items from this scale were included in the questionnaire they completed. The percentages of alumnae and seniors agreeing with each of these statements are given in Table 13.6.

One final comparison can be made of the students and alumnae. Each group was asked to list the magazines that they read regularly. The magazines were classified by the investigators as either serious or nonserious (cf. pp. 71–72). When one compares the reading preferences of the student group and the alumnae group, the most striking finding is the comparatively large amount of reading reported by the alumnae. Every alumna reported reading some magazine regularly, whereas 36% of the students said that they read none. More than 50%

Table 13.6   Percentages of Alumnae and Seniors Agreeing with Estheticism Statements

Estheticism Statements	Alumnae (N = 106)	Seniors (N = 43)
I analyze what I like or dislike about a movie or play which I have seen.	84%	92%
I enjoy reading essays on serious or philosophical subjects.	77	83
* Trends toward abstractionism and the distortion of reality have corrupted much art of recent years.	23	4
* If I were a university professor and had the necessary ability, I would prefer to teach chemistry and physics rather than poetry.	21	8
* I think I take primarily an esthetic view of experience.	29	60

* These differences are significant.

Table 13.7   A Comparison of the Types of Magazines Read
by Alumnae and Students

| Type of Magazine | Number of Magazines | | | |
	0	1–2	3 or more	N
Serious				
Students	48%	39%	13%	307
Alumnae	11	39	50	128

$X^2 = 85.0; \; p < .001$

Nonserious				
Students	57	32	11	307
Alumnae	11	47	42	128

$X^2 = 81.2; \; p < .001$

of the alumnae reported reading five or more magazines regularly.

Tables 13.7 and 13.8 compare the alumnae and students in terms of the types of magazines read. The alumnae listed a significantly greater number of serious magazines, and a significantly greater number of nonserious magazines than the students. However, when only those students who read magazines are considered, approximately the same proportion of students (45%) and alumnae (49%) read more serious than nonserious magazines; the types of magazines read by the two groups do not differentiate them; only the number of magazines read by the two groups is a discriminating variable.

Table 13.8   Ratio of Serious to Nonserious Magazines

	None	More Serious than Nonserious	Equal	Fewer Serious than Nonserious	N
Students	36%	29%	10%	25%	307
Alumnae	0	49	13	38	128

Summary

The Bennington College alumnae, classes of 1938–1940, and the students, classes of 1960–1963, have very similar political points of view.

A slightly greater proportion of alumnae than of students preferred Nixon to Kennedy in 1960. There was no difference in the proportions of the two groups approving of the Negro student sit-ins. Other statements which discriminated the two groups rather typically dealt with the political process. Thus a greater proportion of alumnae than of students indicated that they felt that voting was important, that they could influence their congressmen, and that they were committed to a political party.

In a related area, the average score on the Nonauthoritarianism Scale for the alumnae was higher than the average score for the students, indicating that the alumnae were less authoritarian, as measured by this scale.

In the areas of estheticism, the students reported greater interest in esthetic pursuits than the alumnae. Again, although the students expressed the greater interest in the area, a large number of alumnae were primarily interested in esthetic matters. (A comparison of the rank ordering of the six Spranger values shows that 44% of the alumnae and 59% of the students ranked Estheticism either first or second.)

Finally, both groups read serious magazines in preference to nonserious magazines, but the alumnae reported doing more reading than the students.

Thus more of the alumnae are involved in the political sphere, whereas more of the students are involved in esthetic pursuits. Both groups value intellectualism, estheticism, and liberalism, and express similar points of view. The two generations are more similar than either of them believe. They have stereotyped impressions of each other which exaggerate their differences, but, at least in terms of the questions put to them in this study, they express similar attitudes.

14. Images, Environments, and the Persistence of College-Influenced Attitudes

During the 1930's some hundreds of students sought admission to Bennington College, were accepted, and chose to go there. Its public image was faint, but to those who had heard about the new institution it undoubtedly stood not only for educational novelty, but also for respectability. After all, its founders and most of its early students came from "good families," and it seemed to be in the New England tradition of "good colleges for women." Few if any of the prospective students could have had very accurate premonitions of the kind of college in which they were about to be caught up. It turned out to be a community most of whose members, both faculty and students, defined an adequate liberal education in terms that included attention to depression at home and war clouds abroad. Awareness, even to the point of concern, of social and international conditions responsible for the awesome state of affairs—with which most of the incoming students had relatively little familiarity—came to be one of the college's educational objectives.

Many of those who stayed to graduate from the college had, during the interim, developed a self-image that incorporated such a criterion of a good liberal education. The information that we were able to gather about them, nearly a quarter-century later, has led us to conclude that, for most of this majority of the early graduates, this component of the self-image was important enough to have influenced certain aspects of the environments that they later created for themselves, including husbands, friends, and coworkers in public or community activities. If so, the attitudes that they developed in the college environment were maintained, not *in vacuo*, but by way of supporting environments that were initially congenial to those attitudes and later supportive of them.

Such a sequence of events—initial image unrelated to what they were about to find; community involvement intense enough to change both views of the college norms and related aspects of self-images; subsequent selection of environments congenial to changed conceptions of self—such a chain of psychological events could account for the general nature of the persistence of attitudes acquired or strengthened during college years.

❊   ❊   ❊   ❊

Freshmen entering the college around 1960 were pretty well aware of existing student norms, as described in Chapter 9. About two months after their arrival in the fall of 1959, nearly all freshmen, together with most of the other students, responded to a list of 106 adjectives by checking those that they regarded as distinctive of

Bennington students, as compared with those from other colleges.
Bennington seniors, as compared with other Bennington students.
Bennington freshmen, as compared with other Bennington students.

Let us assume that seniors, in checking these adjectives for the college as a whole, reflected its norms more or less faithfully. If so, the general "correctness" of freshman judgments is shown by the fact that, of 18 adjectives checked by more than 60% of 45 seniors, all but two were also checked by a majority of freshmen. Conversely, of 20 checked by more than 60% of 120 freshmen, all but one were checked by a majority of seniors.

Of the 106 adjectives on the list, 39 were more or less directly related to the dominant college norms of individualism, intellectuality, and unconventionality. Among these, the 16 adjectives listed in Table 14.1 were checked by more than 60% of the seniors as distinctive of the college; their percentages, together with those of freshmen, are also noted.

Freshmen of two months thus agreed very closely with seniors about the distinctiveness of these "normative" characteristics at Bennington. They were less nearly unanimous, however, than were seniors; counting the numbers of items checked by all freshmen and all seniors, these differences are highly significant ($p < .001$).

The same conclusions are supported by a comparison of freshmen and senior selections of adjectives as distinguishing freshmen, and distinguishing seniors, from other Bennington students. Seniors checked every one of these 16 adjectives more frequently as distinctive of seniors than of freshmen, by differences ranging from 2% ("sensitive") to 60% ("independent"), and so did freshmen, with the single exception

Table 14.1   Percentages of Freshmen and Seniors Who Check "Normative" Adjectives as Distinctive of Bennington Students

	Freshmen	Seniors
Esthetic	68%	78%
Clever	57	69
Creative	96	100
Critical	68	87
Independent	94	91
Individualistic	91	96
Introspective	62	89
Liberal	73	89
Original	83	83
Outspoken	76	73
Progressive	83	78
Reflective	48	64
Resourceful	78	80
Self-centered	31	69
Sensitive	76	85
Unconventional	75	69
Mean	72.4%	81.2%

of "sensitive," which 37% of freshmen considered distinctive of themselves, whereas only 32% checked it for seniors. Also, larger proportions of seniors than of freshmen considered the "normative" adjectives more applicable to seniors than to freshmen. This difference, which applies to 15 of the 16 adjectives (the exception is "self-centered"), is highly significant: $p < .001$.

We have provided this detailed evidence in order to document two points: (1) The characteristics listed in Table 14.1 are indeed considered normative; not only are they considered distinctive of this particular college by large majorities, but this is particularly true of seniors, who have been there longest and who have most prestige. Furthermore, seniors regard these same characteristics as more distinctive of themselves than of freshmen. And (2) although freshmen are less "normative" than seniors, the difference is a matter of relatively small (though significant) degree.

Since, as shown in Chapter 9, there is little or no change in freshmen's images of the college during their first two months, we must therefore conclude that most Bennington students now arrive at the college with fairly accurate notions of what is expected of them there. This was not true in the mid-thirties, when the quite different features of distinctiveness at Bennington were not well recognized by most incoming freshmen.

✿   ✿   ✿   ✿

As of the 1930's, we conclude that the processes of initial self-selection and subsequent influence by college norms were somewhat as follows. At that time, the public image of the college—and hence, presumably, the processes of student self-selection—were for the most part unrelated to the influences toward nonconservatism that awaited them there. It might therefore be said that attitude change then represented, for a large number of students, processes of "conversion," that is, of shifting from a generally conservative point of view in terms of then-relevant public issues, to a nonconservative position. Perhaps this rather considerable impact was made possible by the very fact that the environment with which they were confronted was irrelevant to the considerations by which they selected themselves to go to Bennington. If so, a strong identification with a community whose norms were unexpected facilitated "conversion."

A quarter-century later, the college had achieved a public image such that the self-selection of students was made on more realistic grounds. Entering freshmen were now, in the main, as politically "liberal" as the older students whom they were to meet, and by whom they were likely to be influenced. The college appears to have earned a reputation for welcoming individual differences and encouraging creativity and intellectual independence. This was probably not the whole of its reputation; it did attract a sizable minority of freshmen who were rather rapidly absorbed into "deviant" subcultures. But the great majority of the new students pretty well understood the dominant norms of the community into which they were moving. (More than 90% of them, within two months, checked, as distinctive of Bennington students as compared with others, "creative," "independent," and "individualistic"; and 75% of them checked "unconventional.")

Thus the 1959 freshmen did not, like those of their mothers' generation, differ from the "normative" seniors in direction, but only in degree. They were already distinguished from freshman women in most other colleges in ways approaching such norms as independence and unconventionality. There was no possibility of conversion-like changes toward those norms; their changes, rather, accentuated already existing tendencies.*

        ✻   ✻   ✻   ✻

It is tempting, finally, to speculate about the probable persistence of the effects of their Bennington years upon these students of the early 1960's. Certain features of their college experience are so different from that of Bennington students in the 1930's that a prediction of comparable persistence of changed attitudes on the part of the later population hardly seems justified.

As we have noted, the later students changed *less* than the earlier ones during their college years. Whatever the degree of persistence in their college-influenced attitudes, it could still be argued that most of them were predisposed, before coming to Bennington, in intellectual, independent, and unconventional directions. Moreover, even a slight "regression" from their attitudes, on graduation, during the following quarter-century would lead to a verdict of "no persistence of changes effected by college experience."

It may be important, also, that the *content* of typical attitude changes was quite different during the two periods. Oversimplifying somewhat, the earlier students' changes were in attitudes toward public concerns, and those of the later students toward personal ones. With respect to the former, we have reasoned that the persistence of graduates' changed attitudes over the years was in part attributable to the effects of their attitudes on their subsequent selection and creation of supportive environments. We are simply not sure whether the same reasoning applies equally well to the domain of more personal attitudes. We have few doubts that most of the graduates of the early 1960's will find or create supportive environments for their preferred ways of life. But this may be no more than a truism that applies to everyone, and so we cannot be sure that such adaptations are in any important way an outcome of college experience.

It may be true, furthermore, that some of the relatively pronounced characteristics of Bennington graduates of the early 1960's are peculiar to youth—unconventionality, in particular. Insofar as this is true, and insofar as the other normative characteristics of the recent Bennington community are psychologically bound up with unconvention-

---

* We are indebted to Professor Kenneth Feldman and to Stanley Morse, of The University of Michigan, for stimulating discussions of "conversion," "accentuation," and other modes of change that are related to students' initial status.

ality, we would not necessarily expect that changes attributable to the years there would persist.

There is another sense, however, in which the Bennington experience may prove to have had lasting effects. It could well be that the precollege characteristics of the Bennington students, if they had not gone to college or had gone to different kinds of colleges, might have languished in those other environments. It is at least possible that those characteristics, if they were to persist, needed the nurturing soil of a community like Bennington. It is, in fact, altogether likely that at least some of the students—even including those whose attitudes on entrance rather closely resembled the college norms—would have succumbed to other norms in other climes. Some of them, we know, suffered conversion-like experiences; others, we suspect, experienced reinforcement of initial attitudes congruent with the college norms. These two kinds of students, we venture to predict, if no others, are likely to find for themselves environments (including supportive husbands) that in years to come will continue to support Bennington-induced or Bennington-reinforced attitudes.

With an eye both on our alumnae in their mid-forties and on our two sets of graduating students more than two decades separated in time, we bring this study to a close. We conclude that dominant community norms at Bennington were and are potent. Depending on the correctness of prevailing precollege images, the effects of that potency are conversion-like (as typically in the 1930's) or reinforcing (as often in the early 1960's) in nature. In either case, we have observed (in the earlier instance) or we predict (for the later period) that when the effects of the college environment have been powerful enough to influence individuals' self-images, and thereby to affect their subsequent environments, the college influences are likely to persist.

Appendix A

Alumnae Interview Schedule

As you may remember, the study in which you participated while you were at Bennington was pretty much centered on public affairs, especially on the national scene. A large part of today's interview will center on public affairs, but I am also interested in a little history of yourself—the type of interests and activities you have participated in since leaving Bennington College.

1. First of all, after you graduated from Bennington did you continue with graduate work or professional training elsewhere?
   IF YES:
   1a. Where did you enroll?
   1b. How long did you continue your training (studies)?
   1c. Did you earn an advanced degree? Specialization?
2. Since you have graduated, have you ever followed a career, or profession, or were you ever employed either part-time or full-time?
   IF NO: Skip to Q. 4
   IF YES:
3. What was the nature of your first employment or position after leaving Bennington?
   3a. Where were you employed?
   3b. When was this? (Continue asking for every job R has held.)
   3c. What type of work?
   3d. Where were you employed?
   3e. When was this?
4. TO ALL THOSE NOT PRESENTLY EMPLOYED:
   If you had to become employed at the present time, what type of work do you think you would do?
5. Women have various reasons for working—what are (would be) your main reasons for working?
6. Now, how about your leisure-time interests—what do you like to do when your regular responsibilities are done? (Probe for crafts, hobbies, etc.)

Card 1

R active	Impor-tant	No. of years a member	Inter-ested in college	Be-longed first 5 yr	Organizations
——	——	——	——	——	Labor unions
——	——	——	——	——	Church-connect-ed groups
——	——	——	——	——	Fraternal organi-zations or lodges
——	——	——	——	——	Business or civic groups
——	——	——	——	——	Parent-teachers; educational
——	——	——	——	——	Cultural groups (art, music)
——	——	——	——	——	Youth-serving groups (Scouts)
——	——	——	——	——	Sports groups
——	——	——	——	——	Professional groups
——	——	——	——	——	Political clubs or organizations (specify the type)
——	——	——	——	——	Neighborhood improvement
——	——	——	——	——	Social clubs, card clubs
——	——	——	——	——	Charitable and welfare organiza-tions
——	——	——	——	——	Other (please specify)

7. In general, would you say you have become more active and interested in organizations, activities, and causes since you left Bennington, less active, or what?

8. Here is a list of clubs and organizations that many people are active in. Please look at this list (show Card 1) and tell me which of these kinds of organizations you are active in, if any.

IF ANY, ASK FOR EACH GROUP R IS IN:

8a. Which of these are really important to you? (Check in Col. 2)

8b. How long have you been a member of this group? (Write in Col. 3)

9. Which of these types of organizations were you interested in while you were in college? (Check in Col. 4)

10. Which of these kinds of groups were you especially active in the first few years after you graduated from Bennington? (Check in Col. 5)

IF SEVERAL MENTIONED:

10a. Which of them was the most important to you at the time?

11. Are there any other types of clubs or organizations which you have been active in since leaving Bennington College?

12. Whether they belong to organizations or not, many people at some time in their lives work for various committees or causes or fund-raising groups. Here is a list of some of the types of activities and causes that many people become involved in. (Show Card 2.) Please tell me the type of committees and causes you have participated in since leaving Bennington College.

13. IF MENTION ANY, ASK FOR EACH ACTIVITY:

When did you work on that committee (for that cause)? Before 1945; 1945–1950; 1951–1955; 1956–to present. Record in Col. 2.

14. Which of these activities is most important to you? (Try to get a first choice.)

15. Which, if any, were you active in while you were at Bennington? Record on chart.

16. During your life you have probably contributed financial support to several organizations, fund-raising drives, institutions, or causes. At the present time, what type of activity or cause are you most interested in giving money to?

16a. How about the first few years after graduating from college —at that time what activities were you most interested in supporting?

IF BENNINGTON COLLEGE HAS NOT BEEN MENTIONED IN Q. 8–16a:

Card 2

R active	When?	Impor-tant	Active while at Benning-ton	Type of activity
——	——	——	——	Work for a political party or candidate (specify party)
——	——	——	——	Other political activity
——	——	——	——	Work for educational groups
——	——	——	——	Charity drives (Community Fund, Red Cross)
——	——	——	——	Medical drives
——	——	——	——	Civic improvement
——	——	——	——	Work for racial integration
——	——	——	——	Civil defense, war-bond drives, other government sponsored activities
——	——	——	——	Civil-liberties committees
——	——	——	——	Work for disarmament and pacifist groups
——	——	——	——	Church committees
——	——	——	——	Cultural committees (art, theater, music)
——	——	——	——	Other type of committees (please specify)

17. Have you ever participated in Bennington College activities, committees, fund-raising drives, or meetings since graduation?

IF BENNINGTON COLLEGE WAS MENTIONED IN Q. 8–16a:

17. You mentioned . . . ; have you ever participated in other Bennington College activities?

18. I have asked you about your present and past interests and activities. Have you thought about what you would like to do in the next ten years or so? What are your plans?

One of the major concerns of the study is to get a brief history of your interest and activity and attitudes in the area of public affairs and political events, both at the present time and when you were in college.

19. First of all, let's go back to the period when you were at Bennington—did you change your political opinions and attitudes while you were at college? How?

19a.   What do you suppose were the reasons why you changed? (Why you did not change?)

20. While you were in college did you become more interested, remain the same, or become less interested in public affairs than you were before?

21. You mentioned that your political opinions changed (did not change) at Bennington. As far as their political opinions were concerned, did most students at Bennington change more than you did, about the same as you, or less than you did?

22. As far as your present political opinions and attitudes are concerned, have you changed them since you left Bennington?

22a. How would you account for these changes (or lack of change)? What do you suppose are the principal reasons?

Probe: I mean, have there been any special persons, or special experiences that you have had, or special events that have had a good deal to do with these changes?

23. Could you give a brief description of your present political opinions?

24. Have you become more interested, remained the same, or become less interested in public affairs since you were in college?

25. How do you think you compare with your contemporaries from Bennington College—do you think that most of them share your political opinions or do you think that most of them have different political opinions from you? (If different, in what way are they different?)

26. Do you think that the majority of your Bennington contemporaries are more interested in public affairs, the same as you, or less interested in public affairs than you are?

27. How informed do you think most of the Bennington students of your day are—more informed than you, the same as you, or less informed than you?

28. When you get together with your friends, how frequently do you dicuss politics or current events on the national and international scene? Frequently, occasionally, seldom, never?

29. Are most of your friends more interested in public affairs, the same, or less interested in public affairs than you are?

30. Do you think that most of your friends are more informed, the same as you, or less informed than you are about public affairs?

31. Do most of your friends have political opinions which are similar to yours, or are they different? (If different, in what way?)

Now I have a few questions that are more specific, about persons and issues that have been prominent during the past 20 years or so.

32. First, would you tell me how you felt about each of the presidential campaigns since you were at Bennington. Let's begin with 1940.

Which candidate did you prefer?
Would you say you preferred him rather strongly, or just slightly?
Did you actually cast a vote for him?
How did you feel about the other candidate?
1940 preference:
_____strong
_____slight
_____voted
_____did not
Do you remember who the other candidate was?
[Identical questions for elections of 1944, 1948, 1952, 1956, 1960.]

33. If married: How did your husband feel about each of the candidates? (Strong or slight, voted or did not vote, for same six elections.)

34. I have a list of persons who have been prominent during these years. A few of the presidential candidates that you have just mentioned are on this list, but now I'm interested in your present opinions about them. Would you make a brief comment about each one of them? [As listed in Q. 35.]

35. Now just to be sure that I interpret your comments correctly, would you take this card and tell me whether you are very favorable,

slightly favorable, slightly unfavorable, or very unfavorable about each of these persons (Card 3).

Card 3

	Very favor- able	Slightly favor- able	Slightly unfavor- able	Very unfavor- able
a. President Roosevelt	____	____	____	____
b. Senator Taft	____	____	____	____
c. President Truman	____	____	____	____
d. Senator McCarthy	____	____	____	____
e. Walter Reuther	____	____	____	____
f. President Eisenhower	____	____	____	____
g. Senator Kennedy	____	____	____	____
h. Vice-President Nixon	____	____	____	____
i. Gen. Douglas MacArthur	____	____	____	____
j. Adlai Stevenson	____	____	____	____

36. How does your husband feel about each of these persons? [Format as in Q. 35.]

37. Now I am going to ask you to play a guessing game of sorts. I want you to guess or make an estimate of how your close friends feel about some of these people. I just want you to tell me whether you feel most of your friends are favorable or unfavorable about:

	Favorable	Unfavorable
a. President Roosevelt	____	____
b. Senator McCarthy	____	____
c. President Eisenhower	____	____
d. Senator Kennedy	____	____
e. Vice-President Nixon	____	____
f. Adlai Stevenson	____	____
g. Democrats	____	____
h. Conservatives	____	____

38. People who graduated from Bennington about the same time you did. [Format as in Q. 37.]

39. Now some similar questions about recent *issues*. Each "issue" refers to some event that has occurred, or some policy that has been proposed. Tell me how you feel about each.

Issues	Very favor-able	Slightly unfavor-able	Slightly unfavor-able	Very unfavor-able
a. The Supreme Court's decision about de-segregation in schools	___	___	___	___
b. The administration's handling of the U-2 incident	___	___	___	___
c. Increasing social se-curity taxes for med-ical needs of the aged	___	___	___	___
d. Admitting Red China to the U.N.	___	___	___	___
e. Use of the 5th Amendment in re-fusing to answer a Congressional Com-mittee's question about other people's allegedly subversive activities	___	___	___	___
f. Making greater con-cessions than the U. S. has offered toward the objective of nuclear disarma-ment	___	___	___	___

40. How does your husband feel about each of these issues? [As in Q. 39.]

41. How do you guess most of your closest friends feel about each of these issues? [As in Q. 39.]

42. How do you guess most of the people who graduated from Ben-nington the same time you did feel about each of these issues? [As in Q. 39.]

43. Now back to you—how would you describe yourself and where you stand on public affairs, briefly? (*Probe:* Ask about conservative and liberal dimension, if it isn't mentioned.)

44. Now I have a few statements that may amuse you. They are the ones that you replied to, perhaps several times, when Mr. Newcomb was carrying on the original study in the 1930's. Many of them seem terribly dated, even quaint; they may seem like the relics of a bygone age. Because these statements just aren't relevant for the present day, we are not asking you to indicate how you feel about them *now*, but we would like to have you indicate how you *think* you probably answered them at the time you were in Bennington. We don't expect you really to remember after all these years, of course; just make the best guesses you can. (Give PEP scale to R.) [See Appendix B, Q. 22.]

      ❋   ❋   ❋   ❋

Up until now we haven't talked much about Bennington College. I have a few questions about the college and about the students. Let me remind you again that your comments will be kept confidential.

45. Most people had a few very close friends when they were in college. Who were your closest friends then?

46. The first few years after you graduated, did you keep in close touch with any Bennington graduates, either by correspondence or by visiting?

IF YES:

    46a. Who were they?

47. At the present time, are there any Bennington people whom you write to or keep in touch with? (Yes, No)

IF YES:

    47a. Who are they?

48. Are there any members of the faculty whom you keep in touch with?

49. When was the last time you heard from . . . ? (Ask for each person mentioned in Q. 45.)

50. About how many Bennington students of your own day could you get in touch with now without looking them up in the directory?

51. About how many students do you know by their married names?

52. I want you to comment briefly on your Bennington College education. Do you suppose your years there have made any difference in your later life? (In what way?)

53. How well satisfied are you with the education you obtained at Bennington College? (Very satisfied, satisfied, unsatisfied)

54. Are there or were there any special sources of dissatisfaction with Bennington College?

55. Would you recommend Bennington College to a friend's daughter or to your own daughter? Why or why not?

56. Do you think there is anything special or distinctive about Bennington College or its students? Explain.

57. Do you think Bennington students today are different from the students of your day?

58. Some people think of Bennington College as a "liberal" college whose students are unconventional, or maybe even bohemian or beatniks. Do you think the college should do something to change this image?

59. (Ask only of those whose marital status is unknown) What is your marital status? (Single, married, widowed, divorced, separated)

IF SINGLE: Skip to Q. 68.

IF PRESENTLY MARRIED:

60. When did you get married?

61. Is this your first marriage?

IF NO:

   61a. When were you married before?

IF WIDOWED, DIVORCED, OR SEPARATED, PRESENTLY:

60. When were you married?

   60a. How long were you married?

61. Had you ever been married before?

   61a. When?

62. Do you have any children? List them by age and sex.

63. Where are they going to school?

64. What colleges or universities have you considered for your children? (If they are of appropriate age.)

65. How is (was) your husband employed?

66. Has he held any other positions since you have been married? (List in sequence from most recent to earliest.)

67. Does (did) he have any degrees? What degrees and where did he earn them?

68. Have you spent most of the time since college in one place, or have you moved around a good deal? (If mobile, about how many places? Far apart?)

We would like to make some comparisons between the present student body of Bennington and the alumnae. Therefore we are asking some of the questions which we gave the students.

69. What magazines, if any, do you read regularly?

70. Listed here are six important areas, or interests in life. People differ in the emphasis or degree of importance that they attribute to each of these interests.

Please rank the six interests in terms of their *importance to you.* Insert "1" before the area of greatest importance, "2" before the next most important one, and so on down to "6," representing the least important of all to you.

Please note: Your response should be made to the *complete* statement about each of the interests, and not just to the first word, which is only a convenient label; what that word means to you may not correspond at all to the statement following.

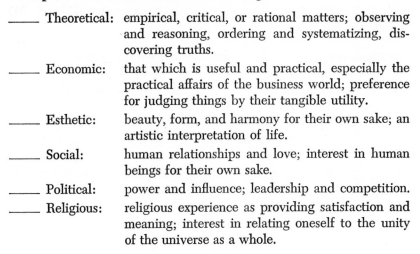

_____ Theoretical: empirical, critical, or rational matters; observing and reasoning, ordering and systematizing, discovering truths.

_____ Economic: that which is useful and practical, especially the practical affairs of the business world; preference for judging things by their tangible utility.

_____ Esthetic: beauty, form, and harmony for their own sake; an artistic interpretation of life.

_____ Social: human relationships and love; interest in human beings for their own sake.

_____ Political: power and influence; leadership and competition.

_____ Religious: religious experience as providing satisfaction and meaning; interest in relating oneself to the unity of the universe as a whole.

71. One essential part of this research is to make some comparisons between Bennington alumnae and two other kinds of groups: present-day students at Bennington and elsewhere; and alumnae from other colleges. In order to do this, it is necessary to include some "standard" questions that are being widely used, following a process of selecting a few items from a very long list of them by research procedures. We have looked long and hard to find a set of questions that will both be *brief* and will enable us to make some direct comparisons with other groups of students and alumnae. The ones that we finally selected have been developed over several years by the Center for the Study of Higher Education at the University of California, in Berkeley.

These questions are quite different from all of the preceding ones. You may feel that you could answer some of these questions in different ways because they have more than one possible meaning. If you do feel that way about some of them, I hope you'll tell me so *after* you have finished, but not while you are answering them. The best way to answer them is to give your first, impulsive response, rather than to stop and ponder about them. If you are willing to do it that way—in spite of any misgivings you may have—then we'll be able to make the comparisons that are so important to this study. There are, of course, no "right" or "wrong" answers; what we are interested in is a frank expression of your feelings.

Next to each statement appear the letters SA, A, D, SD. Encircle A if you *agree* with the statement. Encircle SA if you *strongly agree* with it. Encircle D if you *disagree* with the statement. Encircle SD if you *strongly disagree* with it.

Circle one   Please answer every question

SA A D SD   1. I analyze what I like or dislike about a movie or play which I have seen.

SA A D SD   2. When someone talks against certain groups or nationalities, I always speak up against such talk even though it makes me unpopular.

SA A D SD   3. An urge to jump from high places is probably the result of unhappy personal experiences rather than anything inborn.

SA A D SD   4. I enjoy reading essays on serious or philosophical subjects.

SA A D SD   5. Only a fool would try to change our American way of life.

SA A D SD   6. Books and movies ought to give a more realistic picture of life even if they show that evil sometimes triumphs over good.

SA A D SD   7. Disobedience to the government is sometimes justified.

SA A D SD   8. Sex crimes, such as rape and attacks on children, deserve more than mere imprisonment; such criminals ought to be publicly whipped or worse.

SA A D SD   9. I discuss the causes and possible solutions of social, political, economic, or international problems.

SA A D SD   10. Human nature being what it is, there will always be war and conflict.

SA A D SD   11. Trends toward abstractionism and the distortion of reality have corrupted much art of recent years.

SA A D SD   12. Every person should have complete faith in a supernatural power whose decisions he obeys without question.

Circle one	Please answer every question

SA A D SD 13. All groups can live in harmony in this country without changing the system in any way.

SA A D SD 14. I believe I can influence my congressman if I want to.

SA A D SD 15. Nowadays more and more people are prying into matters that should remain personal and private.

SA A D SD 16. My conversations with friends usually deal with such subjects as mutual acquaintances and social activities.

SA A D SD 17. I would be willing to give money myself in order to right a wrong even though I was not mixed up in it in the first place.

SA A D SD 18. I will probably belong to more than one political party in my lifetime.

SA A D SD 19. Most of our social problems could be solved if we could somehow get rid of the immoral, crooked, and feeble-minded people.

SA A D SD 20. One of the most important things children should learn is when to disobey authorities.

SA A D SD 21. Political authority really comes not from us, but from some higher power.

SA A D SD 22. I would enjoy showing foreigners around my town or state.

SA A D SD 23. Most people don't realize how much our lives are controlled by plots hatched in secret places.

SA A D SD 24. The artist and professor are probably more important to society than the businessman and the manufacturer.

SA A D SD 25. Maybe some minority groups do get rough treatment, but it's no business of mine.

SA A D SD 26. Young people sometimes get rebellious ideas, but as they grow up they ought to get over them and settle down.

SA A D SD 27. If I were a university professor and had the necessary ability, I would prefer to teach chemistry and physics rather than poetry.

Circle one	Please answer every question
SA A D SD	28. It is essential for learning or effective work that our teachers and leaders outline in detail what is to be done and how to do it.
SA A D SD	29. The findings of science may some day show that many of our most cherished beliefs are wrong.
SA A D SD	30. I am *uninterested* in discussions of the ideal society or Utopia.
SA A D SD	31. I believe it is the responsibility of intelligent leadership to maintain the established order of things.
SA A D SD	32. Most honest people admit to themselves that they have sometimes hated their parents.
SA A D SD	33. In spite of what you read about the wild sex life of people in important places, the real story is about the same as for any group of people.
SA A D SD	34. What youth needs most is strict discipline, rugged determination, and the will to work and fight for family and country.
SA A D SD	35. No normal, decent person would ever think of hurting a close friend or relative.
SA A D SD	36. I enjoy listening to debates and discussions on social, economic, or political problems.
SA A D SD	37. You can change human nature.
SA A D SD	38. Communism is the most hateful thing in the world today.
SA A D SD	39. It is highly unlikely that astrology will ever be able to explain anything.
SA A D SD	40. No weakness or difficulty can hold us back if we have enough will power.
SA A D SD	41. People ought to pay more attention to new ideas, even if they seem to go against the American way of life.
SA A D SD	42. I think I take primarily an esthetic view of experience.
SA A D SD	43. I would be ashamed not to use my privilege of voting.

Circle one	Please answer every question

SA   A   D   SD   44. Our way of doing things in this nation would be best for the world.

SA   A   D   SD   45. If it weren't for the rebellious ideas of youth there would be less progress in the world.

❁   ❁   ❁   ❁

Interviewer's Rating of the Respondent

1. Level of information about political and public affairs
    1. very poorly informed
    2. uninformed in some aspects
    3. average
    4. better informed than most
    5. very well informed
2. Degree of conservatism
    1. less conservative than most
    2. about the same as most
    3. more conservative than most
3. Interest and involvement in the interview
    1. disinterested
    2. interest varies
    3. very interested
4. Attitude about Bennington
    1. very unfavorable
    2. unfavorable
    3. indifferent
    4. favorable
    5. very favorable
5. Length of interview

Appendix B

May, 1961

The accompanying letter explains the nature of the follow-up study of Bennington College alumnae. We have sent a questionnaire to everyone who had participated in the study in the 1930's. The whole value of the survey depends on the frankness and care with which you answer the questions. So please read each question carefully before you answer it.

Your replies will be confidential; all reports of the findings in the study will respect the anonymity of the respondents. We ask you to write your name at the bottom of this page only so that we may have a record of your participation and so that we may compare your present opinions and attitudes with your earlier responses. We will remove your name from the questionnaire and will replace it with a code number. Your questionnaire will be seen and processed only by the research people connected with this project.

Instructions:

1. In some questions we have left lines for written answers. If you need more space, please feel free to use the space at the bottom of the page.

2. In many cases, no writing is required. Just check the answer that fits your case best. Questions which require several checks include instructions to that effect.

3. Please feel free to write in any comments or explanations.

To return the questionnaire, please use the enclosed postage-paid envelope. Your cooperation in returning this as quickly as possible will be greatly appreciated.

Name   Date

    1. When did you attend Bennington College?

        From _____ to _____

2. Did you continue your formal education after you left Bennington College?

    ___ Yes   ___ No

    If Yes, Please list the colleges and universities you have attended and indicate the degrees you have obtained.

Name of institution	Dates attended	Degree (for example, A.B., B.S., etc.)
_____	_____	_____
_____	_____	_____
_____	_____	_____

3. Please list the types of employment you have held, either full-time or part-time, since leaving Bennington College.

Type of employment	Date of employment
_____	_____
_____	_____
_____	_____
_____	_____

4. What is your marital status?

    ___ single   (Skip to Q. 9)
    ___ married
    ___ widowed
    ___ separated

5. When did you get married? _____

6. Have you been married more than once? _____ (If yes, when?) _____

7. How is (was) your husband employed?

_____
_____

8. If your husband attended college, please list the colleges or universities your husband attended and the degrees he obtained.

_____
_____
_____

9. Please list the types of activities, committees, or organizations in which you have participated since leaving Bennington College which are particularly important to you.

_____
_____

_____

_____

_____

10. Check those Bennington College activities in which you have participated since leaving the college.

___ Member of Alumnae Board   ___ Arranged teas, meetings, etc.

___ Raised money, contacted alumnae   ___ Attended teas, meetings, re-unions

___ Interviewed prospective students   ___ Other (please specify)

___ Served as class secretary

11. What type of interests or activities would you most like to pursue in the next ten years or so?

12. What magazines do you most like to read?

13. Have you become more interested or less interested in the area of public affairs since you were at Bennington?

     ___ more interested now
     ___ remained the same
     ___ less interested now

14. When you get together with your close friends, how frequently do you discuss politics or current events on the national and international level?

     ___ frequently
     ___ occasionally
     ___ seldom
     ___ hardly ever

15. Are most of your close friends more interested or less interested in public affairs than you are?

     ___ more interested than I am
     ___ the same as I am
     ___ less interested than I am

16. Do most of your close friends have political opinions which are similar to yours, or are they different? (If different, in what way are they different?)

17. Please indicate the candidate whom you preferred in each of the six presidential campaigns going back to 1940. In the second column indicate whether you voted in the election or not.

Preferences		Vote	
1960	__ Kennedy	1960	__ Voted
	__ Nixon		__ Did not vote
1956	__ Stevenson	1956	__ Voted
	__ Eisenhower		__ Did not vote
1952	__ Stevenson	1952	__ Voted
	__ Eisenhower		__ Did not vote
1948	__ Truman	1948	__ Voted
	__ Dewey		__ Did not vote
1944	__ Roosevelt	1944	__ Voted
	__ Dewey		__ Did not vote
1940	__ Roosevelt	1940	__ Voted
	__ Willkie		__ Did not vote

IF MARRIED:

18. Please indicate you husband's preference in the past six elections.

1960	( ) Kennedy	or	( )	Nixon
1956	( ) Stevenson	or	( )	Eisenhower
1952	( ) Stevenson	or	( )	Eisenhower
1948	( ) Truman	or	( )	Dewey
1944	( ) Roosevelt	or	( )	Dewey
1940	( ) Roosevelt	or	( )	Willkie

19. Here is a list of persons who have been prominent during the past 20 years. Please indicate how you feel about their work in public affairs. Indicate whether you are very favorable, slightly favorable, slightly unfavorable, very unfavorable about these persons at the present time.

	Very favorable	Slightly favorable	Slightly unfavorable	Very unfavorable
a. Pres. Roosevelt	__	__	__	__
b. Pres. Truman	__	__	__	__
c. Sen. Joseph McCarthy	__	__	__	__
d. Pres. Eisenhower	__	__	__	__
e. Pres. Kennedy	__	__	__	__
f. Vice-Pres. Richard Nixon	__	__	__	__
g. Gen. Douglas MacArthur	__	__	__	__
h. Adlai Stevenson	__	__	__	__

20. Each of the following statements refers to some event or issue that has recently become prominent. Indicate whether you strongly approve, approve, disapprove, or strongly disapprove of the action taken or the policy proposed.

Issues	Strongly approve	Approve	Disapprove	Strongly disapprove
a. Negro student sit-ins and picketing	—	—	—	—
b. The Eisenhower administration's handling of the U-2 incident	—	—	—	—
c. Increasing social-security taxes for medical needs of the aged	—	—	—	—
d. Admitting Red China to the United Nations	—	—	—	—

21. With respect to which, if any, of the four issues listed in Q. 20, would most of your close friends disagree with you?

22. Below are 26 statements about public issues of the 1930's. [These items constitute the PEP scale, referred to in the text.] They are the same ones that you replied to, perhaps several times, when Mr. Newcomb was conducting the original study in the 1930's. Many of the statements seem terribly dated now—almost like the relics of a bygone age. You will probably agree with some of the statements, disagree with some, and be uncertain of others. There are no "right" or "wrong" answers. Whatever you happen to think about it is the right answer for you.

Please indicate your reply as follows:

Encircle A if you *agree* with the statement: SA Ⓐ ? D SD
Encircle SA if you *strongly agree* with the statement: (SA) A ? D SD
Encircle D if you *disagree* with the statement: SA A ? Ⓓ SD
Encircle SD if you *strongly disagree* with the statement: SA A ? D (SD)
Encircle ? if you are *uncertain* about the statement: SA A Ⓟ D SD

SA   A   ?   D   SD   1. The only true prosperity of the nation as a whole must be based upon the prosperity of the working class.

SA   A   ?   D   SD   2. Recovery has been delayed by the large number of strikes.

SA   A   ?   D   SD   3. Some form of collective society, in which profits are replaced by reimbursements for useful mental or manual work, is preferable to our present system.

SA   A   ?   D   SD   4. The depression occurred chiefly because the working classes did not receive enough in wages to purchase goods and services produced at a profit.

SA   A   ?   D   SD   5. A "planned economy" is not enough unless it is planned for the welfare of workers rather than of business men.

SA   A   ?   D   SD   6. Most labor trouble happens only because of radical agitators.

SA   A   ?   D   SD   7. The people who complain most about the depression wouldn't take a job if you gave it to them.

SA   A   ?   D   SD   8. The standard of living of the working class can be kept above the poverty line only as workers force it up by the use of strikes.

SA   A   ?   D   SD   9. Labor organizations have as much right to bring in outside agitators as do businessmen to import outside technical experts.

SA   A   ?   D   SD   10. Any able-bodied man could get a job right now if he tried hard enough.

SA   A   ?   D   SD   11. Most people on relief are living in reasonable comfort.

SA   A   ?   D   SD   12. The budget should be balanced before the government spends any money on "social security."

SA   A   ?   D   SD   13. Our government has always been run primarily in the interests of big business, and so it is those interests which were chiefly responsible for the depression.

SA   A   ?   D   SD   14. Labor unions are justifiable only if they refrain from the use of strikes.

SA A ? D SD   15. Since it is impossible for working people to have any substantial savings, they have fully earned their rights to old-age pensions.

SA A ? D SD   16. It is all right to try to raise the standard of living of the lower classes, provided that existing property rights are continually safeguarded.

SA A ? D SD   17. Most employers think only of profits and care little about their employees' welfare.

SA A ? D SD   18. Unemployment insurance would saddle us with a nation of idlers.

SA A ? D SD   19. Organizations of the unemployed are just a group of chronic complainers.

SA A ? D SD   20. We have no true democracy in this country because only business and industrial concerns have economic opportunity.

SA A ? D SD   21. If the government didn't meddle so much in business everything would be all right.

SA A ? D SD   22. You can't expect democracy to work very well as long as so many uneducated and unintelligent people have the vote.

SA A ? D SD   23. The vast majority of those in the lower economic classes are there because they are stupid or shiftless, or both.

SA A ? D SD   24. Those who have the ability and the foresight to accumulate wealth ought to be permitted to enjoy it themselves.

SA A ? D SD   25. The middle classes will never enjoy security or prosperity until they understand that their welfare is identified with that of the working class, and not with that of business and industrial groups.

SA A ? D SD   26. The real threat to prosperity in this country is the repressive activities of those who wish to keep wealth and economic power in the hands of those who now possess them.

FOR GRADUATES OF 1936, 1937: (All others skip to Q. 24.)

23. Now go back over each of the 26 statements in Q. 22 and try to answer them in terms of how you think you might have answered them when you were a senior at Bennington. We don't expect you *really* to remember after all these years, of course; just make the best guesses you can. *Place a check* (√) over the letter which corresponds to the way you think you answered the statement when you were a senior.

24. Many of the Bennington alumnae whom we have interviewed have spontaneously used such terms as conservative, moderate, liberal, in describing their general political points of view. With respect to each of the following five situations, *place an X on the line* which

a. Most closely represents your political point of view when you entered Bennington College.

| L_____ | _____ | _____ | _____ | _____ |

Liberal   Conservative

b. Most closely represents your political point of view when you left Bennington College.

| L_____ | _____ | _____ | _____ | _____ |

Liberal   Conservative

c. Most closely represents your *present* political point of view.

| L_____ | _____ | _____ | _____ | _____ |

Liberal   Conservative

d. Represents your best guess about the political point of view of the *majority* of your Bennington College contemporaries. (Please guess.)

| L_____ | _____ | _____ | _____ | _____ |

Liberal   Conservative

IF MARRIED:

e. Most closely represents your husband's political point of view.

| L_____ | _____ | _____ | _____ | _____ |

Liberal   Conservative

25. As you think about how your *present* opinions and attitudes about public affairs happened to become what they are, what seem to be the most important influences (events, experiences, persons) which have helped to shape your present point of view?

The fifteen items that follow are selected from a long list that has been used recently in many colleges and universities, including Bennington. Even though this list is short, your replies will provide a basis for comparing Bennington alumnae with alumnae from other colleges, and also with present-day Bennington students.

Standard instructions for these fifteen items (which we must follow in order to make comparisons) are to indicate either that you "tend to agree" or "tend not to agree" with each one.

Circle "Yes" or "No" before each item

Do you tend
  to agree?

Yes   No   26. Human nature being what it is, there will always be war and conflict.

Yes   No   27. When someone talks against certain groups or nationalities, I always speak up against such talk even though it makes me unpopular.

Yes   No   28. My conversations with friends usually deal with such subjects as mutual acquaintances and social activities.

Yes   No   29. Most people don't realize how much our lives are controlled by plots hatched in secret places.

Yes   No   30. I will probably belong to more than one political party in my lifetime.

Yes   No   31. One of the most important things children should learn is when to disobey authorities.

Yes   No   32. The artist and professor are probably more important to society than the businessman and the manufacturer.

Yes   No   33. The findings of science may some day show that many of our most cherished beliefs are wrong.

Yes   No   34. I believe it is the responsibility of intelligent leadership to maintain the established order of things.

Yes   No   35. What youth needs most is strict discipline, rugged determination, and the will to work and fight for family and country.

Yes   No   36. Communism is the most hateful thing in the world today.

Yes   No   37. If it weren't for the rebellious ideas of youth there would be less progress in the world.

Yes   No   38. No weakness or difficulty can hold us back if we have enough will power.

Yes   No   39. No normal, decent person would ever think of hurting a close friend or relative.

Yes   No   40. Trends toward abstractionism and the distortion of reality have corrupted much art in recent years.

41. Listed here are six important areas, or interests in life. People differ in the emphasis or degree of importance that they attribute to each of these interests.

Please rank the six interests in terms of their *importance to you.* Insert "1" before the one of greatest importance, "2" before the next most important one, and so on down to "6," representing the least important of all to you.

Please note: Your response should be made to the *complete* statement about each of the interests, and not just to the first word, which is only a convenient label; what the word means to you may not correspond at all to the statement following.

__ Theoretical: empirical, critical, or rational matters; observing and reasoning, ordering and systematizing, discovering truths.

__ Economic: that which is useful and practical, especially the practical affairs of the business world; preference for judging things by their tangible utility.

__ Esthetic: beauty, form, and harmony for their own sake; an artistic interpretation of life.

__ Social: human relationships and love; interest in human beings for their own sake.

__ Political: power and influence; leadership and competition.

__ Religious: religious experience as providing satisfaction and meaning; interest in relating oneself to the unity of the universe as a whole.

42. About how many Bennington College students of your own day do you know by their married name? Check one.

     __ none   __ 4–6   __ 11–15   __ 26 or more.
     __ 1–3   __ 7–10   __ 16–25

43. At the present time are there any Bennington alumnae whom you write to or keep in touch with?   __ Yes   __ No

If Yes: Please list them by name.

_____   _____

_____   _____

_____   _____

44. How well satisfied are you with the education you obtained at Bennington College?

     __ very satisfied   __ satisfied   __ unsatisfied

45. We would like you to comment on your Bennington College education. Do you suppose your years there have made any difference in your life? (In what way?)

Thank you very much. (Did you sign your name on the cover?)

Appendix C

The 1964 Presidential Campaign

(Questionnaire mailed to interview respondents)

Which of the two major candidates would you prefer as the next President? (Check one.)

Goldwater ___   Johnson ___   No preference ___

Now please answer the same question for the persons listed. If you do not feel at all sure, just insert a "?" instead of a check to indicate that your answer may not be much better than a guess. Please insert either a check or a "?" in every row of lines unless there is no such person. If no such person exists, please write "none." If there is more than one such person (two sisters, for example), enter more than one check or "?" on the same row of lines.

Your:	Prefers Goldwater	Prefers Johnson	No preference
Husband	—	—	—
* Sister	—	—	—
Brother	—	—	—
Sister's husband	—	—	—
* Brother's wife	—	—	—
* Husband's sister	—	—	—
Husband's brother	—	—	—

* In the case of sister, brother's wife, and husband's sister, would you indicate whether she was ever a Bennington student? If so, please circle the response that you have entered for her—one circle if she attended, but did not graduate, and two circles if she graduated. Like this:

Ⓠ or Ⓟ Bennington student, but not a graduate

Ⓠ or Ⓟ Bennington graduate

Appendix D

Guess Who Rating Scale

(Administered in 1939)

The conditions under which these ratings were made are described in Chapter 9, *Personality and Social Change* (Newcomb, 1943). Raters were first handed the following mimeographed sheet of directions.

❂   ❂   ❂   ❂

Do Not Sign Your Name to This Paper

The questions asked on the following pages have to do with some personality characteristics of Bennington College students. The form of the questions is that which has been found to be the most satisfactory of all "rating" techniques. It is commonly referred to as the "guess who" technique.

I am concerned with only three Bennington College classes, those graduating in 1938, 1939, and 1940, respectively. You will be given lists of the members of these three classes, as this will make it easier for you to answer the questions.

Each question begins with the word "most" or "least," followed by some adjective. Each question is followed by three blank spaces for each of the three classes. You are asked to write in the names of the three individuals in each class who seem to you best to illustrate the characteristic mentioned. It is not compulsory to include three names for each class in response to each question. Two names of which you feel fairly sure are better than three of which you do not feel sure.

No one actually *knows* the answers to these questions. There are no "true" answers. You are asked for your *opinions*. It is therefore hoped that you will fill in every blank. If you feel that to reply with a certain name would be sheer guesswork, leave it blank; but if that name represents something between guesswork and certainty, please include it.

Suggested procedure. Previous experience indicates that the following procedure works best, though you may find a better one. Start with the list of names in one class. Answer all the questions for this one class. During this procedure names from other classes will occasionally occur to you as particularly fitting; fill in those names as they occur to you. Then repeat the procedure for a second class, adding those names which have not previously occurred to you. Then go through the list of questions once more for the third class.

Your identity will never be known. I am interested only in group replies, not in individual replies.

        ✿   ✿   ✿   ✿

Accompanying the sheets of directions was a mimeographed list of the names of all students in the three classes referred to. The raters were then given the list of characteristics for which students from each of the three classes were to be nominated. It was in the following form (Item 1 is here reproduced for sample purposes; the other items followed in exactly the same form):

Class graduating '38   Class graduating '39   Class graduating '40

1. *Most absorbed* in social life, weekends, etc.

The 28 Guess Who items were as follows:
1. *Most absorbed* in social life, weekends, etc.
2. *Most absorbed* in home and family affairs
3. *Most absorbed* in college studies, academic work
4. *Most absorbed* in college community affairs
5. *Most absorbed* in national and international public affairs
6. *Most critical* of college educational policies
7. *Most critical* of individual members of faculty or administrative staff
8. *Most critical* of student committees (E.P.C., Community Council, etc.)
9. *Least concerned* about basic educational policies of the college
10. *Least concerned* about activities of student committees (E.P.C., etc.)
11. *Most anxious* to be left alone to follow individual pursuits
12. *Most anxious* to hold positions of community responsibility
13. *Most resistant* to community expectations regarding codes, standards, etc.

14. *Most influenced* by community expectations regarding codes, standards, etc.
15. *Most resistant* to enthusiams of the crowd
16. *Most influenced* by enthusiasms of the crowd
17. *Most resistant* to appeals regarded as moving or emotional
18. *Most influenced* by appeals regarded as moving or emotional
19. *Most resistant* to faculty authority
20. *Most influenced* by faculty authority

The following items have to do with attitudes during the first four or five years after leaving college.

21. *Most likely* to be enthusiastic supporters of the college
22. *Least likely* to be enthusiastic supporters of the college
23. *Most likely* to engage actively in pursuits related to college interests
24. *Least likely* to engage actively in pursuits related to college interests
25. *Most likely* to lead life of sheltered leisure
26. *Least likely* to lead life of sheltered leisure
27. *Most likely* to be deterred from some interesting pursuit because of family disapproval
28. *Least likely* to be deterred from some interesting pursuit because of family disapproval

Appendix E

I. Factors, principal axes solution

Variables	1	2	3	h²
Attitude toward:				
1. Roosevelt	−.66	−.16	.26	.53
2. Taft	.51	−.05	−.19	.29
3. Truman	−.72	.10	−.10	.54
4. McCarthy	.56	.21	.21	.40
5. Reuther	−.53	−.04	−.27	.36
6. Eisenhower	.78	−.31	.00	.70
7. Kennedy	−.49	−.19	−.26	.35
8. Nixon	.82	−.15	−.13	.71
9. MacArthur	.63	−.03	−.27	.47
10. Stevenson	−.69	−.08	.06	.48
11. Supreme Court decision	−.51	−.23	.06	.32
12. U-2 incident	.40	−.41	.00	.33
13. Medicare	−.61	−.05	−.11	.38
14. Red China in U.N.	−.59	−.12	.00	.36
15. Fifth amendment	−.51	−.31	−.03	.35
16. Disarmament	−.55	−.02	.16	.33
17. Coder's rating of awareness	.51	−.27	.30	.43
Total variance	36%	4%	3%	43%
Common variance	84%	9%	7%	100%

II. Factors, varimax rotation

Variables	1	2	3	h²
1. Roosevelt	−.26	−.64	−.21	.53
2. Taft	.33	.42	.07	.29
3. Truman	−.56	−.34	−.33	.54
4. McCarthy	.25	.27	.51	.40
5. Reuther	−.37	−.15	−.45	.36
6. Eisenhower	.73	.37	.17	.70
7. Kennedy	−.23	−.19	−.51	.35
8. Nixon	.62	.54	.19	.71
9. MacArthur	.38	.57	.09	.47
10. Stevenson	−.37	−.49	−.32	.48
11. Supreme Court decision	−.15	−.44	−.32	.32
12. U-2 incident	.56	.10	−.06	.33
13. Medicare	−.38	−.32	−.37	.38
14. Red China in U.N.	−.29	−.40	−.33	.36
15. Fifth amendment	−.11	−.40	−.43	.35
16. Disarmament	−.31	−.46	−.15	.33
17. Coder's rating of awareness	.59	.01	.28	.43
Total variance	17%	15%	10%	43%
Common variance	40%	36%	23%	99%

Appendix F

Voting Preferences in Six Presidential Elections

(Mailed Questionnaire Sample)

1940 Vote

Questionnaire sample	Republican	Democratic	Other	None	Total
Graduates	52 (48%)	46 (43%)	2 (2%)	8 (7%)	108
Nongraduates	46 (56%)	30 (37%)		6 (7%)	82
Total	98 (52%)	76 (40%)	2 (1%)	14 (7%)	190

1944 Vote

	Republican	Democratic	Other	None	Total
Graduates	41 (37%)	70 (62%)		1 (1%)	112
Nongraduates	40 (47%)	44 (51%)	1 (1%)	1 (1%)	86
Total	81 (41%)	114 (58%)	1	2 (1%)	198

1948 Vote

	Republican	Democratic	Other	None	Total
Graduates	48 (44%)	50 (46%)	6 (5%)	6 (5%)	110
Nongraduates	50 (57%)	32 (36%)	4 (5%)	2 (2%)	88
Total	98 (49%)	82 (41%)	10 (5%)	8 (4%)	198

1952 Vote

	Republican	Democratic	Other	None	Total
Graduates	58 (52%)	53 (47%)		1 (1%)	112
Nongraduates	58 (66%)	30 (34%)			88
Total	116 (58%)	83 (41%)		1 (1%)	200

	1956 Vote				
	Republican	Democratic	Other	None	Total
Graduates	54 (48%)	57 (51%)		1 (1%)	112
Nongraduates	56 (64%)	31 (35%)		1 (1%)	88
Total	110 (55%)	88 (44%)		2 (1%)	200

	1960 Vote				
	Republican	Democratic	Other	None	Total
Graduate	49 (44%)	63 (56%)			112
Nongraduates	45 (52%)	40 (46%)		2 (2%)	87
Total	94 (47%)	103 (52%)		2 (1%)	199

Appendix G

Relationships between Final PEP Score and Political Attitudes

I. Vote in six presidential elections (interview sample)

1940 Vote

Final PEP Score	Republican	Democratic	Other	N.A.	Total
Above median	46 (71%)	17 (26%)	1 (1%)	1 (1%)	65
Below median	18 (25%)	50 (68%)	1 (1%)	4 (6%)	73
Total	64 (46%)	67 (49%)	2 (1%)	5 (4%)	138

Chi-square (Rep. vs. Dem. only) = 26.51; $p < .001$; 1 df

1944 Vote

	Republican	Democratic	Other	N.A.	Total
Above median	31 (48%)	29 (45%)	1 (1%)	4 (6%)	65
Below median	6 (8%)	63 (86%)		4 (6%)	73
Total	37 (27%)	92 (67%)	1 (1%)	8 (6%)	138

Chi-square (Rep. vs. Dem. only) = 27.39; $p < .001$; 1 df

1948 Vote

	Republican	Democratic	Other	N.A.	Total
Above median	36 (55%)	22 (34%)	2 (3%)	5 (8%)	65
Below median	16 (22%)	46 (63%)	6 (8%)	5 (7%)	73
Total	52 (38%)	68 (49%)	8 (6%)	10 (7%)	138

Chi-square (Rep. vs. Dem. only) = 15.9; $p < .001$; 1 df

1952 Vote

	Republican	Democratic	Other	N.A.	Total
Above median	43 (66%)	22 (34%)			65
Below median	16 (22%)	53 (73%)	2 (3%)	2 (3%)	73
Total	59 (43%)	75 (54%)	2 (1%)	2 (1%)	138

Chi-square (Rep. vs. Dem. only) = 23.9; $p < .001$; 1 df

1956 Vote

	Republican	Democratic	Other	N.A.	Total
Above median	39 (60%)	26 (40%)			65
Below median	17 (23%)	56 (77%)			73
Total	56 (41%)	82 (59%)			138

Chi-square = 18.2; $p < .001$

1960 Vote

	Republican	Democratic	Other	N.A.	Total
Above median	40 (61%)	24 (37%)	1 (2%)		65
Below median	13 (18%)	59 (81%)	1 (1%)		73
Total	53 (38%)	83 (60%)	2 (2%)		138

Chi-square (Rep. vs. Dem. only) = 25.12; $p < .001$; 1 df

1964 Vote

	Republican	Democratic	No Pref-erence	N.A.	Total
Above median	8 (12%)	49 (75%)	3 (5%)	5 (8%)	65
Below median	2 (3%)	62 (85%)		9 (12%)	73
Total	10 (7%)	111 (81%)	3 (2%)	14 (10%)	138

Chi-square (Rep. vs. Dem. only) = 3.39; $p < .10$; 1 df

II. Relationship of final PEP score and 1960 conservatism index (mailed questionnaire sample)

	1961 Conservatism Index		
Final PEP Score	Above median	Below median	Total
Graduates			
Conservative	31 (53%)	27 (47%)	58
Nonconservative	5 (17%)	25 (83%)	30

Chi-square = 9.6; $p < .01$; 1 df

Nongraduates			
Conservative	29 (54%)	25 (46%)	54
Nonconservative	7 (26%)	20 (74%)	27

Chi-square = 4.54; $p < .05$; 1 df

III. Relationship of PEP score to the index of favorability to conservative figures (mailed questionnaire sample)

	Favorability to Conservative Figures		
Final PEP Score	Above median	Below median	Total
Graduates			
Conservative	37 (61%)	24 (39%)	61
Nonconservative	6 (20%)	24 (80%)	30

Chi-square = 11.7; $p < .001$; 1 df

Nongraduates			
Conservative	40 (71%)	16 (29%)	56
Nonconservative	8 (31%)	18 (69%)	26

Chi-square = 10.5; $p < .01$; 1 df

Appendix H

Differences in 1960 Conservatism between Interview
Respondents and Their Friends (Wilcoxon Matched-Pairs Test)

Conservatism since college	Total pairs	Mean difference in 1960 conservatism *	Sum of negative ranks of differ- ence (T)	p value
Remained conservative	27	2.33	46.5	<.001
Became conservative	14	2.71	4.5	<.01
Became non- conservative	15	5.53	0	<.001
Remained non- conservative	31	3.61	9.5	<.001

* The direction of the difference is that the friends were reported to be more conservative than the respondents.

Appendix I

Student Interview Schedule

I. Interview questions used in the spring of 1961

1. One of the things we are quite interested in is the significant experiences students have while they are at Bennington. Some students feel that their college years are a period of great change in themselves, while others feel that they have hardly changed at all. Where do you think you would come with regard to these two extremes? In other words, how much and in what ways do you think you have changed since coming to Bennington?

2. Do you think that having gone to Bennington will make any difference in your later life? (In what way?)

3. Have you ever given thought to whether there are implicit social standards that other students expect you to uphold? (PROBE FOR EACH OF THE FOLLOWING.)

   a. Sometimes students feel that they are under pressure to conform in certain ways in order to be accepted by other students.

   b. Sometimes students feel that there is a lack of tolerance for certain individual behavior or personal beliefs.

   c. Sometimes students feel they cannot maintain their own values and standards and remain a part of the community.

   d. Sometimes students feel that if they maintain the values of their family or their religion they are relegated to a minority status in the community.

4. President Fels has said: "The college has a reputation for being unconventional." Do you think that anything should be done to change this reputation?

   a. Are there any respects in which you think of yourself as particularly unconventional? (What might these be?)

II. Interview questions used in the spring of 1962

1–4. Some students feel that their college years are a period of great change in themselves, while others feel that they have hardly changed at all. Are there any ways in which you have changed since coming to Bennington? (What might these be?)

    a. FIRST MENTIONED CHANGE: When do you feel this particular change began?

    b. What do you feel brought about this change—can you recall any particular people, experiences, or events that were responsible for initiating this change? (PROBE PARTICULARLY FOR PEOPLE, AND FOR DETAILS OF EXPERIENCES.)

(IF R HAS NOT MENTIONED ALL OF THE FOLLOWING WHEN SHE FINISHES, PROBE WITH REGARD TO EACH, AS FOLLOWS.) Some students have told us that they have experienced important changes with respect to their

    a. Intellectual development

    b. Ideas about themselves

    c. Attitudes toward their fellow students

    d. Attitudes toward the society outside Bennington

    e. Political attitudes.

Do you think this has been an important area of change for you?
    __ Yes   __ No

IF YES: In what way have you changed in this area? (REPEAT FOR a–e.)

5. Since you have come to Bennington have you noticed any ways in which your values and beliefs have differed from those of certain groups of students here? (PROBE FOR WHAT THE DIFFERENCES WERE AND WITH WHOM R DIFFERED.)

    a. IF YES: When did you first notice these differences?

    b. How were these differences brought to your attention? (PROBE FOR SPECIFIC INSTANCES AND EXPERIENCES OF PRESSURE.)

    c. How did you feel when you became aware of these differences?

    d. How have you reacted to these differences? (What did you do about them?) (PROBE: Sometimes students are disturbed if fellow students disagree with them about important matters.)

6. Since you've come to Bennington have you noticed any important differences between your own values and beliefs and those of your parents? (PROBE FOR CONTENT OF DIFFERENCES AND WHICH PARENT.)

    a. IF YES: Do you think either parent wanted you to change? How was this brought to your attention?

    b. How did you feel when you became aware of these differences?

    c. What did you do about them?

Appendix J

Comparisons of the PEP Scores of the
Participants and Nonparticipants

I. Graduates, 1938, 1939, 1940	N	Mean PEP scores
Interview respondents	129	64.4
Questionnaire respondents	9	58.7
Total Participants	138	64.1
No longer living	· 6	60.3
Address unknown	4	52.0
Not contacted	1	69.0
Refused or did not return questionnaire	9	68.0
Total Nonparticipants	20	62.5
Total in classes of 1938, 1939, 1940	158	63.9

II. Alumnae mailed questionnaire (Graduates 1936, 1937, 1941, 1942, and all nongraduates)

Graduates	Completed questionnaire in 1961		Did not complete questionnaire in 1961		
	N	Mean PEP scores	N	Mean PEP scores	t
I	65	63.8	20	66.4	0.33
II	24	68.0	12	73.8	1.12
III	22	70.0	8	78.5	1.60
Year of last PEP unknown	6	69.0	4	71.5	
Total	117	66.1	44	71.1	
Nongraduates					
I	13	65.2	11	68.4	0.63
II	37	68.8	27	70.7	0.6
III	34	72.4	34	74.4	0.63
Year of last PEP unknown	6	67.2	4	80.5	
Total	90	69.5	76 *	72.6	

I = Last PEP score as a junior or senior.
II = Last PEP score as a sophomore.
III = Last PEP score as a freshman.

* There were no PEP scores for two women from this group.

Appendix K

Ceiling and Regression Effects in Indices of Change

Indices of change that are based upon earlier and later responses to the same questions are subject to two kinds of artifactual limitations. *Ceiling* effects refer to the fact that the more extreme the initial score, the less "room" there is for change toward greater extremeness. *Regression* effects refer to the fact that, because of irrelevant sources of "error" in responding, extreme scores at either time tend to be less extreme at the other time. For either reason, or both, the probabilities are therefore against greater extremeness of the later than of the earlier scores. When greater extremeness does occur, the changes cannot be attributed to ceiling or regression effects, but when changes occur toward lesser extremeness their interpretation is apt to be uncertain.

We conclude that such effects are not responsible for most of the change reported in Table 10.5 (p. 158), for example, for the following reasons. (1) An analysis of the patterns of change within the "Incongruent" and "Congruent" groups as well as the total sample shows that the prediction of change is better *within the extreme groups* than in the total sample. When the possibility of regression effects is reduced to a minimum by carrying out the analysis within the extreme groups, the multiple correlations between various predictors and change in Developmental Status are *greater* than comparable correlations obtained within the total sample; and (2) the magnitude of the correlations obtained within the extreme groups suggests that much more is at work than a simple regression toward the mean. With only four predictor variables it is possible to obtain a correlation of .60 with change in Developmental Status for the students initially incongruent, and a parallel figure of .63 for those initially congruent. The correlation between the four best predictors and change for the total group is only .39.

Appendix L

The Omnibus Personality Inventory

This instrument, commonly known as the OPI, was constructed at the Center for the Study of Higher Education (University of California, Berkeley) for purposes of identifying "nonintellective" or personality factors related to the observed or anticipated effects of colleges upon their students. It has been shown to differentiate among students in diverse colleges, among categories of more and less "successful" students, and among those pursuing different interests and academic majors.*

The OPI includes several distinctively labeled scales, although in the version that we used, several of the items reappear in two or more different scales, so that there are built-in intercorrelations. The scales that we have used, in whole or in part, are listed here, together with their abbreviations and brief descriptions of the characteristics they are designed to measure.†

AA	Atheism-Agnosticism	Skepticism about religious beliefs and practices; tendencies to reject those that are orthodox or fundamentalist.
DS	Developmental Status	Questioning of authority, as of family, school, church, or state, together with freedom of impulse expression.
Es	Estheticism	Diversity of artistic interests and activities: literature and dramatics as well as music and the visual arts.
TO	Theoretical Orientation	Preference for scientific, logical, rational, critical approach to problems.

---

* See Heist (1960); Heist, McConnell, Matsler, and Williams (1961); Heist and Webster (1960).

† These descriptions are based upon information provided in the Manual for the *Omnibus Personality Inventory* (Center for the Study of Higher Education, 1962). The scales have subsequently been revised to eliminate item overlap and, in some cases, renamed.

273

NA   Nonauthoritarianism   Freedom from thought patterns associ-
                              ated with convention, rigidity, preju-
                              dice, and suppression of introspection.

Or   Originality   Independence of thought; creativeness
                              or novelty in expression; tendency to
                              seek patterning in experience.

Li   Liberalism   Absence of conservatism in social and
                              public affairs; openness toward change.

Each of these scales has been named so that *higher* scores are more typical of seniors than of freshmen (for example, freshmen are apt to be more "religious" and less "agnostic" or "atheistic" than seniors, less interested in esthetic matters, and more authoritarian). Each of them was originally constructed, in preliminary form, on the basis of theoretical considerations, then repeatedly revised following analyses of the responses of many students in diverse institutions. In general the "meaning" of the individual items is not self-evident to the student, that is, she was not likely to know the purposes for which either a "true" or a "false" choice would be used.

Instructions were as follows:

This is not a test of ability or achievement, but a questionnaire for reporting your own feelings and opinions. It is a result of extensive studies of college students and other groups.

Do Not Write Your Name [each sheet had a code number]. Read each of the numbered statements [258 of them in the case of undergraduates at Bennington between 1959 and 1962] and decide whether it is *true or mostly true as applied to you,* or *false or mostly false as applied to you.* Do not leave any blank spaces if you can avoid it. [See Heist and Williams (1957) for manner of scoring replies.]

Sample items appear in Appendix A. In the case of one scale (TO), we used only a portion of the items included in the full scale, as originally developed.

Appendix M

The OPI and Bennington Norms

We are reasonably sure that the OPI constituted a valid measure of norm-acceptance at Bennington. There are several criteria which can be used to establish an attitude scale as a valid measure of conformity with the norms of a group. The questions one would ask about the scale include these:

1. Does the scale differentiate the members of the group in question from other comparable groups with different norms?

2. Do individuals who have been in the group longest tend to maximize the trait measured by the scale as compared with new entrants to the group?

3. Is performance on the scale related to status in the group?

4. Does the scale correlate with other measures of norm-acceptance?

If these conditions hold with respect to the OPI scales then we shall assume that an individual's position on these scales reflects her position with respect to the norms of the college, and that changes in her score are likely to reflect changes in her position with respect to the norms.

1. Bennington Students Are Differentiated from Students at Other Colleges

We have already reported data (see p. 127) indicating that OPI scales discriminate Bennington students from a sample of students in California, from Vassar students, and National Merit Scholarship winners. In all cases, the differences obtained were in directions expected on the basis of Bennington's norms. These data demonstrate that Bennington attracts students with certain highly distinctive attributes, and that the OPI scales are capable of measuring at least some of these attributes.

2. The OPI Reflects Differences between Freshmen and Seniors

If a particular cluster of attitudes or attributes is normative, then we would expect those who have been in the group longest to be more likely to exhibit these attitudes and traits than new entrants. This, in part, would be due to processes of socialization, and also to the fact that persons lacking in the trait tended to leave the group. Table 1 presents comparative data on all the OPI scales for students at each class level in 1959.

Using a t-test of the significance of differences between means, differences between freshmen and seniors were found to be significant at or beyond the .01 level for Developmental Status, Estheticism, Liberalism, and Originality; and for Theoretical Orientation at the .05 level. Two scales, Agnosticism-Atheism and Nonauthoritarianism, did not yield significant differences between freshmen and seniors—a fact, incidentally, which helped to determine our decision to drop these scales in a final revision.

3. Scores on the OPI Are Related to Status

Previously, data were mentioned which indicated that status at Bennington was related to scores on the OPI (see pp. 178–179). These data showed that high-prestige students (as measured by number of nominations received for "community representative" or as "most admired") tended to score above the median on Estheticism, Theoretical Orientation, Liberalism, and Originality, whereas students who received no nominations tended to score below the median on these scales. Comparable results, showing a significant relationship between scores on the OPI and status, are presented in Table 2. These data, gathered in 1959, show that juniors and seniors receiving ten or more nominations for "community representative" were generally higher

Table 1   OPI Means by Class at Bennington (1959)

Year Level	AA	DS	Es	Li	NA	Or	TO	N
			Scale Means					
Freshmen	33.4	42.3	33.6	56.6	13.4	63.0	35.7	108–121
Sophomores	36.6	45.4	36.2	58.3	13.8	65.4	38.2	69–71
Juniors	35.9	45.6	34.2	58.8	13.8	65.7	36.5	46–49
Seniors	35.4	47.7	37.4	61.4	13.9	67.5	38.2	41–44

Table 2   Mean OPI Scores by Status and Class Level

	Scale Means							
	AA	DS	Es	Li	NA	Or	TO	N
High-status sophomores	39.6*	48.2*	40.0*	62.8*	15.0	67.7	41.3*	6
Total sophomores	36.6	45.4	36.2	58.3	13.8	65.4	38.2	69–71
High-status juniors	38.6*	48.0*	38.1*	64.6*	14.9	71.8*	42.6*	8
Total juniors	35.9	45.6	34.2	58.8	13.8	65.7	36.5	46–49
High-status seniors	38.1*	47.4	39.3*	62.8	13.1	73.6*	40.7*	12
Total seniors	35.4	47.7	36.5	61.4	13.9	67.5	38.2	41–44

* Denotes mean which is significantly higher ($p < .05$) than class mean.

on the OPI scales than the mean for their class. The same is true for sophomores receiving five or more votes. What is particularly impressive about this table is that in all but one of the 21 comparisons (Developmental Status for seniors) the mean score of high-status students exceeds that for all students in the same class.

4. Correlates of the OPI

Our view of the OPI as an index of the norms would be considerably reinforced if the scales were found to correlate with other variables which were logically connected with the Bennington norms as we have defined them.

A 51 x 51 intercorrelation matrix, containing a number of quantitative indices derived from the Bennington data, was put through a factor-analysis program. The first rotated factor, called "norm-acceptance," contained all the OPI scales finally used, plus a number of other variables which seem to be closely related to the norms of the student body. This first factor, and the variables which loaded on it, is presented in Table 3.

Table 3 is interesting for a number of reasons. First, it demonstrates the high degree of interrelationship among the OPI scales, despite the fact that they purportedly measure disparate traits. This high intercorrelation is partially explained by the fact that there is considerable item overlap among the scales (for example, our sample of TO items is entirely composed of items from other scales). But the fact that all

Table 3   Variable Loading on Factor I

	Loading
Theoretical Orientation	−.88
Originality	−.82
Estheticism	−.78
Liberalism	−.77
Developmental Status	−.45
Change: Theoretical Orientation	−.34
Intellectualism index	−.32
"Small Talk" index	.37
"Serious Talk" index	−.32
Perceived similarity: self and Bennington mode	−.28
Perceived similarity: self and admired student	−.22
Perceived similarity: self and Bennington friends	−.21
Perceived similarity: Bennington and nonBennington friends	−.21
Unconventionality index	−.20
Individualism	−.21

the scales load on a single factor may also mean that they are measuring the same thing at Bennington, namely, acceptance of the norms of the student culture. This interpretation is supported by the fact that various measures of perception of Bennington as a reference group tend to load on the same factor. Thus scores on the OPI are related to rating oneself in a similar fashion to the way the modal Bennington student rates herself, perceiving similarity between one's self-rating and the self-rating of "someone admired by most Bennington students," seeing oneself as similar to one's Bennington friends, and perceiving similarity between one's Bennington friends and friends not at Bennington.

Finally, Table 3 indicates that the OPI scales are correlated with indices compiled from self-ratings on three clusters of traits: "intellectualism," "individualism," and "unconventionality." Since these self-rating measures were explicitly designed to measure norm-acceptance, one would expect that the OPI would correlate with them, if the OPI scales are to be taken as measures of conformity with the norms.

The high loadings of the OPI scales on the same factor would seem to justify the procedure of combining the OPI scales into a single measure of norm-acceptance and attitude change, thus ignoring the discrete trait names attached to the separate scales. On the other hand, some data from Bennington suggest that the individual scales do measure somewhat different attributes. Both the overlapping and distinctive characteristics of each scale are illustrated in Table 4. This table is a summary of correlations obtained between each OPI scale and some of the rating scales mentioned earlier. Only correlations of .20 or above are indicated.

Table 4 suggests that although all the OPI scales are roughly equivalent in their relationship to measures of "individualism" (conventionality, conservatism, compliance, attitude toward rules), Estheticism and Originality are related to measures of "intellectualism" (intellectual, absorbed in academic life) and unrelated to measures of "emotionality" (tenseness, impulsiveness); whereas Developmental Status and, to some extent, Liberalism are unrelated to "intellectualism" and more strongly related to the emotionality scales. These differences in emphasis are quite consistent with the scale descriptions and validation results offered by the authors of the test (Center for the Study of Higher Education, 1958, 1962).

Thus the OPI seems a reasonably adequate instrument for quantitatively ascertaining agreement with the norms of the Bennington student culture. The scales we used, especially those used in the final version of the test (which excluded the Atheism-Agnosticism, and Non-authoritarianism scales) adequately met the criteria for validity which we set up. It should be emphasized that these criteria of validity did not include tests of whether or not each scale was an adequate measure of what it purported to measure (and, in the case of Developmental Status, it is by no means clear what is purportedly measured). Rather, our main interest was whether or not the test as a whole adequately discriminated between those who accepted and those who did not accept Bennington's norms. The results presented suggest that, in fact, this purpose was fulfilled by the scales.

Table 4   Correlations between OPI Scales and Self-Ratings

Self-rating as:	DS	Es	Li	Or	TO
Conventional in dress	−.38	−.40	−.37	−.28	−.36
Conventional in opinion	−.34	−.38	−.40	−.30	−.37
Intellectual	—	.24	.21	.27	.23
Tense	.32	.20	—	—	.21
Conservative	−.46	−.31	−.39	−.32	−.31
Impulsive	.30	—	.21	—	—
Compliant	−.36	−.35	−.34	−.34	−.36
Critical of rules	.34	.27	.26	.24	.25
Absorbed in academic life	—	.23	—	.21	—

References

Adorno, T. W., Frenkel-Brunswik, E., Levinson, D. J., and Sanford, R. N., *The Authoritarian Personality.* New York: Harper and Row, 1950.

Bushnell, J. H., Student Culture at Vassar, in N. Sanford (Ed.), *The American College.* New York: John Wiley and Sons, 1962, pp. 489–514.

Center for the Study of Higher Education, *Manual for the Omnibus Personality Inventory,* Berkeley: University of California Press, 1959.

Center for the Study of Higher Education, *Manual for the Omnibus Personality Inventory,* Berkeley: University of California Press, 1962.

Christie, R., Havel, J., and Seidenberg, B., Is the F Scale Irreversible?, *Journal of Abnormal and Social Psychology,* 1958, **56**, pp. 143–164.

Cohen, A. K., *Delinquent Boys: The Culture of the Gang.* New York: The Free Press, 1955.

Cohen, A. K., The Study of Social Disorganization and Deviant Behavior, in R. K. Merton, L. Broom, and L. Cottrell (Eds.), *Sociology Today.* New York: Basic Books, 1959, Ch. XXI.

Coleman, J. S., *The Adolescent Society.* New York: The Free Press, 1961.

Erikson, E. H., Identity and the Life Cycle, *Psychological Issues,* 1959, **1**, pp. 1–171.

Flacks, R., Adaptations of Deviants in a College Community. Unpublished doctoral dissertation. University of Michigan, 1963.

Freedman, M., The Passage through College, in N. Sanford (Ed.), Personality Development during the College Years, *Journal of Social Issues,* 1956, **12**, pp. 13–28.

Freedman, M., Studies of College Alumni, in N. Sanford (Ed.), *The American College.* New York: John Wiley and Sons, 1962, pp. 847–886.

Friedan, B., *The Feminine Mystique.* New York: W. W. Norton, 1963.

Goldsen, R. K., Rosenberg, M., Williams, R. M., and Suchman, E. A., *What College Students Think.* Princeton: D. Van Nostrand, 1960.

Gump, P. V., Anti-Democratic Trends and Student Reaction to President Truman's Dismissal of General MacArthur, *Journal of Social Psychology,* 1953, **38**, pp. 131–135.

Handlon, B. and Squier, L. H., Attitudes toward Special Loyalty Oaths at the University of California, *American Psychologist,* 1955, **10**, pp. 121–127.

Heider, F., *The Psychology of Interpersonal Relations.* New York: John Wiley and Sons, 1958.

Heist, P., Diversity in College Student Characteristics, *Journal of Educational Sociology,* 1960, **33**, pp. 279–291.

Heist, P., McConnell, T. R., Matsler, F., and Williams, Phoebe, Personality and Scholarship, *Science,* 1961, **133**, pp. 362–367.

Heist, P. and Williams, Phoebe, *Manual for the Omnibus Personality Inventory*. Berkeley: Center for the Study of Higher Education, University of California, 1957.

Jacob, P. E., *Changing Values in College*. New York: Harper and Row, 1957.

Kelley, H. H., Two Functions of Reference Groups, in Swanson, G. E., Newcomb, T. M., and Hartley, E. L. (Eds.), *Readings in Social Psychology* (Rev. Ed.). New York: Holt, Rinehart, and Winston, 1952.

Milton, O., Presidential Choice and Performance on a Scale of Authoritarianism, *American Psychologist*, 1952, 7, pp. 597–598.

Newcomb, T. M., *Personality and Social Change*. New York: Dryden, 1943.

Newcomb, T. M., Attitude Development as a Function of Reference groups: The Bennington Study, in G. E. Swanson, T. M. Newcomb, and E. L. Hartley (Eds.), *Readings in Social Psychology* (Revised Edition). New York: Holt, Rinehart and Winston, 1952.

Newcomb, T. M., *The Acquaintance Process*. New York: Holt, Rinehart, and Winston, 1961.

Pace, C. R., Characteristics of Bennington College as Seen by Its Students. Unpublished paper. Bennington College, 1961.

Simos, I., Ethnocentrism and Attitudes toward the Rosenberg Case and the Republic of Korea, *Journal of Social Psychology*, 1956, 43, pp. 181–185.

Slater, Carol, Weiss, R., and Goldhaber, R., *Participation in Voluntary Associations: A Preliminary Report of Findings from a Study of Married Non-Farm Women*. Ann Arbor: Survey Research Center, University of Michigan, 1957.

Stern, G. G., Environments for Learning, in N. Sanford (Ed.), *The American College*. New York: John Wiley and Sons, 1962, pp. 690–730.

Stern, G. G., Characteristics of the Intellectual Climate in College Environments, *Harvard Educational Review*, 1963, 33, pp. 5–41.

Survey Research Center, *Who Votes and For Whom*. Ann Arbor: Institute for Social Research, The University of Michigan, 1965.

Trow, M., Cultural Sophistication and Higher Education. Unpublished paper. Berkeley: Center for the Study of Higher Education, University of California, 1959.

Trow, M., The Campus Viewed as a Culture, in H. T. Sprague (Ed.), *Research on College Students*. Boulder, Colorado: WICHE, 1960, pp. 106–123.

Warwick, D. P., Socialization and Value Change in a College Community. Unpublished doctoral dissertation. University of Michigan, 1963.

Webster, H., Freedman, M., and Heist, P., Personality Changes in College Students, in N. Sanford (Ed.), *The American College*. New York: John Wiley and Sons, 1962, pp. 811–846.

Webster, H. and Heist, P., Construction of a Multiple Trait Personality Test for Use with College Populations. Unpublished paper. Berkeley: Center for the Study of Higher Education, University of California, 1959.

Index

Activities index, 126
Adolescents, identity problems, 213
Adorno, et al., "F-scale," 16
Age, as factor in nonauthoritarianism, 221
Agnostics, students (1960 compared with alumnae), 218
Alumnae Interview Schedule, 231–244
Alumnae office, 13
American Association of University Professors, 49
American Civil Liberties Union, 84, 86, 87, 91
American Heritage, 93
Americans for Democratic Action, 84, 90
Atlantic Monthly, 91
Attitude Change Scores for deviants, 203–204
  for "quasi-deviants," 204
Attitude differences, 39
Attitudes, political, *see* Political attitudes
Attitudes of husbands of Bennington respondents, affecting change, 104, 192
  indirect influence, 65
  party preferences, 60
  political preferences, 43, 46
  spouses' effect on each other, 54–61
  toward public figures, 56
  voting patterns, 58–59
  voting preferences, 43, 46
  wives' agreement with, 55
    college attitudes, related to, 60–61
    compared with four groups of, 56

Attitudes, liberal, 4, 31, 39
  of Bennington, 125–126, 217
  deviants and, 192, 193, 203
  in educational policies, 225
  families and, 52
  of freshmen, 228
  OPI Scale and, 220
  predisposition to, 51
  self-selection, 52
  students (1960) compared with alumnae, 221, 225
  see also Political attitudes
Attitudes, patterns of changing and nonchanging, 5
  see also Conservatism, Nonconservatism, Political attitudes
Attitudes, religious, 124
  freshmen, 116
  see also Religion as direction of change
Attitudes of students, conservatism, 4, 5, 17, 23, 24, 25, 26, 27
  liberalism, 4, 5, 16, 21, 24
  nonauthoritarianism, 16, 23
  nonconservatism, 4, 5, 24

Bennington College, study (1935–1939), data from, 17–19
  description of, 3–5, 8
  faculty, 4
  liberalism at, 4
  nonconservatism at, 5
  respondents from classes 1932–38, 42
  social environment, 3–4
  sociometric ratings, 18

283